Developing Countries in the World Trading System

Developing Countries in the World Trading System

The Uruguay Round and Beyond

Edited by

Ramesh Adhikari

Senior Capacity Building Specialist
Asian Development Bank Institute

Prema-chandra Athukorala

Professor of Economics
Research School of Pacific and Asian Studies
Australian National University

Edward Elgar

Cheltenham, UK • Northampton MA, USA

Published by
Edward Elgar Publishing Limited
Glensanda House
Montpellier Parade
Cheltenham
Glos GL50 1UA
UK

Edward Elgar Publishing, Inc.
136 West Street
Suite 202
Northampton
Massachusetts 01060
USA

A catalogue record for this book
is available from the British Library

Library of Congress Cataloguing in Publication Data
Developing countries in the world trading system : the Uruguay round and beyond / edited by Ramesh Adhikari, Prema-chandra Athukorala.
    p. cm.
    "This volume contains updated and edited versions of selected papers presented at a capacity building and training program on Trade Policy Issues held at the Asian Development Bank Institute in Tokyo during 16–25 July 2000." Foreword.
    Includes index.
    1. Developing countries—Foreign economic relations—Congresses.
2. Developing countries—Economic conditions—Case studies—Congresses.
3. Produce trade—Government policy—Case studies—Congresses. 4. Clothing trade—Government policy—Case studies—Congresses. 5. International trade—Social aspects—Congresses. 6. International trade—Environmental aspects—Congresses. 7. World Trade Organization—Congresses. 8. World Trade Organization—Asia—Congresses. 9. Uruguay Round (1987–1994)—Congresses.
I. Adhikari, Ramesh, 1951– II. Athukoralge, Premachandra.

HF2580.9 .D48 2002
382'.09172'4—dc21   2001054780

ISBN 1 84064 724 8

Printed and bound in Great Britain by MPG Books Ltd, Bodmin, Cornwall

Contents

Figures

Tables

Contributors

Ramesh Adhikari, Senior Capacity Building Specialist, Asian Development Bank Institute, Tokyo, Japan

Kym Anderson, Professor, Department of Economics and the Centre for International Economic Studies, University of Adelaide, Australia

Prema-chandra Athukorala, Professor of Economics, Division of Economics, Research School of Pacific and Asian Studies, Asia Pacific School of Economics and Management, Australian National University, Canberra, Australia

Arnab Basu, Assistant Professor, Department of Economics, College of William & Mary, Williamsburg, VA 23187, USA

Nancy Chau, Assistant Professor, Department of Agricultural, Resource, and Managerial Economics, Cornell University, Ithaca, NY 14853, USA; and Senior Research Fellow, Federal Agricultural Research Centre, Braunschweig, Germany

Claus Deblitz, Federal Agricultural Research Centre, Germany

Ulrike Grote, Senior Research Fellow, Centre for Development Research, University of Bonn, Germany

Jayant Menon, Economist, Regional Economic Monitoring Unit, Asian Development Bank, Manila, Philippines

T.N. Srinivasan, Samuel C. Park Jr Professor of Economics, Yale University, USA

Susanne Stegmann, Senior Research Fellow, Centre for Development Research, University of Bonn, and the Society for Agricultural Policy Research and Rural Sociology E.V. (FAA), Germany

Kerrin Vautier, Consulting Research Economist, Auckland, New Zealand

Yongzheng Yang, Economist, International Monetary Fund, Washington DC, USA

Foreword

Trade openness is a key component of a country's economic policy mix for growth and general well-being. Experience suggests that trade openness has contributed substantially to the remarkable growth of the industrialized countries, as well as to that of Asia's newly industrialized economies. However, for various reasons many developing countries in the Asia and Pacific region have not yet been able to integrate successfully into global markets and realize the growth-inducing and poverty-reducing benefits of trade.

While trade liberalization by developing countries progressed subsequent to the Uruguay Round, new rules were being developed in the multilateral trading system pertaining to a variety of domestic policy and regulatory areas that affect trade and investment flows in a less direct manner than traditional tariffs and quotas. The World Trade Organization (WTO) seeks to promote a rules-based multilateral trading system. This initiative should be seen as beneficial for the developing countries. After all, developing countries are heavily represented in the WTO, accounting for about four-fifths of its membership. Nevertheless, the multilateral trading system could be improved to make it work more effectively for the interests of developing countries.

For this reason developing-country policymakers should have a good understanding of the economic implications of the various policies, standards and regulatory regimes associated with national and international trade. They should also understand the timing, sequencing and costs of trade policy reforms and the appropriate institutional arrangements required for their effective implementation. Furthermore, as standard trade policy instruments such as tariffs and quotas are becoming increasingly less relevant, the reform of domestic markets and the need to strengthen local institutional capacity for policy development in new areas have become urgent. This includes not only the need for building local capacity to implement international agreements, but also to assess policy initiatives. Given that the welfare implications of many of the policies that are now emerging on the international negotiating agenda may depend on identification and consideration of impacts on local stakeholders, the choice of a policy mix that reflects the right assessment of local interests and concerns becomes increasingly important. Similarly, the institutional dimensions of trade policy formation and implementation have become more important.

Such understanding and related actions are therefore of fundamental importance if developing countries are to participate fully and successfully in multilateral trade negotiations and safeguard their interests, and at the same time promote international trade and investment flows. Donors and national governments are working towards achieving the international target of halving poverty by 2015. Given this goal and the important role of international trade in assisting in this regard, WTO-related policy developments and actions must contribute meaningfully to achieving the international development target of poverty reduction through the promotion of more open international trade. Clearly, developing countries need more access to industrialized countries' markets. WTO members must provide increased access to their markets for goods and services on the basis of more predictable and non-discriminatory rules. International trade rules must remain relevant to the 21st century's challenges and opportunities.

At the Asian Development Bank Institute, in addition to ongoing research in post-crisis development paradigms for Asia, our new challenge is to intellectually support the overarching poverty reduction goal recently set by the Asian Development Bank. We want to clearly identify concrete development mechanisms whereby growth and globalization can be compatible with the least income disparity and the largest reduction in poverty. In the international trade area our research activities include export competitiveness in precrisis East Asia; trade and foreign direct investment in a post-Asian crisis environment; impact of information technology on conventional comparative advantage-based development strategy; and new dimensions of education, learning and skills formation linkages in Asia.

This volume contains updated and edited versions of selected papers presented at a capacity building and training programme on Trade Policy Issues held at the Asian Development Bank Institute in Tokyo during 16–25 July 2000. I hope that the views and information presented in this volume will enhance readers' understanding of these important emerging trade policy issues and that they will eventually make some contribution towards the promotion of a more open and rules-based multilateral trading system and through this mechanism assist in achieving the international development target of poverty reduction.

Masaru Yoshitomi
Dean, Asian Development Bank Institute
May 2001

Acknowledgements

First of all we are most grateful to the contributors to this volume for their discerning papers and for patiently complying with our tight editorial timetable. We also acknowledge with gratitude the encouragement provided by S.B. Chua, Naoki Kajiyama, M.G. Quibria, Grant Stillman and Masaru Yoshitomi of the Asian Development Bank Institute. Finally, we thank Alice Faintich for a great editorial job on the manuscript.

Views expressed in this volume are the authors' own and do not necessarily represent the views of the organizations they belong to.

Ramesh Adhikari
Prema-chandra Athukorala

Abbreviations and acronyms

ADB	Asian Development Bank
AFTA	ASEAN Free Trade Area
APEC	Asia Pacific Economic Cooperation
ASEAN	Association of Southeast Asian Nations
ATC	Agreement on Textiles and Clothing
CEPT	common effective preferential tariff
CP	competition policy
DSM	Dispute Settlement Mechanism
DSU	Understanding on Rules and Procedures Governing the Settlement of Disputes
EU	European Union
FTA	free trade area
GATS	General Agreement on Trade in Services
GATT	General Agreement on Tariffs and Trade
GDP	gross domestic product
GMO	genetically modified organism
GSP	Generalized System of Preferences
ILO	International Labour Organization
IMF	International Monetary Fund
Lao PDR	Lao People's Democratic Republic
MFA	Multi-Fiber Arrangement
MFN	most favoured nation
NGO	nongovernmental organization
NIE	newly industrializing economy
NTB	nontariff barrier
OECD	Organization for Economic Co-operation and Development
PECC	Pacific Economic Cooperation Council
QR	quantitative restriction
RTA	regional trading arrangement
SEATE	Southeast Asian transition economy
SPS	sanitary and phytosanitary
SPSA	Sanitary and Phytosanitary Agreement
TRIPs	Agreement on Trade-Related Aspects of Intellectual Property Rights
TRQ	tariff rate quota

UNCTAD	United Nations Conference on Trade and Development
UR	Uruguay Round
URAA	Uruguay Round Agreement on Agriculture
WTO	World Trade Organization

1. Developing countries in the world trading system: an overview

Ramesh Adhikari and
Prema-chandra Athukorala

The Uruguay Round (UR) of multilateral trade talks, which formally concluded on 15 August 1994 in Marrakesh, Morocco, after eight years of intense and often contentious negotiations, was a landmark in the evolution of the global trading system. The Uruguay Round Agreement signed at Marrakesh embodied three key outcomes, which were crucial for laying the foundation for an effective, rules-based trading system, namely: (a) providing for the establishment of the World Trade Organization (WTO) as the successor to the General Agreement on Tariffs and Trade (GATT); (b) laying down provisions to ensure participation by developing countries as equal partners in the world trading system; and (c) broadening the coverage of international trade rules to encompass virtually all economic activities relevant to economic interaction.

For almost fifty years following World War II the global trading system functioned without a fully fledged organization with well-defined rules of decisionmaking and enforcement to deal with trade issues among countries. The GATT, which came into being in 1947 on the basis of the Protocol of Provisional Application signed at the United Nations Conference on Trade and Employment in Havana, Cuba, on 21 November in that year,[1] did not have the international standing of the International Monetary Fund (IMF) or the World Bank, both of which were international organizations. Instead the GATT, as its name implied, was a multilateral agreement among its contracting parties rather than a treaty among sovereign nations (Jackson 1989). By contrast, the WTO, which came into being on 1 January 1995 on the basis of a treaty ratified by GATT members at the conclusion of the UR, has the same legal and organizational standing as the IMF and the World Bank. As an organization the WTO has the potential and the opportunity to play an active role in the international trading system, compared with the passive role of the GATT Secretariat, which simply implemented decisions made by the contracting parties. The WTO has at its disposal a much stronger enforcement and dispute

1

settlement mechanism than what prevailed under the GATT. In other words, the WTO provides the world trading system with an effective institutional and legal framework for the design and enforcement of trade rules (for details on the nature of, and challenges faced by, the WTO as an international organization see Krueger 1999).

The developing countries had participated in previous rounds of multilateral trade negotiations generally as observers (for a succinct history of the role of developing countries in the multilateral trading system and how their concerns were reflected in the GATT see Srinivasan 1999). They benefited as free-riders from any reductions in trade barriers undertaken by the industrial countries on a most favoured nation (MFN) basis. At the same time they insisted on special and differential treatment within the GATT on the grounds that they were too weak to compete, and therefore needed special exemptions from general trade rules applicable to the industrial countries. The special and differential privileges 'won' through these demands included the Generalized System of Preferences (GSP), which permitted unilateral discrimination in the form of tariff remissions for developing countries and the ability to continue applying quantitative restrictions (QRs) and other protectionist measures without entering into reciprocal negotiations with the industrial countries. For the first time in the history of multilateral trade negotiations, developing countries participated in the UR not as observers, but as active members, and they signed the WTO Agreement as full-scale members. Under the WTO Agreement trade preferences to developing countries are to be phased out. The conditions under which countries can evoke the balance of payments exception to the requirement that QRs be eliminated have been made far more stringent, and countries using this exception will be subject to more frequent and critical surveillance than in the past.

With regard to extending the coverage of multilateral discipline to international trade, the UR succeeded in bringing agriculture and textiles and clothing – two areas of great significance for the developing countries – back under multilateral trade discipline. It also succeeded in extending multilateral rules and discipline to trade in services, trade-related aspects of intellectual property rights and international investment. While the actual extent of liberalization achieved under these various initiatives is likely to be extremely modest, they do provide for more far-reaching changes under future WTO negotiations about protectionism in these product areas than could realistically have been anticipated before the negotiations began.

The period between the establishment of the WTO and late 1999 was one of unprecedented enthusiasm about achieving a more liberal world trading system. By the end of 2000 the WTO had 135 member countries (compared with total GATT membership of 65 at the beginning of the UR), and some 30 more countries were negotiating entry. Developing countries now accounted for four-fifths of total WTO membership. The first two WTO Ministerial Meetings (in Singapore in 1996 and in Geneva in 1998) succeeded in creating a process to analyse and exchange information on implementing the UR and to identify items for a new round.[2] Both meetings concluded with greater enthusiasm for further reform. The implementation of the UR also boosted trade liberalization in the developing countries by providing a mechanism to link reform to an international commitment to guard against possible slippage in response to domestic protectionist lobbies. Various international organizations, in particular the World Bank, the Food and Agriculture Organization of the United Nations and the World Health Organization, began to join hands with the WTO by embarking on various programmes to develop the capacity of developing countries to implement the new international trade rules.

By 1999 these developments had led to high expectations that the third Ministerial Meeting, to be held in Seattle in December 1999, would decide to launch a new round of world trade negotiations that would address the UR's unfinished reform agenda and new challenges to liberal trade policies emanating from the international trading environment. However, the Seattle meeting broke down in acrimony on 3 December, shattering these expectations.[3]

The failure in Seattle is not unique in the history of world trade negotiations. The multilateral trading system has survived such setbacks before. For instance, an effort to launch a round in 1982 failed, and the UR, launched in 1986, broke down repeatedly. However, the damage the Seattle fiasco has done to the credibility of the WTO and to the process of global trade opening was so severe that it will take some time to regain the lost momentum and set the stage for a new round. In March 2001 the WTO announced that its members had decided to hold the fourth WTO Ministerial Meeting in Doha, Qatar, on 9–13 November 2001.

The Seattle collapse has worsened the deep division between the developing and the industrial countries about the future course of multilateral trade liberalization, which undoubtedly played a part in the collapse of the Seattle meeting. Worse still, the WTO's main critics, notably the trade unionists and environmentalists who brought Seattle to a standstill and who have increasingly come to see themselves as the real 'saviours' of the poor, are more powerful than ever. The halt to multilateral trade liberalization has also given new impetus to regional and bilateral efforts by an increasing number of developing countries (Moore 2001). These developments clearly illustrate that 'one size fits all' is not a good rule of thumb when it come to global trade negotiations. It is therefore vital that the implications of the implementation of UR agreements to date for developing countries and the factors constraining these countries' effective participation in the WTO are assessed carefully to set the background for a new round of multilateral negotiations.

To this end, this volume brings together ten papers by prominent economists and practitioners in the field on key facets of the post-UR debate on the world trading system as they relate to developing countries and to new challenges to liberal trade. As background, the next two sections of this chapter review WTO rules and the issues developing countries face in participating in the WTO system. The final section summarizes the main inferences arising from each chapter.

THE WTO AND NEW TRADE RULES

The WTO Agreement states that the WTO's objective is

> To provide a common institutional framework for the conduct of trade relations among its members ... with a view to raising standards of living, ensuring full employment and a large and steadily growing volume of real income and effective demand, and expanding the production of and trade in goods and services, while allowing for the optimal use of the world's resources in accordance with the objective of sustainable development. (WTO 1995, p. 1)

The agreement also emphasizes the need for the WTO to make 'positive efforts designed to ensure that developing countries, and especially the least developed among them, secure a share in the growth in international trade commensurate with the needs of their economic development'. (WTO 1995, p. 2).

As noted, while the GATT operated on a provisional basis, the WTO is a permanent international organization with a solid institutional framework. The MFN principle of the WTO requires that each member country treat all other members as most favoured as regards levying import duties, so as not to discriminate between them. Likewise, national treatment secures equal treatment between imported and domestic goods in the case of trade in goods. To provide the security and predictability of market access, members cannot change their concessional rates of duty agreed to and specified in their schedule annexed to the WTO Agreement. Duty is the sole instrument of regulating trade, and the introduction of QRs is generally prohibited. To promote fair trade, the WTO permits the use of some trade remedy instruments under specific circumstances, such as antidumping and countervailing duties, as well as general safeguards. There are, however, no special and differential treatment provisions in favour of developing country members.

The WTO administers 13 agreements regulating trade in goods and services and trade-related aspects of intellectual property. Under the GATT, a member had the discretion to accede to a particular agreement, but a country wishing to join the WTO must accept all the agreements under the 'single undertaking' concept. Of these agreements, the Uruguay Round Agreement on Agriculture (URAA) is aimed at liberalizing world trade in this sector in a gradual and progressive manner. Core elements in the agreement are, first, the so-called tariffication, which means that any form of QRs must be converted to tariff measures, either *ad valorem* or specific rates of duty. Second, industrial country members must make a 36 per cent tariff cut within six years. Third, the current import amount must be maintained. Fourth, as a trade remedy in this sector, a special safeguard measure may be introduced under certain conditions. Fifth, domestic support must be reduced by 20 per cent within six years and export subsidies must be reduced by 36 per cent in terms of expenditure on such subsidies.

The Agreement on Textiles and Clothing (ATC) provides new rules on trade in this sector. While trade in the sector was, and still is, subject to the Multi-Fiber Arrangement (MFA), it must be integrated into the GATT rules within ten years in four phases. All members who impose MFA quotas must increase their quota amounts by a given percentage during the progressive integration period. Given certain conditions, such members may invoke transitional safeguard measures under the surveillance of the Textiles Monitoring Body.

On issues relating to trade in goods, a number of agreements relate to nontariff measures, and aim at promoting and expanding international trade. The Agreement on Technical Barriers to Trade provides rules on international standards and conformity assessment systems, including packaging, marking and labelling requirements, that may create unnecessary obstacles to international trade. The Agreement on Trade-Related Investment Measures governs measures member governments have adopted to promote and regulate foreign direct investment. It prohibits measures inconsistent with GATT rules, namely, Article III on national treatment and Article XI on the elimination of QRs. The Agreement on Customs Valuation provides a set of precise methods for determining customs value for the purpose of collecting customs duties. Because many developing countries depend heavily on customs duties for their national revenues, a number of developing-country members have requested an extension of the deadline for implementing the agreement.

The Agreement on Preshipment Inspection stipulates rules for preshipment services that may give rise to unnecessary delays in shipment, such as verifying the quality, quantity, price and commodity classification of a particular good to avoid under- or overinvoicing at the time of shipment. The Agreement on Rules of Origin provides a set of rules on determining the country of origin of tradable goods and a framework for a plan to develop a precise method for determining the country of origin of all tradable goods within three years. The WTO and the World Customs Organization are still working on the methods to be applied to nonpreferential trade.

Under GATT rules two trade remedies are available against so-called unfair trade practices, namely, dumping and export subsidies. The 1994 Agreement on Implementation of Article VI of the GATT, also known as the Agreement on Antidumping, provides detailed rules and procedures. If the export price of a product is less than its normal sales price in the exporting country (the home market price), the product in question is considered to be dumped. The last three multilateral trade negotiations (Kennedy, Tokyo and Uruguay) have clarified and elaborated antidumping rules and procedures. The Agreement on Subsidies and Countervailing Measures defines various types of subsidies and provides a set of rules and procedures to invoke countervailing duty measures. A subsidy is defined as a financial contribution by a government or any public body to the nation's exporters with a view to making their products 'competitive' in world markets, and that thereby confers a benefit. A countervailing duty is a special duty levied by the government of an importing country to offset the artificial competitiveness created by subsidies.

With the rapid increase in trade in services, particularly among the industrial countries, the trading nations recognized the importance of this sector in economic activities and the need to establish discipline over this trade in a multilateral framework. The service sector was negotiated at the UR as one of the new areas, despite the negative position of developing countries in general that domestic service industries were still at an early stage of development, and thus they should not be subject to a variety of regulations. Nevertheless, the General Agreement on Trade in Services (GATS) provides a framework for governing trade in various services.

GATS has the following objectives: expanding trade in services; liberalizing such trade progressively through successive rounds of negotiations; achieving transparent rules and regulations; and increasing participation by developing countries. GATS covers all measures that affect trade in services. These are divided into cross-border supply of services (services that come from abroad into the territory of the member, for example, telecommunications), consumption abroad (delivery outside the territory of the member, for instance, tourism), commercial presence (local establishment of legal entities such as corporations), and the presence of so-called natural persons (the physical presence of a service supplier such as a doctor or lawyer).

WTO members' obligations under the GATS take two forms: unconditional and conditional. Unconditional obligations include MFN treatment, transparency and domestic regulation. In the case of conditional obligations, an important one is not to restrict international transfers and payments for current transactions. The GATS does provide certain exceptions, such as restrictions to safeguard the balance of payments and general and security exceptions. Commitments to liberalize trade in services by individual members are specified in their schedule of specific commitments for which national treatment and other obligations are imposed. For this reason, it is vital to expand specific commitments with increased participation by the developing countries. To this end, this services trade was treated in the Uruguay Round Agreement as one of the built-in agenda items (that is, an item to be further negotiated before the next round of multilateral trade talks), and negotiations have just started.

At the Tokyo Round, participating countries attempted to establish rules on trade in counterfeit goods, but such rules did not materialize. In the UR countries did agree to the Agreement on Trade-Related Aspects of Intellectual Property Rights (TRIPs). TRIPs, which stipulates minimum standards, covers seven intellectual property rights, namely: copyright and rights related to copyright; trademarks; geographical indications/origins; industrial designs; patents; layout designs (topographies) of integrated circuits; and undisclosed information. The two most important principles of the GATT, that is, MFN and national treatment, are applicable to TRIPs. A set of enforcement provisions is available, including those at the border as well as civil and administrative measures. Disputes concerning TRIPs are settled under the WTO dispute settlement framework.

Developing-country members and members whose economies are in transition can defer implementation of TRIPs for five years, while the least developed countries have ten years. Given the complexity of the issues TRIPs covers, many developing-country members are still not in a position to fully implement TRIPs, and further extensions to implementation of the agreement are being discussed at the WTO. The WTO and the World Intellectual Property Organization are providing developing countries with technical assistance in relation to TRIPs.

While GATT and WTO rules impose a number of obligations on members, such as applying MFN rates of duty and adhering to agreements on nontariff measures, instances arise when some members fail to comply with these obligations. As a result, the rights of other members may be nullified and impaired, for example, the European Union's (EU's) bananas case, Malaysia's automobile case, and India's QRs. For such cases, GATT provides two simple articles (XXII and XXIII) for the settlement of disputes. As a rule, the WTO regime respects efforts made by the parties to settle disputes through bilateral consultations. Only if this process fails, cases are taken up at the WTO. Even though the GATT did not provide precise and detailed rules and procedures for implementing the two articles, it developed and accumulated such rules and procedures on a *de facto* basis, in particular, panel proceedings, through cases over time. In the UR, practices for dispute settlements were codified in an international agreement known as the Understanding on Rules and Procedures Governing the Settlement of Disputes (DSU).

The DSU provides a single set of rules for all disputes arising from the implementation of all UR agreements. When a member has recourse to the DSU, a panel is convened to examine the case and to report its findings and recommendations to the General Council. Once the report has been approved, the party concerned takes WTO-consistent actions on the basis of the report. If action is not taken within a reasonable period of time, compensation may be provided to the party. If the party fails to take WTO-consistent action, a retaliatory action may be approved. Thus the DSU provides security and predictability to the multilateral trading system.

Major characteristics of DSU include detailed procedures established through experience, automatic application of the proceedings, the setting of clear-cut deadlines at each stage of panel proceedings, and implementation aimed at securing conformity of measures. When a member country requests the establishment of a panel consisting of three to five panelists, the Dispute Settlement Body decides to do so by 'reverse' consensus. A panel report is generally submitted six months after the panel's establishment. Third parties with substantial interest in a particular case may join the proceedings. The parties to the dispute may appeal the case to the Standing Appellate Body of seven members in relation to the legal interpretations developed by the panel. With the exception of appeal cases, a panel report is adopted by reverse consensus within 60 days of circulation of the report. The Dispute Settlement Body regularly monitors the implementation of panel reports by the parties concerned. Since the inception of the WTO, panels have been convened for almost 200 cases. Generally, the DSU works satisfactorily.

THE UR AND BEYOND: KEY ISSUES FOR DEVELOPING COUNTRIES

Many critical observers believe that to a large extent the UR's outcome has so far been tilted against the developing countries (Finger and Schuler 2000; Srinivasan 1998; Stiglitz 2000). Certain WTO agreements, most notably those related to TRIPs, were not necessarily in the interests of low-income countries. The phase-out of the MFA and the implementation of tariff reduction commitments under the URAA would create short-run adjustment costs for these countries. In general, the commitments developing countries have undertaken to reduce trade barriers and to reform trade procedures and regulations far outweigh the gains from market access commitments given by the industrial countries in areas where developing countries have a comparative advantage, particularly agriculture and textiles and clothing. Moreover, the costs involved in implementing reform obligations in trade procedures (for instance, import licensing procedures and customs valuation) and in many areas of regulation (such as technical, sanitary and phytosanitary standards and intellectual property law) are prohibitively costly, particularly for low-income countries.

When the implementation of the UR has been completed by 2005, agricultural protection in the industrial countries will still remain twice as costly as protection in manufacturing, even though manufacturing will have a much bigger share of the value of world production and trade than agricultural products, including processed food. Similarly, the abolition of the MFA quotas under the ATC will still leave high tariff barriers in the industrial countries, which will be far more discriminatory against the developing countries compared with their industrial-country counterparts in world trade in manufactured goods. Another possibility is that potential gains from market opening will soon be significantly reduced, if not completely erased, by the use of antidumping, country of origin and safeguard restrictions by industrial countries in the post-MFA era.

The new Dispute Settlement Mechanism (DSM) aims to play a key role in providing security and predictability to the multilateral trading system, and is envisaged to help eliminate the industrial-country bias embodied in the old system under the GATT. However, experience with the DSM over the last five years suggests that unilateralism in setting world trade rules has not altogether disappeared. In particular, smaller and poorer developing countries complain that settling disputes under the DSM is extremely costly (Hudec 1999).

As concerns the agenda for a future WTO round of trade negotiations, on balance, the case put forward by the developing countries for a limited 'development-oriented' agenda consisting of the built-in UR agenda relating to agriculture and services, the problems with implementing the UR commitments, the issues related to accessing the DSM for dispute settlement and the WTO's decisionmaking process seems strong. However, to make the next round a reality, the developing countries may have to concede some items from the broader agenda proposed by the industrial countries, such as competition policy, international investment rules, and the multifunctionality of agricultural reform.

The introduction of a social clause relating to labour standards and environmental issues in the WTO needs further consideration. The industrial countries should envisage discussing such development-related issues in other appropriate international forums, such as the International Labour Organisation (ILO) and the United Nations Environment Programme. Sanctions on formal sector employment of children in developing countries could well encourage them to seek employment in the informal sector, leading to more, not less, exploitation. There is little to recommend social labelling and codes of conduct as alternatives to trade sanctions. Of course, several alternative measures could be more effective in ensuring children's welfare, for example, flexible school hours, stipends to parents of children attending school, and incentives for employers to provide better working conditions for child workers that could include schooling and medical facilities.

Beginning negotiations on the movement of natural persons is important. This is an area where developing countries have a comparative advantage in the supply of skilled, semiskilled and unskilled labour. International development agencies, in particular the World Bank and regional development banks, should develop appropriate emergency safeguard mechanisms to cushion developing countries against excessive adjustment costs incurred in the process of opening up the services sector to foreign competition.

If properly designed and implemented, regional trading arrangements (RTAs) under various economic co-operation groupings can bring about dynamic economic gains by promoting competition and expanding markets and can facilitate multilateral trade liberalization. However, the proliferation of RTAs with overlapping membership and complicated operational norms relating to rules of origin could be counterproductive. The monitoring of RTAs by the WTO (under Article XXIV of the GATT) should, therefore, be strengthened. It should be streamlined to avoid costly tariff preferences and to ensure that regional trade preferences provided under each RTA be extended within a specified period to all WTO members on an MFN basis. However, the increasing trend in bilateral free trading arrangements appears to be a growing concern, and also a potential digression from the primary aim of achieving a comprehensive and rules-based multilateral trading system. While economic gains from the Association of Southeast Asian Nations (ASEAN) Free Trade Area (AFTA) in the areas of harmonizing customs procedures and tariff nomenclature and speeding up customs valuation methods among new members have been significant, one should be cautious in generalizing from this experience, because specific geopolitical factors have contributed to AFTA's success. The South Asian Association of Regional Cooperation has so far yielded few tangible benefits, but its members' commitment to economic co-operation has gained momentum in recent years in reaction to the changing global economic environment. Thus wider and deeper economic co-operation may develop.

Subregional economic co-operation promoted in Southeast Asia has succeeded in promoting common infrastructure development projects, and such co-operation should be encouraged to expand further. Another possibility is horizontal integration of such economic co-operation or of groupings, for example, across Southeast Asia, South Asia, Central Asia and the Pacific countries, to encourage the mobility of labour, capital and technology and to maximize trade creation. Ultimately, these initiatives could and should be instrumental in promoting a fairer and genuinely rules-based multilateral trading system.

There is a clear need for international initiatives to assist the least developed countries and the small economies in the process of global integration. To be effective, such initiatives should take the form of providing overt development support, such as helping with human capital development, promoting institutional reforms and enhancing the quality of governance, to enable these countries to grow faster and reap the benefits of being integrated within the global economy, rather than developing under the old-fashioned 'special and favourable treatments', such as debt write-offs and favoured market access, which invariably lock these countries into perpetual dependence.

Growth achieved through greater openness and nondiscriminatory domestic policy is an effective means to reducing poverty. However, some of the concerns about the adverse short-term effects of globalization and openness on certain vulnerable groups are legitimate and must be addressed through appropriate government policy. Trade openness leads to faster economic growth and economic growth leads to poverty reduction. Poverty-reducing growth may take place through economywide resource reallocation effects and exposure and access to foreign markets, capital and technology, but the extent of poverty reduction will also depend on other factors, such as initial conditions, socio-political structure, and governance. In the immediate term, however, trade liberalization may negatively affect the income growth of the poor, and thus appropriate social safety nets will have to be provided.

CONTRIBUTIONS IN THIS VOLUME

The rest of the book is organized in nine chapters. In Chapter 2, T.N. Srinivasan provides a comprehensive overview of the trade policy issues the developing countries face in the context of the world trading system. The chapter starts by noting that growth acceleration is an effective, if not the most effective, way to alleviate poverty, and that greater openness is an efficient way to achieve rapid growth. Srinivasan argues that while no simple one-to-one relationship exists between trade and poverty reduction, the evidence suggests that trade liberalization is generally a positive contributor to poverty alleviation. Redistribution without economic growth would simply redistribute poverty; it would not reduce poverty. Similarly, poverty reduction associated with growth generated through costly domestic and foreign borrowing, for instance, as occurred in India during the 1980s, is not sustainable.

Commenting on the current state of the world trading system, Srinivasan observes that despite significant trade liberalization under the GATT and WTO, there are still significant barriers to trade in primary commodities and labour-intensive manufacturing, the major areas of interest to developing countries. While barriers to capital flows have come down rapidly, barriers to labour flows and to transfers of technology and knowledge, both of which are extremely important to developing countries, have remained. He argues that the commitments under the UR agreements relating to a number of key aspects of the proposed reform agenda were tilted against the developing countries. The developing countries undertook several unprecedented obligations not only to reduce trade barriers, but also to implement significant reforms, both in trade procedures and in many areas of regulation, and established the basis for an appropriate business environment in their domestic economies. In return they obtained only a few commitments from the industrial countries to phase out GATT-inconsistent MFA quotas and to achieve limited liberalization of GATT-inconsistent intervention in agricultural trade. Moreover, the agreed phase-out of the infamous MFA by 2005 was a qualified benefit; since the UR Agreement was concluded, actions by the United States and the EU have created serious doubts about their commitment to liberalize trade in textiles and apparel. For example, they have either invoked or recommended safeguard and antidumping provisions to limit imports of textiles and apparel. Srinivasan also notes that for the developing countries, in particular the smaller and poorer developing countries, accessing the DSM is prohibitively costly. Thus the unilateralism in world trade rule setting that the strengthened DSM was intended to curb has not entirely disappeared.

As regards the possible agenda for a new round of world trade negotiations, Srinivasan discusses the advantages and disadvantages of a broad and a limited agenda. He notes that on balance, the case for a limited negotiating agenda consisting of the issues left over from the UR, the problems with implementing UR commitments and issues relating to the WTO's decisionmaking process is strong. He is emphatic that developing countries must remain united in resisting the introduction of a social clause relating to child labour standards into the WTO, while remaining receptive to reasoned discussions of labour standards in the ILO. In addition, they should strive to take environmental issues and TRIPs out of the WTO altogether and outlaw antidumping measures. Developing countries should not fall into the trap of once again asking for preferential access to world markets. On the contrary, they have much to gain from participating fully and as equal partners with the industrial countries in a nondiscriminatory, liberal world trading system. While engaging in such constructive negotiations, developing countries that still maintain high protection levels should continue to liberalize unilaterally. The pursuit of a liberal trade policy is always in the self-interest of developing countries.

Chapter 3 by Kym Anderson specifically focuses on liberalization initiatives in world agricultural trade, emphasizing achievements to date under the UR and the interests of and options for developing countries in the next round of negotiations. The chapter also examines some 'new' agricultural trade issues, in particular the sanitary and phytosanitary standards governing the world food trade and the debate on the multifunctionality of agricultural reforms. As concerns potential gains from the removal of farm subsidies, Anderson notes that about half of the estimated global economic welfare gains would come from reforms in countries of the Organization for Economic Co-operation and Development (OECD), with one-sixth coming from reforms in the developing countries. Developing countries as a group have a major stake in reform in the industrial countries, because distortionary farm and food policies in the industrial world account for 40 per cent of the cost to developing economies of global goods trade distortions. Full liberalization of OECD farm policies would boost global agricultural trade by more than 50 per cent, but would cause real international food prices to rise by only 5 per cent, given the potential global farm supply response to liberalization.

The issue of agricultural trade should also be looked at from the developing countries' side. Much of the distortion to incentives facing internationally competitive farmers stems from their own countries' nonagricultural policies. Export-oriented farmers have a negotiating interest not only in better access to food markets abroad, but also in more competition from abroad in their own economies' markets for nonfarm products. This applies not only to industrial goods, but also to services. The inclusion of new trade agenda issues in the next round would have the advantage of participation by more OECD nonagricultural groups that, depending on the issue, could counterbalance forces favouring agricultural and other sectoral protection. Anderson observes that almost all developing countries have an interest in the agricultural component of the next round of multilateral trade negotiations, either directly or indirectly. Even if a country's national economic welfare were to decline following the change in its terms of trade resulting from global trade liberalization, that does not imply that the country would be better off by not participating in the round. On the contrary, failure to liberalize would result in welfare falling even more, because the country would forego the economic efficiency gains resulting from reforming its own policies. The net economic gain from liberalization is likely to be greater the wider the sectoral and commodity coverage of liberalization, because wider coverage reduces the possibility that reform is confined to sectors and commodities that are not the most distorted.

To further the agricultural reform process, Anderson proposes banning farm export subsidies, further decoupling of farm income support measures, tightening the 'green box' criteria to reduce the loopholes they provide for continuing output-increasing subsidies and reducing the aggregate measure of support. However, the most important area requiring attention concerns import market access. Tariffication appeared to be a great step forward; however, the combination of dirty tariffication by the industrial economies (setting bound rates well above applied rates) and the adoption of extremely high ceiling bindings by the developing economies allows many countries to continue varying their protection as they wish in response to changes in domestic or international food markets. Reducing bound tariffs from the current range of 50 to more than 150 per cent to 0 to 15 per cent is one of the major challenges that lie ahead.

Anderson proposes that developing countries with significant interest in agricultural trade should be proactive and take the high ground in the next round by demanding faster reform of both farm and textile trade in return for opening up their own trade. Their wish list should include the following:

- removing tariffs on tropical agricultural products, including processed food;
- replacing specific tariffs with *ad valorem* tariffs on imports of interest to developing-country exporters, because the former (which currently apply to 42 per cent of US and EU agricultural tariffs) discriminate against products of lower quality and those whose international price is declining over time;
- using the Swiss formula approach for rationalizing declared bound tariffs with a view to reducing tariff peak escalation cost;
- seeking a firm phase-out date for agricultural tariff quotas, as was obtained for textiles and clothing in the UR, but with limits on the extent to which safeguards can replace the QRs at the end of the phase-out period;
- seeking firm commitments, preferably written into OECD countries' schedules, on the extent of economic and technical assistance that they will provide to help developing countries cope with adjustment to reforms, especially the least developed countries and the net food-importing countries;
- supporting the liberalization of trade in maritime services, given the potential for the cartelized OECD firms that own most liners to extract much of the exporters' gains from liberalization in goods trade via higher markups.

As regards the so-called multifunctionality of agricultural reforms, Anderson argues for accommodating the nontrade concerns of security of food supplies, the protection of the environment and the viability of rural areas in the agricultural reform process. He also discusses effective ways to ensure that the reform process continues or accelerates in the years to come. Access to traditional agricultural markets is likely to remain the main priority for the next round, because agricultural protection rates in OECD countries will still be huge. Less precise (dirty) tariffication and the introduction of tariff rate quotas in the URAA mean that large commitments in terms of bound tariff cuts and/or quota expansions will be needed if agricultural protection is to be reduced significantly. The chapter concludes by reviewing some of the options facing developing-country negotiators. The millennium round thus offers probably the best prospects ever for developing countries in general – and their rural communities in particular – to secure growth-enhancing reforms. Note that the so-called concessions that are offered are actually a win–win game in terms of nations' economic welfare. The liberalization of access to traditional agricultural markets should be the key priority issue in the next WTO round, given the enormous potential for global and developing-country welfare gains from reducing agricultural protection. From an agricultural development perspective, attention should also focus on reducing protection granted to other manufacturing and services industries. Protection in those sectors still bestows a significant anti-agricultural bias in many developing countries, making it more difficult for them to benefit from the agricultural and textile trade reforms of OECD countries.

In Chapter 4 Prema-chandra Athukorala examines agricultural trade liberalization and the phasing out of the MFA in the light of the experiences of the Asian developing countries. He also focuses on post-UR issues in these areas and provides a number of suggestions for the future reform agenda. The UR was concluded at a time when most Asian developing countries had already embarked on significant unilateral trade liberalization reforms. However, in all countries reforms in agricultural trade have generally lagged behind those in manufacturing. The contribution of the URAA to redress the imbalance in the reform process has so far been marginal, but the new WTO regime does offer opportunities for domestic reform and effective engagement in multilateral negotiations to further the liberalization process and to keep the policies from regressing to the old QRs. Likewise, the agreed abolition of the ATC is important for the effective integration of labour-surplus countries into a rules-based trading system in line with their comparative advantage.

To be effective, planning to free agriculture in the developing countries should involve simultaneous reforms of import and export regimes and domestic production support mechanisms. The provision of financial support to implement the required social safety net measures can play an important role in making the required comprehensive reforms politically palatable and feasible. While overloading the WTO with matters that fall beyond its purview may be counterproductive, there is certainly a case for a co-ordinated approach involving the WTO and international financial institutions, including regional development banks, in this sphere. The policy options for world agricultural reforms suggested in the light of South Asian experience include: reducing bound tariffs rapidly to realistic levels, with a view to providing an effective anchor for the ongoing liberalization process; providing developing countries with more institutional support for making the best use of the DSM; and engaging in effective consultative efforts to improve the capacity of developing countries in meeting international standards required under the Sanitary and Phytosanitary Agreement.

In the area of textiles and clothing, the abolition of the MFA quota regime, despite inevitable short-run adjustment problems that may be created for some developing countries, is important for the effective integration of developing countries into a rules-based world trading system. Thus these countries should make every effort to see that the industrial countries honour their commitments under the ATC through active engagement in multilateral trade negotiations. At the same time, they should prepare themselves to face competitive market conditions in the post-MFA era by speeding up domestic liberalization reforms. The other issue discussed in the chapter includes the possible relocation of clothing production from the high-cost newly industrializing economies (NIEs) to Asia's labour-surplus countries following the abolition of MFA quotas, and the complementary role of trade liberalization and foreign direct investment liberalization in the expansion of clothing and other labour-intensive export product lines in latecomer countries.

In Chapter 5, Ulrike Grote, Claus Deblitz and Susanne Stegmann address the often-voiced concern in trade policy debate that the costs of higher environmental standards give the industrial countries an unfair competitive advantage over the developing countries. The chapter focuses on an in-depth comparative study of the production and processing of vegetable oils, grain and broilers in Brazil, Germany and Indonesia. The results of their empirical study are presented against the backdrop of a succinct survey of the literature on environmental standards and competitiveness and an overview of the importance of the selected agricultural products in international trade and in the export trade of the countries under study.

Based on the results of their firm-level investigation, the authors argue that for the typical firm, the impact of environmental standards on production costs is relatively small compared with the total cost differences due to wage levels and the prices of land, machines, buildings and equipment. Such costs could be binding only in the presence of small profit margins resulting from other firm- and country-specific factors. The authors also stress that country-specific differences in environmental standards are not only determined by climate, but also by population density, national economic and social conditions, and differences in the scarcity of environmental goods. Thus the current emphasis on the possible adverse effects of imposing environmental standards seems misguided.

Arnab Basu, Nancy Chau and Ulrike Grote critically review the widely debated issue of labour standards and social labelling in Chapter 6. Since the world trade negotiations failed in Seattle in December 1999, the conflict about social dimensions in the context of trade liberalization has become evident. While the industrial countries ask for the inclusion of minimum labour standards, referring to hours of work, safety at the workplace and/or the employment of child labour, in a multilateral trading system, the developing countries are strictly opposed to this idea and consider labour standards as disguised protectionism. The authors review the broader issues related to the inclusion of minimum labour standards in the form of a social clause under the WTO by looking at opposing arguments regarding the benefit of imposing a set of minimum labour standards on developing countries. They further analyse whether social labelling offers an alternative to raising low labour standards.

On the issue of child labour, the authors argue that even if trade sanctions improved the working conditions of a small percentage of child workers in developing countries, such measures could ultimately do more harm than good to the poor. Working children contribute a substantial proportion of their family income in these countries. More important, sanctions affecting formal sector employment could well encourage children to seek employment in the informal sector, leading to more, not less, exploitation.

The authors are sympathetic to the view expressed by the developing countries that the inclusion of a social clause in the WTO as proposed by some industrial countries would play into the hands of the protectionist lobby in the industrial countries, leading to a loss of international competitiveness and market access by developing-country exporters. They also stress that any concerns about labour rights and the exploitation of labour should be dealt with through the ILO's regulatory procedures. The enforcement mechanisms would be limited to international pressure and persuasion, and there would be no explicit sanctions, such as import bans for traded goods, as would be possible under the WTO. The authors note that if properly implemented through the ILO (and not as part of international trade policy), higher labour standards would have some positive effects by helping governments that find it difficult to implement such standards for domestic political reasons and by promoting the development of democratic institutions. As to the efficiency and equity effects of higher labour standards, the authors observe that the literature provides no clear answers.

Different labour standards are perfectly legitimate for countries with different preferences, technologies and factor endowments. Unless standards are appropriate for the level of development in a country, they are unlikely to improve the situation of workers, and standards that are too high would be widely ignored. Despite the possibility of a joint welfare gain, whether industrial and developing countries will simultaneously adopt high labour standards endogenously depends crucially on the nature of competition between them. Trade competition may, under some circumstances, exacerbate the exporting countries' failure to improve labour standards. According to the authors, including a social clause in the WTO is likely to make developing countries worse off. Instead, diverse labour standards should reflect different countries' preferences, technologies and factor endowments.

Social labelling – the provision of information via product labels on the use of acceptable labour standards in the production process – if properly implemented, has the potential to act as a superior, market-based alternative to the direct imposition of labour standards on developing-country producers. It is a corrective policy that aims to discourage unfair labour practices by redressing consumers' lack of information about such practices. However, this instrument suffers from a number of drawbacks. The price premium for labelled products raises incentives for false labelling in the presence of imperfect monitoring and may render social labelling efforts futile. In this case the effect is a lowering of the price premium and a decrease in the number of producers who choose to employ higher standards. Also, explicit labelling renders unlabelled products particularly vulnerable to allegations of unfair trade practices, and provides a lever for interest groups in industrial countries to advocate restrictions on market access. Even if credibly enforced, social labelling may not translate into an improvement of workers' welfare. In particular, wage increases that result from the establishment of social labelling schemes may lead to a decline in the demand for labour. Thus in developing countries that already face high unemployment rates, social labelling has the potential of pushing workers from poverty into destitution. The authors make a strong case against bringing labour standards or social labelling to the international trade policy agenda.

Chapter 7 by Kerrin Vautier is devoted to the issues related to competition policy and provides an excellent overview of the relevant conceptual and policy issues. Following some introductory remarks on the meaning and scope of competition policy and its importance as a new trade-related issue, the chapter explains at length the approaches being taken to competition policy in both the Pacific Economic Cooperation Council and the WTO. The chapter emphasizes the importance of the council's principles on economic policy formation in member countries, as well as their relevance for identifying and dealing with certain competition issues at a multilateral level in the context of the WTO. Competition policy has become an increasingly prominent topic on international agendas and is currently the subject of serious discussion at the regional and international levels. Various initiatives reflect a growing interest in the role of competition in market processes and economic policy. However, there is little prospect for a single workable approach to transnational competition issues, let alone any prospect of multilateral competition rules and supranational enforcement. Vautier notes that while the three major players, the EU, Japan and the United States, agree on the importance of domestic competition law and its enforcement based on common objectives, there is a fundamental divergence of views relating to the WTO's role and how antidumping relates to international discussions on competition policy.

Competition is probably best described as a continual process of discovery by existing and potential suppliers of what customers want and what prices they are prepared to pay, taking product and service quality into account. Competition-driven policies should therefore be directed at creating and maintaining those market conditions that are conducive to this process of discovery, responsiveness and innovation. Encouraging competitive business is about fostering opportunities for businesses to compete on their merits. This welfare-enhancing role is the responsibility of both governments and business. As markets enlarge beyond their traditional country boundaries, the need for government co-operation in promoting business competition in these rapidly globalizing markets increases. A review of efficiency is still necessary to ensure that markets serve as the best guide for the quantity, quality and composition of goods and services to be produced and consumed. In this regard Vautier makes a number of propositions.

Commenting on the relationship between trade measures and competition, Vautier emphasizes that to achieve efficiency and welfare gains, the impacts of trade measures on competition need to be brought within a multilateral framework under the purview of the WTO. Any arguments that international competition issues are confined to anticompetition business practices, and hence to antitrust policy, should be rejected for what they are, namely, an inappropriate narrow approach that risks leaving government measures, including trade measures, off the competition agenda. Lowering border restrictions on trade and exposing trade measures to competition criteria through multilateral initiatives are necessary conditions for stimulating business conduct that favours competition. However, these conditions are unlikely to be sufficient. To be effective, initiatives at the multilateral level need to be reinforced by unilateral policy responses at the national level in accordance with competition principles. Vautier believes that competition policy should be treated as an important element of a comprehensive policy package aimed at creating the pro-competitive incentive structure needed to reap the economic gains resulting from global integration. Based on the experiences of the Pacific Economic Cooperation Council, she also argues that other regional groupings should include competition policy as a priority item in their reform agendas.

In Chapter 8, Yongzheng Yang examines the implications of the emergence of China as a major exporter of labour-intensive manufactured goods on the export competitiveness of other export-oriented economies in East Asia. Although Yang does not directly examine the possible implications of China's imminent entry into the WTO, his results are directly relevant for broadening the understanding of this important issue. Yang begins by discussing the fallacy of composition argument, which casts doubt on the role of export-led industrialization in developing countries. The key message is that such an argument is fundamentally flawed and that export-led industrialization through global integration is the only effective path for sustained, equitable growth. Yang proceeds to examine the implications of export competition from China for the export-led growth process in other countries in the region. Based on simulations using the global trade policy analysis model, which permits capturing economy-wide implications of the issue, he comes out against the widely held view that intense competition from China would crowd out opportunities for others. In a world of differentiated products, argues Yang, developing countries not only compete with, but also complement, one another. The net effect on any particular country of China's success at expanding its manufactured exports would depend crucially on the intensity of its trade with its competitors and partners as well as the extent of competition in third-country markets. Thus the net effect of competition from China could be favourable, rather than negative, for other countries in the region.

Yang also believes that China's decision to stick to the exchange rate peg during the 1997 Asian financial crisis was well thought out, but with the deepening of reform, China will be compelled to move toward greater exchange rate flexibility in the near future. However, from his model simulation results he infers that eventual devaluation of the renminbi would not have a significant negative effect on other countries in the region. China is still a much smaller player in the global economy than the EU, Japan and the United States, which provide markets for the bulk of exports from the countries in the region.

Economic integration is an important subject that has been widely discussed in recent years. In this connection, a recent development in RTAs has been their tendency to both widen and deepen. Of the several economic integration initiatives, ASEAN is relatively active. In Chapter 9, Jayant Menon examines the impacts of widening and the progress of deepening in AFTA. As a result of the widening of AFTA its membership has grown from six countries at its inception in 1992 to ten countries currently. The new entrants will gain from membership in AFTA, with the main benefits likely to come from improved access to markets in the region, and increased foreign investment flows. This widening has increased AFTA's diversity and made it more heterogeneous, but it also threatens to fragment AFTA through the emergence of a two-tier system consisting of a developed and an underdeveloped segment. The AFTA-Plus programme is designed to deepen regional integration. Apart from harmonizing customs procedures and tariff nomenclature, progress has been limited. In services and intellectual property rights, for instance, the multilateral rather than the regional approach would appear to be both more effective and less likely to be subject to distortions. In regard to foreign investment, the preferential access arrangement proposed in AFTA could distort the investment climate and result in unequal gains to old and new members.

The empirical literature suggests that countries with more open (outwardly oriented) economies have grown faster than closed ones. Another observation is that trade openness is generally beneficial for poor people. In this context Chapter 10 by Ramesh Adhikari deals with the debate on the link between trade policy reforms, growth and poverty reduction. He examines conceptual issues on openness, growth and poverty reduction; key effects of trade policy reforms on the poor; and how openness could be made more poverty reducing. Economists have claimed many benefits for greater openness to trade and investment, including a reallocation of resources in line with comparative advantage, increased economic efficiency and faster growth, additional employment opportunities for labour due to the expansion of labour-intensive industries, productivity growth and technological advancement and poverty reduction. Many countries that opted for trade openness have achieved faster economic growth and reduced absolute poverty. However, the benefits arising from trade policy reform also vary depending on the type and extent of reforms and country-specific circumstances. Trade policy reforms could hurt poor people in the short run because of some unavoidable costs during the adjustment period in the form of losses of jobs, traditional businesses and subsidies and reduced public investment in the social and infrastructure sectors. Adhikari observes that empirical evidence on adjustment time and costs subsequent to trade policy reform is limited.

While there is no straightforward answer as to how to make trade policy reform more poverty reducing, some obvious areas of reform could affect the incomes of the poor. Trade policy reform is only one of several important policy variables for poverty reduction. It works more effectively when the reform is comprehensive, markets are liberal and functioning, and institutions are sufficiently market friendly. Adhikari stresses that trade policy reform and poverty reduction issues should be addressed systematically under the overall development strategy of the country concerned and co-ordinated in a comprehensive and integrated manner. Furthermore, he urges that policy-makers should start by removing those policy measures, institutions and practices that hurt the poor the most.

NOTES

1. The purpose of convening the Havana conference was to consider and ratify a charter for an international trade organization with a standing equal to that of the IMF and the World Bank. However, such an organization did not come into existence because the United States and some other countries did not ratify the charter. Consequently the GATT, which was set up under a Protocol of Provisional Application signed by 23 contracting parties as a temporary organization to be subsumed later in the international trade organization, remained the only framework governing world trade until the WTO was set up in 1995 (Srinivasan 1999, p. 1050).
2. The Ministerial Conference is the topmost body of the WTO under the governance structure set up by the WTO Agreement.
3. For discussions on factors that led to the Seattle débâcle see *The Economist* (1999a,b), Rajapatirana (2000) and Sampson (2000). A consensus view from these and other postmortems is that the claim by trade unionists and environmentalists that they single-handedly derailed the Seattle summit is wrong. The key factors included the Clinton administration's last-minute concessions to labour unions and environmental lobbies in an election year; the lack of adequate preparation on the part of the WTO (which remained leaderless during May–September 1999), in particular, in bridging the widening gap between the United States and the European Union over agriculture and that between rich and poor countries over labour standards; and the abrasive style of Charlene Barshefsky, who chaired the talks and acted as the leader of the US negotiating team, which proved ill suited to achieving consensus. Relating to the latter point, *The Economist* (1999b, p. 17) reported: 'Many developing countries bridled at her clumsy attempts to impose an American-drafted deal that ignored their concerns.'

REFERENCES

Economist (1999a), 'A Global Disaster', 11 December, pp. 17–18.

Economist (1999b), 'The Nongovernmental Order: Will NGOs Democratise, or Merely Disrupt, Global Governance?', 11 December, pp. 18–19.

Finger, J. Michael and Philip Schuler (2000), 'Implementation of the Uruguay Round Commitments: The Development Challenge', *World Economy*, **23** (3), 511–25.

Hudec, R.E. (1999), 'The New WTO Dispute Settlement Procedure: An Overview of the First Three Years', *Minnesota Journal of Global Trade*, **8** (1), 34–56.

Jackson, John (1989), *The World Trading System*, Cambridge, MA: MIT Press.

Krueger, Anne O. (ed.) (1999), 'Introduction', in *The WTO as an International Organization*, Chicago: University of Chicago Press, pp. 1–27.

Moore, Mike (2001), 'The WTO: Challenges Ahead', speech at the National Press Club, 5 February, Canberra. Available on http://www.wto.org.

Rajapatirana, Sarath (2000), *The Trade Policies of Developing Countries: Recent Reforms and New Challenges*, Washington, DC: American Enterprise Institution Press.

Sampson, Garry P. (2000), 'The World Trade Organization After Seattle', *World Economy*, **23** (7), 1097–117.

Srinivasan, T.N. (1998), *Developing Countries and the Multilateral Trading System*, Delhi: Oxford University Press.

Srinivasan, T.N. (1999), 'Developing Countries in the World Trading System: From GATT, 1947 to the Third Ministerial Meeting of WTO, 1999', *World Economy*, **22** (7), 1047–64.

Stiglitz, Joseph E. (2000), 'Two Principles for the Next Round or How to Bring Developing Countries in from the Cold', *World Economy*, **23** (3), 437–58.
WTO (World Trade Organization) (1995), *The Results of Uruguay Round*, Geneva.

2. Emerging issues in the world trading system

T.N. Srinivasan

The third Ministerial Meeting of the WTO in Seattle in December 1999 ended in a spectacular collapse without a ministerial declaration, let alone a decision to start a new round of multilateral trade negotiations. Assorted groups consisting of anarchists, die-hard protectionists, well-intentioned but naive individuals genuinely concerned about the welfare of the poor and child workers in developing countries and others for whom the cause of the poor was a cloak for the pursuit of their own self-interests had all converged in Seattle to express their opposition to what they perceived to be the evil juggernaut of globalization.

Undoubtedly the street demonstrations by these groups were disruptive, but they had little to do with the collapse of the ministerial meeting. Odell (2000) points out that the real reasons for the collapse were basically three: the inadequate preparation before the Seattle meeting; the inclusion of too many controversial issues in the negotiating agenda; and the poor management of the meeting, including, in particular, that by the leader of the most powerful delegation, Charlene Barshefsky of the United States, who also served as the meeting chair. In addition, the schedule allowed insufficient time to iron out substantial differences among the delegations. Yet some of the demonstrators mistakenly believe they had succeeded in preventing a successful ministerial meeting, and were thus encouraged to organize protests, albeit less violent than those in Seattle, in Bangkok, Washington, DC, and elsewhere whenever a high-level meeting of the IMF, the United Nations Conference on Trade and Development (UNCTAD), the World Bank, or any such organization was being held. We have not seen the last of such protests.

Clearly many people are uneasy, and perhaps fearful, that the forces of globalization are beyond their control and will inevitably marginalize them. Those who are convinced of the benefits of globalization, among whom I count myself, have been put on the defensive, and the voices of the likely beneficiaries, particularly poor workers and their dependants in developing countries, have not been heard.

In the United States, the American Federation of Labor–Congress of

Industrial Organizations, which claims to speak for the workers of the world, does not even represent a majority of the workers in the United States, let alone those in developing countries. One could also question whether some of the nongovernmental organizations (NGOs) that are active in the antitrade movement represent more than a small segment of the population. Indeed, the uneasiness with globalization has found expression in the writings and speeches delivered at many talk-fests on globalization and the publications resulting from them. It is also evident that the response of institutions such as the IMF, the World Bank and the regional banks and the United Nations to the critics of globalization suggests hastiness and over-reaction (see, for example, Grunberg and Khan 2000).

Some of the concerns about the effects of globalization on the poor are indeed legitimate and must be addressed; however, unqualified pessimism is not only unwarranted, but also counterproductive. Assertions such as those implicit in Grunberg's questions in her introduction (Grunberg and Khan 2000) that globalization is not improving the lot of millions of the world's poor not only have no factual basis, but could hurt the cause of poverty alleviation by delaying needed reforms in developing countries. For example, China in the early 1980s and India in the early 1990s moved away from autarkic development strategies and opened up and liberalized their economies. Both have experienced more rapid growth since that time than in the three preceding decades. These are also the two countries in which an overwhelming majority of the world's poor live, particularly in rural areas. According to national data, in both countries poverty has declined as growth has accelerated.

The association between an acceleration in the rate of economic growth and poverty reduction has also been observed elsewhere and at other times. Even though we are well aware that correlation and association are not causation, economic theory and practical experience provide strong support for the proposition that growth acceleration is an effective, if not the most effective, means to alleviate poverty and that greater openness is an efficient means to achieve rapid growth. Moore, director general of the WTO, has eloquently argued the case for openness from the perspective of the poor, most recently in the *Financial Times* (19 June 2000). A special study commissioned by the WTO on trade, income disparity and poverty (Ben-David, Nordström and Winters 2000) concludes that 'Trade provides an important contribution toward the economic growth of nations – in particular, for those countries that are lagging behind their trade partners – and hence also potentially faster poverty alleviation' (p. 5), and that 'While there is no simple one-to-one relationship between trade and poverty, the evidence seems to indicate that trade liberalisation is generally a *positive contributor* to poverty alleviation' (p. 6, emphasis in the original). Underplaying the roles of growth and openness in alleviating poverty – as some academics, policymakers, senior World Bank officials (Wolfensohn and Stiglitz 2000) and misguided spokesmen from some NGOs have been doing – is self-defeating.

To say that growth and openness are vital for poverty alleviation is, of course, not to say that growth will be associated with poverty alleviation always and everywhere, that greater openness promotes growth and welfare always and everywhere, and that the global trading system has always been responsive and enabling from the perspective of developing countries. On the contrary, growth that is the result of ever greater investment in countries where the incentives for efficient use of an increasing stock of human and physical capital are absent is unlikely to be an effective instrument for poverty alleviation. In any case, such growth is unsustainable. The late, unlamented Soviet Union provides a classic example of such growth. And growth generated by expansionism financed by costly domestic and foreign borrowing, as was the case in India during the 1980s, while alleviating poverty while it lasts, is unsustainable, and hence cannot alleviate poverty in the long run. Also, opening the economy to external investment while high barriers protect inefficient domestic industries is a prescription for the wrong type of tariff-jumping investment to come in. Such investment, which is based on exploiting protected domestic markets of limited size rather than on exploiting large world markets through exports, is unlikely to generate rapid and efficient growth. When it comes to markets for primary commodities and labour-intensive manufacturing and services in which developing countries have a comparative advantage, the global trading system has not been liberal. Finally, while the barriers to capital flows have fallen rapidly, the barriers to labour flows and to transfers of technology and knowledge, both of which are extremely important to developing countries, have remained.

Should we then conclude that developing countries should insulate their economies from the world economy and not participate in the forums that set the rules of the world trading game? Should they abandon policies promoting growth and instead adopt redistributive policies? The answer to both questions is a resounding no. Instead of insulating themselves from the world economy, developing countries should eliminate domestic distortions that prevent them from exploiting the opportunities that the global economy offers fully and efficiently, as well as continue to liberalize their foreign trade unilaterally. Above all, they should participate effectively and on an equal basis in any multilateral negotiations that set global trading rules so that the resulting system is nondiscriminatory and liberal. The issue of growth versus redistribution is a nonissue. The redistribution of income in a nation that is, on average, poor will not alleviate the poverty of many; it will just redistribute the poverty. Without sustained growth there is no lasting solution to the problem of poverty.[1] On the one hand, a domestic environment that is conducive to exploiting the opportunities offered by the global economy is clearly essential for accelerating growth and enhancing its capacity to alleviate poverty. On the other hand, it is equally important that the world trading and financial system do not discriminate against the developing economies, and an effective means for ensuring that it does not is for developing countries to participate fully in the system.

In the context presented above, the following section examines whether the UR Agreement was tilted against developing countries.

THE UR AGREEMENT: WAS IT TILTED AGAINST DEVELOPING COUNTRIES?

Unlike agreements on earlier rounds of multilateral trade negotiations, which largely covered commitments on measures at the border such as tariff and quotas, the UR Agreement involved behind-the-border commitments, many of which required developing countries to undertake major institutional development as well as to create new institutions. They undertook several 'unprecedented obligations not only to reduce trade barriers, but to implement significant reforms both on trade procedures (e.g. import licensing procedures, customs valuation) and on many areas of regulation that establish the basic business environment in the domestic economy (e.g. technical, sanitary and phytosanitary standards, intellectual property law)' (Finger and Schuler 2000, p. 511). For example, 'countries that did not have patent or copyright laws were obliged to enact them, to offer remedies for infringements, and educate officials in how to carry them out' (Odell 2000, p. 3). Under the single undertaking rule, participating countries had to accept all the multilateral agreements relating to goods and services, to trade-related aspects of intellectual property rights, and to understandings on dispute settlement and trade policy review mechanisms. Thus they could not pick and choose which of the many agreements to accept. In fact, only four plurilateral agreements (on civil aircraft, government procurement, the dairy industry, and bovine meat) did not form part of the single undertaking.

Some developing countries had begun liberalizing their trade barriers unilaterally even before the UR Agreement was signed in Marrakesh in April 1994. Indeed, it was very much in their interests to do so, although, in the mercantilist illogic of the GATT negotiations, they did not get credit for these unilateral 'concessions'. Under the agreement, developing countries dramatically increased the percentage of their bound tariffs, from 21 per cent before the agreement to 73 per cent. They also agreed to phase out the QRs on imports of manufactured goods. Clearly, given their high levels of protection from tariffs and QRs before the UR, these commitments to liberalize were certainly in their self-interest. The commitments undertaken under trade-related investment measures include the phase-out of domestic content requirements and export obligations imposed on foreign-owned enterprises and their subsidiaries.

Commitments under TRIPs were far reaching, including major revisions of domestic patent laws, for example, countries that did not grant product patents before TRIPs would have to grant such patents after TRIPs came into force. There is no doubt that but for strong US pressure, TRIPs would not have been included in the UR negotiating agenda, let alone would an agreement have been reached to include it in the WTO. The empirical evidence either on whether patents are even needed to stimulate innovation, or in favour of a uniform 20-year patent life, is not strong. The evidence that a minimum 50-year term for copyrights is excessively long is convincing. Yet the TRIPs agreement imposes a uniform 20-year life span for patents and 50 years for copyrights. Some estimates (Maskus 2000, table 6.1) suggest that because of TRIPs, there will be a massive rent transfer of US$8.3 billion from the rest of the world to just six industrial countries (of which US$5.8 billion will accrue to the United States).

Clearly the range of commitments developing countries undertook under the UR Agreement is far more extensive than those in any of the previous rounds. Even though many of the commitments were in these countries' interests, given the mercantilism of the GATT negotiations, asking what they got in return is not unreasonable. Even after the UR concessions by industrial countries, 'significant trade barriers in the form of high tariff peaks (exceeding 12 percent but in some cases reaching or exceeding 300 percent) and tariff escalation will continue to affect many exports from developing countries' (UNCTAD 1999, p. 41). The decision to bring agricultural trade back into the GATT was indeed an important achievement. However, the attempt to subject it to disciplines similar to those that govern trade in manufactures was only partially successful: export subsidies were reduced but not eliminated; domestic support measures were restricted but not removed; and the process of 'tariffication' of pre-existing nontariff measures became so 'dirty' that the bound levels of tariffs (from which scheduled reductions were to take place) were set way beyond prevailing applied levels. UNCTAD (1999, p. 41) comments that 'In agriculture, exports from developing countries remain severely hampered by massive domestic support and export subsidy programs in developed countries, by peak tariffs and by difficulties in the implementation of the tariff quota system.' To be fair, one should recognize that some developing countries viewed agricultural export subsidies, such as those in Europe, as being in their interest given that they were importers of the subsidized commodities.

An ostensibly major benefit to the developing countries from the UR

Agreement was the phase-out of the infamous MFA by 2005. However, this is a qualified benefit for several reasons. First of all, under the MFA exporters bilaterally negotiate quotas on exports of textiles and apparel with each importer. Such quotas are egregious violations of the GATT's fundamental principles of nondiscrimination and nonuse of QRs. Phasing out a violation of GATT principles cannot possibly be viewed as a concession to developing countries to which they have to respond by granting their own concessions, even if one accepted the mercantilist illogic of the GATT negotiations. Second, even the phase-out is heavily back-loaded: products accounting for as much as 49 per cent of the value of 1990 imports could still be under quota restrictions as of 31 December 2004, just before the phase-out. Third, after the phase-out of quotas the industrial countries would still retain significant tariff barriers on their imports of textiles and apparel.

Since the agreement on the phase-out of the MFA was concluded, actions by the United States and EU have thrown serious doubt on their commitment to liberalize trade in textiles and apparel. Safeguards and antidumping provisions have either been invoked or recommended to limit imports of textiles and apparel. For example, in April 1995 the United States imposed restrictions on imports of women's and girls' wool coats from India. India complained to the Textile Monitoring Body set up under the ATC and a panel was established to decide on the complaint. However, because the United States removed the restrictions before the panel met, further proceedings were terminated at India's request. Based on another complaint by India, a panel was established to examine the imposition by the United States of restrictions on imports of woven wool shirts and blouses. The panel found that the US restrictions violated the ATC. Although the United States lost the case, the fact that it took safeguard actions is indicative of the possibility of such actions by others.

The European Commission (the same one that was tainted by allegations of corruption and some of whose members had to resign in 1999) recommended the imposition of a provisional antidumping duty on imports of unbleached (grey) cotton fabrics originating from China, Egypt, India, Indonesia, Pakistan and Turkey. These imports were subject to bilaterally negotiated MFA quotas, and therefore exporters could not increase their sales by dumping. If they could not increase their sales, they obviously could not hurt their competitors in the EU; hence such antidumping duties had no rationale other than protectionism (Hindley 1997a,b). Fortunately the EU ministers did not accept the Commission's recommendation.

The developing countries became concerned that US restrictions and EU measures might be the first among many such so-called safeguard actions to come. Although such actions have to be terminated by 1 January 2005, in the interim the damage to developing countries could be substantial. A failure to live up to the UR commitments in textiles and apparel would be damaging for yet another reason: the developing countries might then revert to their perception that the WTO, like the GATT, largely serves the interests of the industrial countries. Ruggeiro, the former director general of the WTO, was clearly aware of the dangers of failing to adhere to the agreed pace of implementation of the phase-out of the MFA.[2]

In mid-1996 Pakistan, acting for a group of developing countries, the United States, the EU and others, presented a paper to the WTO Goods Council on the issues relating to the implementation of the ATC. The paper stated that 'the developed importing members were not living up to the liberalizing spirit of the agreement and the interests of the developing countries were not being served. Industrialized members countered that they had fully met the commitment that they had made and argued that some exporting countries retained high import barriers' (WTO 1997, pp. 22–3).

The issues most debated in the papers submitted by Pakistan and other countries to the Goods Council related to the pace of the phase-out of the MFA, with the developing countries complaining that importing countries were using the four-step procedure to postpone the integration of textiles into the GATT until the last day, with only one quota being removed in the first step. The industrial countries pointed to the agreed rise in the growth rates of quotas and noted that such accelerated growth should make the enlarged quotas nonbinding long before the end of the transition period. The industrial countries complained that the high existing tariffs, the newly raised applied tariffs and the nontariff barriers in developing countries limited their market access. The response of the developing countries was that they had complied with the commitment they had made with respect to market access, and in any case they opposed linking market access to the quota phase-out. There is, of course, no reason to presume that the industrial countries will necessarily use other WTO-sanctioned means to protect their textile industries after the MFA phase-out, but by raising such a possibility, the developing countries may have sensitized the industrial countries against contemplating such action.

To implement the UR with respect to customs valuation, licensing processes, TRIPs and sanitary and phytosanitary standards many developing countries have to invest a significant amount of scarce resources. According to Finger and Schuler (2000, p. 511) of the World Bank:

> Implementation will require purchasing of equipment, training of people, establishment of systems of checks and balances, etc. This will cost money and the amounts of money involved are substantial. Based on Bank project experience in the areas covered by the agreements, an entire year's development budget is at stake in many of the least developed countries.

Their analysis suggests that 'for most of the developing and transition economies – some 100 countries – money spent to implement the WTO rules in these areas would be money unproductively invested' (Finger and Schuler 2000, p. 511).

Clearly a rules-based, rather than a power-based, trading system is in the interests of developing countries, which undoubtedly are the less powerful members of the system. However, a rules-based system would be of little use if the rules were not observed. Thus a mechanism to interpret and enforce rules is an integral part of any rules-based system. The UR Agreement included an understanding on dispute settlement and established the DSM in the WTO. Many view the DSM to be an improvement and strengthening of the mechanism that existed in the GATT, though others (for example, Hudec 1999) see more of a continuity than a radical difference between the two mechanisms.

Since the creation of the WTO in January 1995 until the end of May 2000, 194 disputes were brought before the system (WTO 2000b). As of 12 September 2000 the total was 205. Developing countries as a group registered 50 of them, with Brazil, India, Mexico and Thailand playing the most active roles. As expected, the world's major traders, the United States and the EU, have registered the most complaints, 60 and 50, respectively. Of the 77 disputes that were resolved during 1995–99, as many as 41 were resolved without going to adjudication, and compliance with the rulings of panels and the appellate body in those disputes that went to adjudication, particularly those that went against the powerful members, though far from full, is none the less encouraging. However, the unilateralism that the strengthened DSM was meant to curb has not altogether disappeared.

A major concern of the smaller and poorer developing countries about the DSM is that accessing it is costly. It takes resources to recognize whether a trading partner has violated one or more of the complex set of rules of the system and to mount a strong defence if accused of such violation by a partner. Equally important and costly is the creation of mechanisms for stakeholders to identify potential cases, transmit the relevant information to their governments and get them to act; that is, to take the case to the WTO (Hoekman and Mavroidis 2000a,b). A DSM that can be accessed only by the rich and powerful members is obviously not conducive to building confidence in the rules-based system among its less powerful members. Fortunately, the need to help poorer countries access the system has been recognized and a fund to provide such help has been established within the WTO from voluntary donations by industrial-country members. Hoekman and Mavroidis (2000a,b) suggest the creation of an independent special prosecutor with the mandate to identify violations of WTO rules that are detrimental to developing countries.

The built-in agenda of GATS included negotiations on telecommunications, financial services, maritime services and the movement of natural persons. Agreements on the first two have been concluded since. However, in 1996 negotiations on maritime services failed and have not been resumed. An agreement on the movement of natural persons has yet to be concluded. Because many developing countries have a comparative advantage in the supply of labour-intensive services such as construction, maritime services and nursing, and because others have developed a comparative advantage in skill-intensive services such as computer software, the failure to agree on the movement of natural persons delays the benefits that developing countries could reap from exporting such services.

A fairly strong case can be made that the UR Agreement was unbalanced: the developing countries undertook many costly commitments, and in return obtained only a few commitments by the industrial countries to phase out GATT-inconsistent MFA quotas and to engage in limited liberalization of GATT-inconsistent intervention in agricultural trade. Indeed, on balance there was virtually no liberalization of agricultural trade in the UR Agreement. Although subsidies on exports of manufactures (which some developing countries offered to their infant manufactured exports) were made WTO-inconsistent, agricultural export subsidies (which were used mainly by industrial countries, particularly the EU) were reduced, but not eliminated. It is true that the developing countries were given longer to implement their commitments than the industrial countries, yet as the implementation began, many developing countries found that even the longer implementation periods might not be long enough. However, UNCTAD (1999, p. 1) perhaps goes too far in asserting that 'the predicted gains to developing countries from the Uruguay Round have proved to be exaggerated'. Be that as it may, while the case for unilateral liberalization of their trade barriers by developing countries is strong, domestic political support for any liberalization, unilateral or multilateral, would be eroded if trade agreements were perceived as placing a heavier burden on developing countries. Thus restoring a balance and avoiding an imbalance of commitments in any future agreements must be the principal objectives for developing countries, both in the discussions about the possible agenda for any future round of multilateral trade negotiations and in the negotiations themselves, were a round to materialize.

The following section discusses whether the new round should be comprehensive or whether it should have a limited agenda.

COMPREHENSIVE VERSUS LIMITED AGENDA FOR A NEW ROUND OF MULTILATERAL TRADE NEGOTIATIONS

Before the Seattle Ministerial Meeting, consensus on the agenda for any future round of trade negotiations was lacking. As Ambassador Bernal (1999, p. 71) points out, the minimalist school argued that a new round of negotiations was unnecessary. The built-in agenda of the UR Agreement, namely, review of the Agriculture and Services agreements, would be complex, time-consuming and call for difficult compromises. The developing countries were mostly of the minimalist persuasion: they wanted to discuss the implementation problems and failures relating to the UR commitments in addition to the built-in agenda.

Those who argued for a comprehensive new round made the case that a broad agenda would offer many options and tradeoffs so that there would be greater gains for the participants. Again as Ambassador Bernal (1999) points out, there was no agreement either among the industrial countries or between the industrial and the developing countries on what the expanded agenda should cover. Among the additional issues proposed, namely, competition policy, government procurement, investment, linkage of market access to enforcement of labour and environmental standards and electronic commerce, the United States accorded high priority to electronic commerce and labour standards. The EU, by contrast, placed investment and competition policy at the top of the agenda. Among services, the industrial countries wanted the focus to be on air transport and financial and professional services, while the developing countries were more interested in maritime transport, entertainment and the movement of natural persons. Institutions concerned with trade and development – such as UNCTAD – forcefully raised the issue of imbalance in the UR commitments and asserted that the gains to the developing countries from the UR liberalization have proved to be limited. They argued that any new round should be a development round devoted to issues of interest to developing countries. The former chief economist and senior vice president of the World Bank, Stiglitz (2000), agrees. In his view any new round should be fair to the developing countries, and also comprehensive in the sense of including issues of critical importance to the industrial countries such as financial market liberalization and information technology, but also those such as construction and maritime services that are important to the developing countries. UNCTAD continues to champion the so-called special and more favourable treatment of developing countries and initiatives such as debt write-off and free market access for exports of the least developed countries.

With Albania's accession on 8 September 2000, the membership of the WTO has reached 138. Most of the members are developing countries, many of them small and poor. The main attraction of a comprehensive round covering many issues is that, in principle, it would enlarge the set of potential bargains among fully informed participants. However, in practice, expecting most members to be able to inform themselves about the gains and losses that would accrue to them under many permutations and combinations of possible 'concessions' across commodities, services and issues is extremely unrealistic.

Even with a well-informed set of negotiators, the process of negotiating among 138 members would be slow and cumbersome. With the so-called civil society advocates pushing for transparency, the negotiators will be under intense scrutiny and relentless pressure. This suggests that negotiations of a narrow agenda are more likely to succeed. However, given such an agenda, interest in future negotiations on excluded issues may wane on the part of those who have little to gain from any agreement on these issues, but have much to gain from any agreement favourable to them on the included issues. Thus the problem of time inconsistency could arise if initially the negotiations are focused too narrowly. Although the time inconsistency problem is logically possible, I am not convinced that it is serious.

On balance, the case for a limited negotiating agenda consisting of the issues left over from the UR, the implementation problems of UR commitments and the issues relating to the WTO's decisionmaking processes is strong. An encouraging start has been made with the first meeting of the special negotiating sessions of the Council of Trade and Services in February 2000, and the second meeting in July 2000 continued the progress (WTO 2000c). Future sessions will continue the mandated reviews of the trade-related investment measures and TRIPs agreements, and in particular, will also address their trade and developmental impact on developing countries (WTO 2000a). The first three meetings of the Agriculture Committee in March, June and September 2000 were fruitful (WTO 2000d). If the future meetings of these two groups continue to be productive, there may be no need for a conventional new round of negotiations with well-defined starting and ending dates. Building on the success of the reviews, negotiations on other issues could be initiated in suitable forums of the WTO, including ministerial meetings.

Clearly several issues of process and substance need to be addressed regardless of whether future negotiations will take place in a new round of the conventional kind, be it limited or comprehensive, or whether they will take place in other formats extending from ongoing mandated reviews of the Agriculture and Trade agreements of the UR.

To begin with process issues, the Seattle Ministerial Meeting exposed the weaknesses of the decisionmaking process in the WTO. In most rounds of GATT negotiations, developing countries did not participate actively in the negotiations and, in effect, were presented with agreements that were negotiated by the few powerful industrial countries on a more or less take-it-or-leave-it basis. The so-called 'green room' process of ministerial meetings controlled by the chair, the few powerful industrial countries and the director general broke down in Seattle. With no discernible criterion for admission to the green room, those not admitted felt disenfranchised. Even the developing countries present in the green room could not claim to represent other developing countries. Thus the legitimacy of any decisions or consensus arrived at became doubtful, with the Caribbean and African countries explicitly dissociating themselves from any consensus that might emerge from such a process. In response, a hybrid system of formal working groups and informal green room meetings emerged, but it satisfied few. The naked exercise of power by the chair, Ambassador Barshefsky, did not help. Bernal (1999, p. 71) quotes her as having said: 'I fully reserve the right to also use a more exclusive process to achieve a final outcome. There is no question about either my right as the chair to do it or my intention as the chair to do it.' Satisfying the principles of transparency and representation, while at the same time ensuring an orderly and efficient decisionmaking process in a body of more than 138 members with diverse interests and resources, is a challenge.

The dispute settlement process set up by the UR Agreement involves hearings by panels and an appellate body. It has been characterized as nontransparent and nonrepresentative. Under the process, 'the proceedings themselves are closed to the public and private parties are not permitted to submit these views or information directly to panels or the Appellate Body' (Hudec 1999, p. 43). There have been demands from various quarters, including NGOs, for doing 'away with most confidentiality restrictions on documents, open hearings to the public, and allow parties to submit briefs to panels and the Appellate Body' (ibid.).

The standard argument against greater transparency is that it will encourage government representatives, particularly those of the defendant, to engage in obstructive behaviour, and even grandstanding, mainly to satisfy domestic constituencies, rather than in co-operative and constructive behaviour. However, as Hudec (1999) points out, public access and transparency would help deflect attacks on the legitimacy of WTO rulings.

Hudec (1999, p. 48) is indeed correct in his view that 'in short, the participation issue is an issue of normative politics and not just a question of process'. It is, in effect, an argument that national governments do not adequately represent the views of private groups in their own countries. The NGOs claim 'that national pursuit of environmental, labour and human rights goals are being deflected by economic considerations', while business interests claim 'that the government's pursuit of the nation's economic interests is being unduly restrained by concerns about more ephemeral political interests' (ibid., p. 47). Because the difference between a nation's NGOs and its businesses is a difference that ought to be resolved in the domestic political process, the claim for representation at an international tribunal is basically an attempt to get around and side-step the domestic political process. Granting such a claim could have potentially serious consequences. However, other aspects of the DSM relating to due process, such as the lack of legal counsel to disputants in a panel proceeding and the difficulties panels can have in settling factual disputes (for example, a complaint by one member about the failure of others to enforce their competition laws as they are required to do by WTO rules) are troubling (Palmeter 1997). The example cited by Palmeter is particularly telling: the WTO panel ousted private lawyers who were advising some Caribbean countries on the US–EU banana dispute after the United States and the EU objected to their presence on the grounds that they were not permanent government officials.

Turning now to substantive issues, first, assuming that after the eight rounds of multilateral trade negotiations under the GATT the traditional issue of market access is no longer important is a mistake. The problem of tariff peaks and tariff escalation relating to developing-country exports and, above all, barriers to trade in textiles and apparel, still remain. Significant agricultural trade barriers also remain, and the GATS is no longer GATT-consistent when it comes to nondiscrimination (MFN) and national treatment, with members permitted to exclude several categories from MFN and national treatment.

Second, developing countries must remain united in resisting the introduction of a social clause relating to labour standards into the WTO, while remaining receptive to reasoned discussion of labour standards in the ILO.

Third, WTO members should attempt to take environmental issues out of the WTO. The WTO's Committee on Trade and Environment should be wound up. This is not to say that environmental issues are not important. They are, but they are better negotiated in other forums such as the United Nations Environment Programme. As Rollo and Winters (2000) argue, linking trade and labour and environmental standards and including these social issues in any future negotiations will detract from negotiating further liberalization of trade in manufactures, agriculture and services and 'can actively undermine the process of negotiation, compromise and ultimate balance' (Rollo and Winters 2000, p. 575).

Fourth, concluding the TRIPs agreement was a colossal mistake. There is no economic logic behind the one-size-fits-all intellectual property protection through a single patent law and system. The TRIPs review should be used, if not to take TRIPs out of the WTO altogether and put it under a strengthened World Intellectual Property Organization, at least to introduce needed diversity in intellectual property protection and longer implementation periods for developing countries.

Fifth, Article XXIV of the GATT on customs unions and free trade areas, which has been incorporated into the WTO, should be replaced with the requirement that all preferences granted to partners of existing or any proposed future preferential trading agreements, such as free trade or customs union agreements, regional or otherwise in geographic coverage, should be

extended to all members of the WTO on an MFN basis within a specified five-
to ten-year period of the coming into force of such agreements.

Sixth, dumping has no economic rationale (other than predation, which is
extremely unlikely). As such, antidumping measures are really discriminatory,
protectionist devices that can be, and have been, used to target particular
exporters, even specific exporting firms. Unfortunately, some developing
countries, such as India, have now begun to use them, while the industrial
countries continue to use them as they have in the past. Antidumping measures
are the analogues of chemical and biological weapons in the armoury of trade
policy instruments. The WTO should make them illegal.

Seventh, it seems premature, at least from the perspective of developing
countries, to negotiate and conclude a multilateral agreement on investment
and related issues such as competition policies. An agreement to make current
policies transparent should be the first step.

Eighth, the legitimate concern of the community of trading nations for
accelerating the economic and social development of the least developed and
less dynamic countries should be appropriately accommodated, with a view to
providing them with the resources, knowledge and technology to enable them
to grow faster and reap the benefits of being integrated into the global
economy. Offering them preferential access to world markets would, in effect,
pit one group of developing countries, the least developed countries, against
other developing countries, thereby creating the potential for trade diversion.
In addition to having only a limited beneficial effect on the growth of the least
developed countries, it will create a sense of complacency on the part of the
rich countries of having done enough for them, and will also, more seriously
and deleteriously, enable the rich countries to persist in maintaining trade
barriers that are detrimental to developing countries as a whole. Indeed, by
demanding and receiving special and differential treatment in the GATT and
agreeing to the creation of the Generalized System of Preferences, which are
exceptions to the GATT's fundamental principle of nondiscrimination,
developing countries have in the past enabled the industrial countries to get
away with their own GATT-inconsistent trading arrangements such as the
MFA. Developing countries should not fall into that trap again. They have
much to gain by participating fully and as equal partners with the industrial
countries in a nondiscriminatory, liberal world trading system.

CONCLUSION

Even though the Seattle Ministerial Meeting of the WTO did not initiate a new
round of multilateral trade negotiations, the UR's built-in agenda and the
problems of implementation the developing countries face is enough to keep

negotiators busy in the immediate future. Rather than rush into a new round
without adequate preparation, a period of constructive engagement between
the industrial and the developing countries in the recently initiated reviews of
the Services and Agriculture agreements would help both groups of countries
engage in a less confrontational approach when discussing the agenda for any
future round. While engaging in such constructive discussions, many
developing countries should continue to liberalize unilaterally their levels of
protection, which continue to be high. The pursuit of a liberal trade policy has
always been, and will continue to be, in the self-interest of the developing
countries, but such pursuit does not preclude their attempting to get as much
as possible for themselves at the international bargaining table.

NOTES

1. In Srinivasan (2000) I discuss the theory and empirics of the relationship between growth,
   poverty and inequality. I stress that first, the data on all three are riddled with measurement
   errors and biases, and second, that postulating and seeking a stable, one-way relationship
   between growth and poverty would be simplistic.
2. According to Ruggiero: 'It is not possible to talk seriously about furthering a relationship
   of mutual confidence with developing countries unless the industrial countries are ready to
   act courageously in this sector. There is considerable anxiety among textile exporting
   developing countries – who also include some of the least-developed – that the major
   importers are not always living up to the spirit of the Uruguay Round agreement, whatever
   their observance of its letter. The developing countries are not seeking to rewrite the rules, but
   they are concerned to have a second integration phase that is more commercially meaningful,
   and they are anxious about what the end-loading of the commitments will mean in terms of
   the pressures importing countries face when they finally come to be implemented' (WTO
   1996, p. 4).

REFERENCES

Ben-David, D., H. Nordström and A. Winters (2000), *Trade, Income Disparity and Poverty*, Geneva: WTO.
Bernal, R. (1999), 'Sleepless in Seattle: The WTO Ministerial of 1999', *Social and Economic Studies*, **48** (3), 61–84.
Finger, M. and P. Schuler (2000), 'Implementation of Uruguay Round Commitments: The Development Challenge', *World Economy*, **23** (4), 511–25.
Grunberg, I. and S. Khan (eds) (2000), *Globalization: The United Nations Development Dialogue*, New York: United Nations University Press.
Hindley, Brian (1997a), 'EC Anti-Dumping: Has the Problem Gone Away?', *Annual Review of Trade Policy 1996/97*, Brussels: Centre for European Policy Studies.
Hindley, Brian (1997b), 'Anti-Dumping in Grey Cotton Fabric: Have the Problems Gone Away?', London School of Economics, London, processed.
Hoekman, B. and P. Mavroidis (2000a), 'Enforcing WTO Commitments: Dispute Settlement and Developing Countries – Something Happened on the Way to Heaven,' paper prepared for the World Bank conference on the World Trading

System Post-Seattle: Institutional Design, Governance and Ownership, 14–15 July, Brussels.

Hoekman, B. and P. Mavroidis (2000b), 'WTO Dispute Settlement, Transparency and Surveillance', *World Economy*, **23** (4), 527–42.

Hudec, R. (1999), 'The New WTO Dispute Settlement Procedure: An Overview of the First Three Years', *Minnesota Journal of Global Trade*, **8** (1), 1–53.

Maskus, K. (2000), *Intellectual Property Rights in the Global Economy*, Washington, DC: Institute for International Economics.

Odell, J. (2000), 'The Seattle Impasse and its Implications for the World Trade Organization', paper presented at the conference on The Political Economy of International Trade Law, 15–16 September, University of Minnesota Law School, Minneapolis, Minnesota.

Palmeter, D. (1997), 'The Need for Due Process in WTO Proceedings', *Journal of World Trade*, **31** (1), 51–7.

Rollo, J. and A. Winters (2000), 'Subsidiarity and Governance Challenges in the WTO: Environmental and Labour Standards', *World Economy*, **23** (4), 561–76.

Srinivasan, T.N. (2000), 'Growth, Poverty Reduction and Inequality', paper presented at the Annual World Bank Conference on Development Economics, 26–28 June, Paris.

Stiglitz, J. (2000), 'Two Principles for the Next Round or, How to Bring the Developing Countries in from the Cold', *World Economy*, **23** (4), 437–54.

UNCTAD (United Nations Conference on Trade and Development) (1999), *Trade and Development Report 1999*, Geneva: United Nations.

Wolfensohn, J. and J. Stiglitz (2000), 'Growth Is Not Enough', *Financial Times*, 22 September.

WTO (World Trade Organization) (1996), 'Director-General's Speech to EU Trade Ministers in Dublin', WTO PRESS/56, 18 September, Geneva.

WTO (1997), *Focus Newsletter*, 15 January, Geneva.

WTO (2000a), Press Release, PRESS/167, 7 February, Geneva.

WTO (2000b), Press Release, PRESS/180, 5 June, Geneva.

WTO (2000c), *WTO News*, 20 July.

WTO (2000d), 'September 2000: Chairperson's report to General Council', document G/AG/NG/3, 3 October, Geneva.

3. Developing-country interests in WTO-induced agricultural trade reform

Kym Anderson

A great achievement of the UR negotiations was to begin at last to bring agricultural policies under mainstream GATT discipline.[1] In 1986 the nonsubsidizing, agricultural-exporting countries formed the Cairns Group with the single goal of ensuring that outcome.[2] The group, together with the United States and other GATT contracting parties, sought successfully for all nontariff barriers to agricultural imports (other than quarantine) to be tariffied and bound, for those tariff bindings to be scheduled for phased reductions, and for farm production and export subsidies to be reduced. The industrial countries committed themselves to implement those reforms between 1995 and 2000 (which they more or less did, but based more on the letter than the spirit of the agreement), while the developing countries have until the end of 2004.

That URAA, together with the Sanitary and Phytosanitary Agreement (SPSA) to limit the use of quarantine import restrictions to cases that can be justified scientifically, the new policy notification and review requirements, and the Dispute Settlement Mechanism (which has greatly improved the process of resolving trade conflicts), ensure that in the future agricultural trade will be much less chaotic than it was before the formation of the WTO in 1995. The Agreement on Textiles and Clothing also has great potential to boost farm exports from the Cairns Group, albeit indirectly.

Much remains to be done, however, before agricultural trade is as fully disciplined or as free as world trade in manufactures. This chapter examines what has been achieved to date, explores the interests of and options for developing countries in the next round of negotiations, and discusses effective ways to ensure that the process of reform continues.

The chapter makes several claims. One is that traditional issues of agricultural market access remain the main priority for the next round, because at the start of the twenty-first century, agricultural protection rates in OECD countries are still huge. However, 'dirty' tariffication and the introduction of tariff rate quotas in the URAA mean that large commitments in terms of bound tariff cuts and/or quota expansions will be needed if agricultural protection is to be reduced significantly. Whether that is done in the same way as in the UR (in the form of percentage cuts to bound tariffs, export subsidies and domestic support and growth in the share of consumption imported) or whether a more radical approach is needed is a moot point.

Second, reforms in other sectors are also important for developing-country agriculture, because having them on the negotiating agenda can bring to the table groups that can counter farm protectionist lobbies. Adding new issues to the agenda can contribute in a similar way, albeit at the risk of diverting attention away from traditional market access issues.

Third, among the other issues that will be raised in the next WTO round are two of concern to some high-income, food-importing countries. They relate to their assertions that stricter technical barriers to farm trade are necessary for food safety reasons, and that agriculture's multifunctional nature requires that the sector be treated differently from other sectors. If handled badly in the millennium round, both could lead to outcomes detrimental to developing-country agriculture.

DEFINING DEVELOPING COUNTRIES' INTERESTS

Almost all developing countries have an interest in the agricultural parts of the next round of multilateral trade negotiations, either directly or indirectly. Consider four groups of such countries. First, the exporters of tropical farm products face relatively low tariffs on most of their primary exports, but with important exceptions, such as bananas. They also face much higher effective tariffs on many of the processed versions of tropical products, which hinders their capacity to export the processing value added component.

Second, developing-country exporters of temperate zone farm products, such as grains, livestock products, sugar and oilseeds, typically face high import tariffs and restrictive tariff rate quotas when trying to export to OECD countries and have a clear interest in seeing those barriers lowered. This group includes a subset of developing countries whose exports of farm products enjoy preferential access into OECD countries' markets. In the short term at least, they may lose sales revenue on those items if the OECD countries lower their MFN tariff rates. However, they may gain enough sales of other farm products whose tariffs have been lowered to more than offset the cut in their margin of preference, and/or they may be able to negotiate compensation.

Third, the net food-importing developing countries fear that cuts in agricultural protection by OECD countries will lead to higher international food prices for their imports, and perhaps fewer concessional imports via food aid or subsidized sales. Yet even these developing countries need not lose from farm support cuts abroad. If, for example, they are almost self-sufficient in food as so many net food importers are, and reform abroad raises the international price of food, they may switch to become sufficiently export oriented that their net national economic welfare rises. A second possibility is that the country's own policies are sufficiently biased against food production that the country is a net importer despite having a comparative advantage in food. In that case, a rise in international food prices can improve national economic welfare even if the price change is not sufficient to turn that distorted economy into a net food exporter (Anderson and Tyers 1993). This occurs because the higher price of food attracts mobile resources away from the more distorted sectors, thereby improving the efficiency of national resource allocation. Thus the number of poor countries for which a rise in international food prices might cause some hardship is much smaller than the number that are currently net importers of agricultural products.

Even within those net food-importing countries, the vast majority of the poor are in farm households that would benefit directly from a food price rise. Most of the rest of the poor would benefit indirectly from farm trade liberalization via a rise in the wage for unskilled labour, which may be sufficient to more than offset the rise in food prices. As the more affluent people would find it relatively easy to pay a little extra for food, the vulnerable group of underemployed poor would be quite small and could be compensated with food aid programmes at low cost. Fourth, for those developing countries that are rapidly accumulating capital, developing their infrastructure and industrializing, their comparative advantage is gradually moving away from primary products to (initially unskilled) labour-intensive manufactures. While that lowers their direct interest in agricultural trade reform abroad, it heightens their interest in reducing barriers to their exports of textiles and clothing. That interest is shared by developing countries that export agricultural products, because if NIEs could export more manufactures, they would tend to become larger net importers of farm products.[3] Conversely, lowered industrial-country barriers to farm trade would reduce the need for the more land-abundant developing countries to move into manufactures in competition with the NIEs. This suggests scope for the two groups to band together and negotiate as a single voice calling for barriers to both farm products and the textile trade to be lowered.

Even if a country's national economic welfare were to decline because of a deterioration in its terms of trade resulting from the next multilateral trade negotiations, that does not mean it would be better off not participating in the round. On the contrary, that country's welfare would fall even more if it did not participate, because it would forego the economic efficiency gains from reforming its own policies.[4] There is also the likelihood that in this next round

- already dubbed the development round by the EU - participating poor economies that lose from multilateral liberalization could secure much more compensation than in previous rounds in the form of technical and economic assistance commitments.

It is thus in the national economic interests of such countries to commit to such reform, painful though that may be politically for their governments. The political pain tends to be less, and the prospect for a net economic gain greater, the more sectors countries involve in the reform, because a wider net gain reduces the possibility that reform is confined to a subset of sectors that are not the most distorted. In the latter case, resources might move from the reformed sector to even more inefficient uses, thereby reducing rather than improving the efficiency of national resource use.

Of course net national economic welfare is not the only criterion that drives governments to act as they do. Indeed, until recently, it may not even have been a major one. However, it is steadily becoming more dominant for at least two reasons. One is the rapid globalization brought about by technological and economic policy changes over the past decade or so, a major effect of which is that economies will be penalized ever more rapidly and severely through capital flight because of bad economic governance. The other reason is the broader mandate of the WTO, which makes it easier for developing countries than before the UR to engage profitably in a cross-sectoral exchange of market access commitments. Both developments add a new, liberalizing dimension to the domestic political market for protection policies (Grossman and Helpman 1995; Hillman and Moser 1995).

TRADITIONAL ISSUES

With the foregoing points in mind, we turn to examining developing-country interests in the traditional market access issues associated with the next WTO round.

The Legacy of the URAA

For most farm products in OECD countries, according to Ingco (1996) actual tariffs will provide just as much protection at the beginning of this century as the nontariff import barriers of the late 1980s and early 1990s did. This is because in most cases, tariffs were bound well above the applied rates (or the tariff equivalents of the quantitative restrictions) in place at the end of the UR. This is true in other sectors also, but to a much lesser extent. Table 3.1 suggests that a bound tariff cut just 40 per cent greater than in the UR would bring the average bound rate down to the applied rate average for

Table 3.1   Depth of UR tariff cuts and post-UR bound and applied tariffs on imports by sector and region

Sector	Depth of UR cut in bound tariff rate t (as a percentage of $1 + t$)	Post-UR bound tariff rate (%)	Post-UR applied tariff rate (%)	Depth of cut needed in bound tariff rate t (as a percentage of $1 + t$) to bring it down to the sector's post-UR applied rate	Proportional cut needed in bound tariff rate t (as a percentage of t) to bring it down to the region's post-UR average applied rate
Agriculture					
OECD countries	1.5	15	14	0.9	83
Developing economies	4.7	60	18	26.3	78
All WTO members	2.6	24	14	8.1	82
Textiles and clothing					
OECD countries	1.4	11	8	2.7	76
Developing economies	4.1	24	21	2.4	45
All WTO members	1.6	12	10	1.8	53
Other manufactures					
OECD countries	1.0	4	3	1.0	35
Developing economies	2.7	20	13	5.8	34
All WTO members	1.3	6	4	1.9	35

Source: Finger and Schuknecht (1999).

manufactures, whereas for agriculture the depth of the cut would need to be three times greater than in the UR to close the gap. The final column of Table 3.1 shows that a one-third cut in the bound tariffs on other manufactures would bring the average down to each region's applied rate average for all goods, whereas for textiles and clothing a cut of about one-half would be needed and for agriculture (including processed food) the cut would have to be about four-fifths.

Binding agricultural tariffs well above applied rates have also allowed countries to vary applied tariffs below the binding so as to stabilize the domestic market in much the same way as the EU has done in the past with its system of variable import levies and export subsidies. This means that little of the reduction in price fluctuations in international food markets that tariffication was expected to deliver will occur in this decade.[5]

Even getting agricultural (and textile) bound tariffs down to currently applied rates on those products would require big cuts. Yet applied rates for textiles and clothing are 2.5 times those for other manufactures and those for agriculture are 3.5 times those for other manufactures. Clearly action is needed on two tariff fronts: getting bound rates down to applied rates; and lowering applied rates on these two outlying industry groups, both of which are of vital interest to developing countries.

As if that were not enough, a third front requires attention. Agricultural-importing countries also agreed to provide minimum market access opportunities, such that the share of imports in domestic consumption for products subject to import restrictions rose to at least 5 per cent (less in the case of developing countries) by 2000 under a tariff rate quota. Even though within-quota imports attract a much lower tariff than out-of-quota imports, such tariff rate quotas (TRQs) have several undesirable features: they legitimize a role for state trading agencies; they generate quota rents; they introduce scope for discriminating between countries; and they can reduce national welfare by much more than similarly protective import tariffs.

More specifically Anderson (1999, appendix) shows that

- In the presence of TRQs, the national welfare cost of agricultural protection can be considerably greater than under a similarly protective tariff-only regime, and cost tends to rise more when a fall in international food prices occurs (as happened in the late 1990s).
- With a TRQ regime, a cut in the out-of-quota bound tariff may have only a fraction of the effect on prices and quantities traded (and possibly none at all) of a cut of the same size under a tariff-only regime, not only when the bound rate exceeds the applied rate, but also when the applied rate is above the prohibitive tariff in the presence of a TRQ.
- The effect of a tariff cut on national welfare, by contrast, may be much

greater when a TRQ rather than a tariff-only regime is in place, depending on how the quota is being administered before and after that reform.

- An expansion of the market access (quota) commitment need not expand trade and welfare, because the quota administrator can always allocate the quotas so as to ensure under-fill such that no more, or even fewer imports in total, flow in.

Models such as the Global Trade Analysis Project (Hertel 1997) are, in principle, capable of handling these complications through careful additional programming, but to generate reliable numbers requires assimilating a much greater volume of policy data than is required when a simple tariff-only regime exists. Until all these data are collected and added to the model databases, model results of the effects of a cut in the bound tariff will necessarily overestimate price and quantity effects, but may underestimate the welfare effects of reform.

Elbehri et al. (1999) present a number of the undesirable features of TRQs in food-importing countries, 1366 of which have been notified to the WTO. Table 3.2 summarizes some of the data from that study. The low in-quota and extremely high out-of-quota tariffs mean that potentially huge benefits are going to those allocated quota licences. In numerous cases quotas are far from being filled, however; one possible reason is that quotas are allocated (inadvertently or deliberately) to imports from high-cost suppliers incapable of making full use of them. The fact that the quota often represents a high proportion, sometimes 100 per cent, of actual imports suggests that some out-of-quota tariffs are virtually prohibitive.

The aggregate level of domestic support for industrial country farmers was to be reduced to four-fifths of its 1986–88 level by the turn of the century. That too should have required only modest reform in most industrial countries, partly because much of the decline in the aggregate level of domestic support had already occurred by the mid-1990s. The need for reductions is modest, because many forms of support can be excluded from the calculation of the aggregate level of domestic support, the most important being direct payments under production-limiting programmes of the sort adopted by the United States and the EU. A risk that needs to be curtailed is that the use of such 'blue box' instruments, as with exempt 'green box' instruments such as quarantine and environmental provisions, may spread to other countries and other commodities as the use of farm income support via trade and direct domestic price support measures is gradually curtailed through the WTO.

Thus despite the UR's achievement of establishing rules for agricultural trade and securing some reform, in the last five years limited progress has been

Table 3.2   *In-quota and out-of-quota tariff rates and estimated maximum TRQ quota rents, selected agricultural products and OECD countries, 1996*

Country/ region and product	In-quota *ad valorem* tariff (%)	Out-of-quota *ad valorem* tariff (%)	Maximum quota rents (US$ billions)	Quota fill ratio (%)	Quota as a percentage of total imports
European Union					
Wheat	0	87	0.0	21	2
Grains	35	162	0.4	74	26
Sugar	0	147	2.4	100	87
Dairy products	24	91	1.1	99	80
Meats	19	128	2.3	100	73
Fruits and vegetables	11	51	0.0	78	20
United States					
Sugar	2	129	1.0	97	76
Dairy products	11	70	0.6	77	95
Meats	5	26	0.0	67	102
Canada					
Wheat	1	49	0.0	27	218
Grains	1	58	0.0	5	2400
Dairy products	7	262	0.3	100	75
Meats	2	27	0.0	124	72
Japan					
Wheat	0	234	3.4	109	95
Grains	0	491	10.8	109	84
Dairy products	29	344	2.8	93	91
Korea, Republic of					
Rice	5	89	0.0	100	53
Grain	3	326	1.9	148	61
Oilseeds	8	545	0.0	157	62
Dairy products	21	106	0.0	85	106
Meats	40	42	0.4	97	77
Fruits and vegetables	47	305	0.0	99	83

Source: Elbehri et al. (1999).

made in reducing agricultural protection and market insulation, and a great deal of reform remains to be undertaken relative even to textiles and clothing, let alone other manufactures.

Potential Gains from Further Trade Policy Reform

When implementation of the UR is complete in 2005, what will be the potential for further gains from reforming the agricultural markets of OECD countries compared with the gains from protection cuts in other sectors, and how large are those potential gains from OECD liberalization compared with gains from developing-country reforms? According to Anderson, Hoekman and Strutt (2001), the gains from removing remaining tariffs and subsidies would be huge.[6] The economic significance of the projected distortions in the different sectors by 2005 depends not only on the size of the price wedges, but also on the size of each sector's production and the importance of its products in consumption. If all merchandise trade distortions were removed globally, almost half (48 per cent) of the estimated global economic welfare gains (ignoring environmental effects) would come from policy reforms related to primary agricultural products and processed foods in OECD countries (Table 3.3), even though such products in those countries contribute only 4 per cent of global gross domestic product (GDP) and less than one-tenth of world trade. Another one-sixth would come from reform of farm and food policies of the developing countries, defined here as in the WTO to include NIEs such as the Republic of Korea (henceforth referred to as Korea). Textiles and clothing reforms appear pale by comparison with agricultural reform: their potential global welfare contribution is barely one-tenth that of agriculture's (7 per cent compared with 65 per cent). This big difference reflects two facts: projected distortions in prices for agriculture are more than twice those for textiles and clothing in 2005; and textiles and clothing contribute only 1.5 per cent to the value of world production and 5 per cent to the value of world trade, half or less the shares for farm products (Anderson, Hoekman and Strutt 2001).

However, two assumptions are crucial in generating the results reported in Table 3.3. One is that China and Taiwan will soon join the WTO and enjoy the same accelerated access to OECD markets under the UR Agreement on Textiles and Clothing as other developing countries that are already WTO members. The other crucial assumption is that OECD countries fully implement the Agreement on Textiles and Clothing. The latter is far from certain to happen, however, particularly if China were to join the WTO soon and phase out its 'voluntary' export restraints on textiles and clothing by 2005. Dropping either of those assumptions reduces the estimated gains from UR implementation substantially (Anderson et al. 1997), and therefore raises

Table 3.3   *Sectoral and regional contributions to the economic welfare gains[a] from completely removing trade barriers globally, post-UR, 2005*

Liberalizing region	Benefiting region	Agriculture and food	Other primary	Textiles and clothing	Other manufactures	Total
		In 1995 US$ billions				
High income	High income	110.5	–0.0	–5.7	–8.1	96.6
	Low income	11.6	0.1	9.0	22.3	43.1
	Total	122.1	0.0	3.3	14.2	139.7
Low income	High income	11.2	0.2	10.5	27.7	49.6
	Low income	31.4	2.5	3.6	27.6	65.1
	Total	42.6	2.7	14.1	55.3	114.7
All countries	High income	121.7	0.1	4.8	19.6	146.2
	Low income	43.0	2.7	12.6	49.9	108.1
	Total	164.7	2.8	17.4	69.5	254.3
		As a percentage of total global gains				
High income	High income	43.4	0.0	–2.3	–3.2	38.0
	Low income	4.6	0.1	3.5	8.8	16.9
	Total	48.0	0.0	1.3	5.6	54.9
Low income	High income	4.4	0.1	4.1	10.9	19.5
	Low income	12.3	1.0	1.4	10.9	25.6
	Total	16.7	1.1	5.5	21.7	45.1
All countries	High income	47.9	0.1	1.9	7.7	57.5
	Low income	16.9	1.0	4.9	19.6	42.5
	Total	64.8	1.1	6.8	27.3	100.0

Note: These calculations do not take into account the welfare effects of environmental changes associated with trade liberalization, which could be positive or negative depending in part on how environmental policies are adjusted following trade reforms.

Source: Anderson and others (1999).

the potential gains from textile and clothing reform in the next and subsequent WTO rounds.

Even so, agricultural protection would remain far more costly to the world economy than barriers to the textiles and clothing trade, and more than twice as costly as protection to other manufactures, despite the latter having much bigger shares in the value of world production and trade than farm and processed food products.

Moreover, if OECD governments did renege on the spirit of the Agreement on Textiles and Clothing, for example by using safeguards such as antidumping measures to limit their textile imports after voluntary export restraints are abolished at the end of 2004, the industrialization of developing countries as a group would slow down, and hence their need to depend on farm products to trade their way out of poverty would be greater.

The distribution of the gains across regions that would result from full trade liberalization is clear from Table 3.3. As always, most of the gains accrue to the liberalizing region. For example, all but one-tenth (12/122) of the gains from high-income countries removing distortions to their trade in farm and food products accrues to those countries. Even so, farm trade reform contributes more than one-quarter of the total welfare gains to developing countries from industrial countries liberalizing their merchandise trade (12/43). As for developing countries liberalizing their own farm and food policies, three-quarters of the benefits stay with the developing countries themselves (31/43), and such policies contribute almost half of the gains from those countries' overall merchandise trade reform (31/65).

WTO members were right, therefore, to insist that agricultural reform must continue into the new century without a pause. In particular, developing countries as a group have a major stake in the process of farm policy reform continuing: according to the model results in Table 3.3, farm and food policies globally contribute 40 per cent (17/43) of the cost to developing economies of global goods trade distortions. Textile and clothing policies also harm them greatly, but nowhere near as much as farm policies.[7]

For reasons explained in the previous section, even many food-importing developing economies would benefit from farm policy reforms by high-income countries. For the subset whose terms of trade would deteriorate, however, the extent of the rise in their food import prices would be small. Anderson, Hoekman and Strutt (2001) found that full liberalization of OECD farm policies would boost global agricultural trade by more than 50 per cent, but would cause real international food prices to rise by only 5 per cent on average, such is the extent of the global farm supply response to liberalization.

What Should be Done to Further the Agricultural Reform Process?

In terms of farm export subsidies, nothing less than a ban is needed to bring agriculture in line with nonfarm products under the GATT. They are, after all, almost exclusively a Western European phenomenon apart from sporadic US involvement: the EU granted five-sixths of all export subsidies in the mid-1990s; and Norway, Switzerland and the United States accounted for all but 2 per cent of the rest (Tangermann and Josling 1999, p. 16).

With respect to domestic subsidies, gradual reform of US and EU policies, in particular further decoupling of farm income support measures from production as with the United States Federal Agricultural Improvement and Reform Act of 1996, may allow removal of the blue box in the next round of talks. The blue box was an anomaly introduced into the UR negotiations in 1992 simply to satisfy two members so the negotiations could proceed. Also efforts could be made to tighten the green box criteria, so as to reduce the loopholes they provide for continuing output-increasing subsidies, and to further reduce the aggregate measures of support.

However, the most important area requiring attention concerns import market access. Tariffication appeared to be a great step forward. However, the combination of dirty tariffication by industrial economies (setting bound rates well above applied rates) and the adoption of extremely high ceiling bindings by developing economies still allows many countries to vary their protection as they wish in response to changes in domestic or international food markets. Reducing bound tariffs from 50 to more than 150 per cent to the 0 to 15 per cent range of tariff rates for manufactures is one of the major challenges ahead. If the steady rates of reduction of the past are used, that gap will not be closed for several decades, and it will be some time even before many of those bound tariffs reach current applied rates.

At least three options for reducing bound tariffs present themselves. One is a large across-the-board tariff cut. Even if as much as a 50 per cent cut were to be agreed, however, many very high bound tariffs would still remain. A second option is the Swiss formula used for manufactures in the Tokyo Round, whereby the rate of reduction for each item is higher the greater the item's tariff level. This has the additional economic advantage of reducing the dispersion in rates that was introduced or exacerbated during the UR. In particular, it would reduce many of the tariff peaks and the extent of tariff escalation that bothers developing countries. A third option is the one used successfully in the information technology negotiations, namely, the zero-for-zero approach, whereby tariffs are eliminated altogether for selected products. In contrast to the second option, this third option would increase the dispersion of tariffs across products, increasing the risk that resources would be wastefully diverted from low-cost to higher-cost activities. While that might appeal as a way of allowing attention to then focus on the politically difficult items such as dairy products and sugar, the manufacturing sector's experience with long-delayed reductions in protection of textiles and automobiles makes it difficult to view this third option optimistically as a quick solution.

These tariff reductions refer to above-quota imports. There is also a pressing need to focus on in-quota imports, that is, those that meet the minimum access requirements in the URAA (generally 5 per cent of domestic sales by 2000 for industrial economies). These quotas were introduced ostensibly to guarantee traditional exporters a minimum level of market access, equal at least to what was available before tariffication, given that tariffs have been bound at rates greatly above applied rates. As many as 36 WTO member countries listed TRQs in their UR schedules, of which at least half actively use them. However, as Anderson (1999, appendix) makes clear, this system of TRQs ensures that agricultural trade policies continue to be complex. In particular, their existence reduces the extent to which future tariff cuts will lead to actual import growth in the medium term, and it is worrying that quotas have, on average, been barely two-thirds filled according to the count of notifications to the WTO Committee on Agriculture during 1995 and 1996 (Tangermann and Josling 1999, p. 26).

Countries exporting agricultural products are understandably reluctant to suggest that TRQs be removed, because they provide at least some market access at low or zero tariffs. Nor would allowing TRQs to be auctioned be seen by all as a solution, because that would be like imposing the out-of-quota tariff on quota-restricted trade that the TRQ was designed to avoid. If banning TRQs is not yet possible, the next best alternative is to expand them, so as to simultaneously reduce their importance, increase competition and lessen the impact of high above-quota tariffs.

One can imagine an outcome from TRQ expansion that is either optimistic or pessimistic from a reformer's viewpoint. On the one hand, optimists may say that if the TRQs were to be increased by, say, the equivalent of 1 per cent of domestic consumption per year, the quota would soon became nonbinding. Expanding the TRQ could thereby potentially be much more liberalizing in the medium term than reducing the high above-quota tariffs. Such an approach may require binding within-quota tariffs at a reasonable level, such as that for manufactures.

On the other hand, negotiators familiar with the tortuous efforts to reform the quota arrangements for textiles and clothing trade see the agricultural TRQs as a way to recycle the acronym MFA before it disappears in 2004, when the last of the textile quotas are scheduled to be removed. In this case it would stand for a multilateral food arrangement (Francois 1999). As the first inception of textile quotas was around 1960, it looks as if it will have taken 50 years or so before they are finally abolished. Is that the expected lifetime of agricultural TRQs?

Those with this more pessimistic view may wish to put the case for a more radical approach to the next round of agricultural negotiations, namely, to bring agriculture more closely in line with the treatment of nonagricultural goods in the WTO. For example, they might call for the total elimination of agricultural TRQs (along with export subsidies and export credits) and a major reduction in bound (out-of-quota) tariffs. To soften the blow of that request, their *quid pro quo* could be to suggest that the WTO put less emphasis on trying to discipline farm domestic measures other than direct output-increasing subsidies. The almost infinite scope for re-instrumentation of domestic price support measures makes disciplining them difficult anyway, and as Snape (1987) has pointed out, tightening constraints on border measures would ensure an increasing proportion of the cost of support programmes would be exposed via the budget, and thereby subjected to regular domestic political scrutiny.

Why Agriculture Needs Other Sectors in the Next WTO Round

Agricultural negotiations and supportive analytical efforts to date have focused primarily on the traditional instruments of agricultural intervention, namely, border measures and producer subsidies. Yet much of the distortion to incentives facing internationally competitive farmers stems from their own countries' nonagricultural policies (Schiff and Valdes 1992). As the WTO negotiations focus on reciprocal exchange of market access concessions, export-oriented farmers have a negotiating interest not only in better access to food markets abroad, but also in more competition from abroad in their own economies' markets for nonfarm products. That applies not only to industrial goods, but also to services.

The WTO's nonagricultural negotiations are relevant to agriculture for at least three reasons. One is that the government of a WTO member that imports farm products and exports nonfarm goods and services will be more interested in lowering its impediments to agricultural imports if agricultural-exporting members lower their impediments to nonfarm imports. This is because the government's loss in political support from farmers will be compensated by political support from nonfood exporters (Grossman and Helpman 1995; Hillman and Moser 1995). The second reason is that farmers need many nonfarm goods and services as intermediate inputs or to get farm products to the final consumer. If because of trade impediments those nonfarm products are more expensive than they need be, costs are raised, so net farm incomes are reduced.[8] The third reason is that farmers compete with nonfarm sectors for mobile factors of production, especially investment funds and labour. To the extent that a country's nonfarm sectors are supported by trade impediments, so its farmers can be disadvantaged by having to pay higher prices for those factors.

Having other sectors on the negotiating table at the same time as agriculture is important for yet another reason: many developing-country WTO members are unable to engage in market access exchange just with agricultural goods, as they have relatively little intrasectoral trade in farm products.

For all these reasons, the probability of the next WTO round delivering further agricultural reforms will be significantly greater if negotiations also seek to achieve protection cuts for other sectors, including services. Fortunately, services are already scheduled to be on the agenda for the next round. Further liberalization of manufacturing industries is also required, especially in developing countries where industrial tariff rates are still high. Further textile and clothing reform, which would give a major boost to developing economies as a group, would encourage labour-intensive industrial production in NIEs. That would be at the expense of agricultural production in those countries in so far as farm household labour is attracted to factories. Hence it would have the flow-on effect of providing new market opportunities for agricultural exporters in other countries. This shows up even in model simulations involving an across-the-board liberalization in all manufacturing globally, as in Hertel and Martin (1999). One of their unreported simulation results shows that when manufacturing tariffs are cut globally by 40 per cent, the agricultural exports of developing countries as a group hardly change, but the net food imports of the developing East Asia subgroup rise by US$2.8 billion per year (in 1995 US dollars), while Latin America's and Sub-Saharan Africa's net agricultural exports rise by US$2.5 billion per year.

AGRICULTURE AND 'NEW' TRADE ISSUES

Some developing-country negotiators consider the inclusion of new trade issues in the agenda of the next round of WTO negotiations to be undesirable, because it would distract attention from the market access issues that they deem to be of greater importance. However, their inclusion could have the advantage that more OECD nonagricultural groups would take part in the round which, depending on the issue, could counterbalance forces favouring agricultural (and other sectoral) protection. Moreover, better rules on some of those new issues would reduce the risk of farm trade measures being replaced or made ineffective by domestic agricultural measures and technical barriers to trade that may be almost as trade distorting, a risk that has grown considerably in recent years.

Such issues as competition policy and investment policy are as relevant for developing-country agriculture as for other groups. However, as they may not be included in the millennium round, and as their implications for agriculture are, in any case, discussed elsewhere (for example, Tangermann and Josling 1999), this section focuses on the interests of developing countries in two emerging issues that directly affect agriculture: the issues surrounding technical standards, including SPS and food safety in the wake of the new biotechnologies; and agriculture's so-called multifunctionality.

Technical Standards, Including SPS and Food Safety Measures

The inability of the Standards Code that came out of the Tokyo Round to adequately address SPS issues, plus the desire to reduce the risk of re-instrumentation of agricultural support to SPS measures in response to reforms committed to under the URAA, gave birth to the SPS Agreement (SPSA) during the UR. That agreement defined new criteria that had to be met if a country chose to impose regulations more onerous than those agreed in international standards-setting bodies. It, together with the UR's strengthening of dispute settlement procedures at the WTO, was bound to raise the profile of SPS matters. That profile has been raised even more dramatically, especially in Europe, with the emergence of several food safety issues: mad cow disease, beef hormones and transgenic food products or genetically modified organisms (GMOs).

Developing countries have a complex set of interests in these developments. One is that the SPSA requires a WTO member to provide scientific justification for any measure that restricts trade more than the appropriate international standard would, and to formally assess the risks involved. At least some technical assistance to help developing countries meet these requirements has been provided, but more may be needed.

A second interest is in maintaining and increasing access to other members' markets that are protected by SPS measures. Again, some technical assistance in meeting those importers' standards is helpful. However, numerous countries use blunt quarantine instruments that excessively restrict imports well beyond what is necessary to protect the health of their plants and animals, or of their citizens in the case of food safety concerns. For example, outright bans exist on imports of many products, including into agricultural-exporting countries seeking to preserve a disease-free image. The levels of protection involved are in some cases equivalent to tariffs of more than 100 per cent. Without some form of notification requirement on WTO members that forces members to disclose the degree to which trade is restricted by such measures, reform in this area is likely to be confined to the small proportion of those cases that are brought before the WTO's dispute settlement body. The resource requirements of such legal proceedings ensure that the pace of reform by that means alone would be glacial, and would be skewed towards the concerns of those richer WTO members able to afford to bring such cases to the dispute settlement body.

Who gains and who loses from an SPS measure varies from case to case, depending on how widespread the externalities affecting production and/or consumption are. In the straightforward situation where the intent of the import restriction is simply to prevent the rise in the cost of disease control for domestic farmers, the latter group gains at the expense of domestic consumers and overseas producers. James and Anderson (1998) provide an example where the cost to consumers is likely to have outweighed any possible benefit to producers, resulting in a net national loss (not to mention the loss to potential overseas suppliers) from apparently excessive protection in a case where broader externalities appeared to be absent.

Domestic consumers are unlikely to be a source of pressure for liberalization of quarantine barriers, however, and not just for the usual reasons, that is, poor information, high costs of collective action because of free-riding and so on. In addition, citizens are often concerned about possible risks to the natural environment from importing exotic diseases and/or about the safety of imported food, and their demands for higher-quality, safer food and for environmental protection are going to continue to rise with their per capita incomes.

However, perceptions about the safety of different foods and food production and processing methods and the quality of conformity assessment procedures differ greatly, even among countries with similar income levels. The WTO dispute settlement case, brought by the United States and Canada against the EU over its ban on imports of beef that had been produced with the help of growth hormones, shows that standards differences across countries are difficult to resolve, even with a great deal of scientific advice. So too does the controversy over the banning of intra-EU beef trade because of the mad cow disease scare. How much more, then, are trade disputes likely to arise over issues for which the scientific evidence is far less complete? Thus not having consumers' concerns represented in the SPSA has been a two-edged sword: on the one hand, it has meant the absence of a voice arguing that domestic consumers should have better access to lower-priced imported food currently excluded by excessive quarantine regulations; but on the other hand, it has kept out of the SPS debate such issues as the consumers' right to know via, for example, labelling. The latter concern is not going to disappear. On the contrary, it is likely to show up in dispute settlement cases under the WTO's Agreement on Technical Barriers to Trade.[9]

Whether or not wealthy consumers are irrational and excessively risk averse when it comes to food safety issues is not really the point. Providing them with more scientific information and improving the reputation of national, regional and international standards-setting bodies may be valuable initiatives, but they may do little to alter consumer opinions in the medium term, and in any case, such information is scarce on new issues (Henson 1998; Mahe and Ortalo-Magne 1998).

In the case of policy dialogues surrounding GMOs, far more heat than light has been generated so far. Attempts to promote science-based assessment of the risks involved have met with extreme versions of the precautionary principle, manifest in the form of compete bans on their production, importation and/or sale in numerous markets. Many consumer groups have rejected proposed solutions, such as segregating GMO products and identifying them via labels on affected food items. They have also been resisted by the major producing countries in North and Latin America, which claim that 'like' products are involved, and so no costly GMO labelling is warranted. The fact that the production of some GMO products is less damaging to the environment than the production of traditional farm products has done little to dissuade civil society groups from their opposition to GMOs.

How are developing countries affected by this issue? Two ways in particular are worth noting: one is via the impact of the new technology in so far as it is lowering the costs of food production; and the other is via any food trade barriers that may be erected in response to consumer concerns in (mostly OECD) countries. The former would benefit those food-exporting developing countries able to attract the new technology, which places a premium on them having sound intellectual property law and enforcement in place (because seed companies would otherwise be wary of selling into or producing in such countries). If they cannot make productive use of the new biotechnologies, however, their competitiveness on international markets may be eroded as international food prices come down. Net food-importing developing countries could benefit from that price fall (subject to the provisos discussed in the first section of this chapter), and perhaps even more so if OECD countries ban imports of GMO products. The likely impact is clouded, however, because a premium might be attached to GMO-free products in international trade. This is clearly an area that requires more empirical economic research,[10] ideally taking into account the impact of the new biotechnology on the competitiveness of the often multinational input-supplying firms to examine the extent to which such firms, rather than farmers or consumers, may capture the gains from the new technology.

While such agricultural issues will arise increasingly under the UR's SPS and Technical Barriers to Trade Agreements, they will also arise in other contexts not related to agriculture. As with state trading, subsidies and competition policies, there is a strong case for developing common disciplines for all types of products, whether agricultural or not. In the case of the Agreement on Technical Barriers to Trade, there is nothing special about food as compared with, say, dangerous chemicals or heavy metals involved in the production or disposal of manufactured goods. A key advantage of having a common set of rules for risk analysis and risk management is that inconsistencies in current arrangements, and the problems that will keep causing a need for dispute settlement, would be reduced.

Multifunctionality

Some OECD countries have paid considerable attention to the term 'nontrade concerns', which appears in Article xx[c] of the URAA. WTO members agreed that in negotiating the continuation of the agricultural policy reform process after 1999, nontrade concerns would be taken into account. While not spelt out in any detail, the preamble to the URAA defines those concerns to include security of food supplies and protection of the environment. A third concern is the viability of rural areas. The governments discussing these three items are characterizing them as positive externalities and, in some cases, public goods that are jointly produced along with food and fibre. Hence their use of the word multifunctionality to describe these features of agricultural production.

Does agriculture deserve more price support and import protection than other sectors because of the nonmarketed externalities and public goods it produces jointly in the process of producing marketable food and fibre? That is, do these unrewarded positive externalities exceed the negative externalities from farming by more than the net positive externalities produced by other sectors? If so, to what extent, if any, are those farmer-produced externalities undersupplied, and where there is underprovision, what are the most efficient ways to boost farmers' production to socially optimal levels?

So-called nontrade concerns are becoming an issue in the WTO in numerous areas, not just with respect to agriculture. They are a direct consequence of the lowering or outlawing of trade barriers: with less natural and government protection from import competition, domestic policies are becoming relatively more important as determinants of the international competitiveness of certain industries. Despite their characterization as nontrade, these concerns need to be dealt with in the WTO because they certainly can affect trade. Ideally they should be handled in the same way for all sectors, for example, under an expanded Agreement on Subsidies and Countervailing Measures, but until that is done they cannot be ignored in the upcoming agricultural negotiations.

These concerns are not really new, but they are being packaged slightly differently than in the past. A key question at stake is whether they require exceptional treatment, or whether WTO provisions are sufficient to cater for them, for example, via the URAA's green box. The short answer appears to be that WTO provisions are adequate for dealing with the main cases raised.

Both economic theory and policy practice have taught us at least five lessons relevant to this issue. First, where there are several policy objectives, an equal number of policy instruments is typically required to deal with them efficiently. Second, the most efficient and lowest-cost policy instrument or measure for achieving a particular objective (such as overcoming a market failure) will be the one that addresses the concern most directly. Third, trade measures in particular are rarely the most efficient instruments for addressing nontrade concerns. Fourth, trade reform will improve welfare so long as optimal domestic interventions are in place to deal with the nontrade concerns. Fifth, whenever governments intervene in a market, even if it is to overcome a market failure, there is a risk of government failure, which could reduce welfare more than the market failure the intervention is trying to offset. The government failure could result simply from a lack of information and analysis to design an appropriate intervention (bureaucratic failure), or it could result from deliberate action at the political level aimed at rewarding particular groups covertly for their political support, even though that intervention may be costly to the community at large.

Every productive sector generates both marketed and nonmarketed products. Some of those nonmarketed products (for instance, the amenity value of animals grazing) are considered more desirable than others, and some (such as pesticide sprays) are considered undesirable. Because tastes and preferences change over time and differ between countries, so too will society's valuation of those nonmarketed products. As technologies, institutions, policy experiences and market sizes change in the process of development, so will the scope for being able to market some of the previously unmarketable products that were jointly produced with each sector's main products.

To make a case for farming to receive more assistance from the government than other sectors, proponents need to demonstrate that agricultural production is not only a net contributor in terms of externalities and public goods, but is also more of a net contributor than other sectors, especially those sectors that would expand if agricultural supports were to shrink. Demonstrating this is an almost impossible task, given the difficulties in obtaining estimates of society's ever-changing evaluation of the myriad externalities and public goods generated by the economy's various sectors and of the marginal costs of their provision. This is the rationale behind the practice of intervening only in the most obvious situations requiring correction.

Even if a clear case could be made for an intervention, the appropriate measure is unlikely to be import restrictions or output price supports for a broad range of marketed farm commodities. Rather, it will be a finely tuned measure to encourage the optimal extra amount of just the public good or external aspect that has been undersupplied (or would be under *laissez-faire*).

The policy task thus involves several steps: obtaining a sense of society's willingness to pay for the nonmarketable by-product; determining the most efficient policy instrument for encouraging farmers or others to supply that by-product for society; and assessing the optimal level of encouragement so as to equate the marginal social benefit with the marginal social cost of that intervention, bearing in mind the risks associated with one or both forms of government failure identified earlier.

Some of the more specific conclusions from a recent review of these issues are worth stressing (Anderson 1998). First, several policy instruments will be necessary to address the numerous policy objectives encompassed in the nontrade concerns efficiently. General agricultural price support programmes are not among the efficient measures. This is true even of direct domestic supports, let alone indirect supports via import barriers or export subsidies (which also distort consumer prices), because those instruments are far too blunt to achieve the specific objectives involved efficiently.

With respect to food security, the most efficient policy instrument for boosting it beyond that provided under free markets is probably subsidies to stockholding staple foods, something already allowed for in annex 2 of the URAA. Import restrictions to boost self-sufficiency, far from helping, may actually diminish food security for vulnerable groups struggling to pay the high price of protected domestic food. Once bound tariffs are lowered to applied rates, greater stability in international food markets will prevail, which will boost food security in all parts of the world.

Environmental protection has many facets, and so requires a range of policy instruments. Reducing farm output price supports, as under the URAA, probably provides the single biggest potential contribution to the rural environment in OECD countries inclined towards agricultural protectionism by lowering the level and intensity of farm production. While those supports are still in the process of being phased down, additional taxes, charges or other regulations should be levied on pollution from farm inputs to offset the extra damage they cause via output price supports. Such input taxes are, of course, permitted under WTO rules. In so far as agriculture provides positive externalities or public goods, appropriate policies are decoupled payments for their specific provision to the optimal level in each location, assuming that the optimal level is higher than the level that would otherwise prevail, bearing in mind the marginal social cost of further provision. Because most of those goods can be provided independently of farming, decoupling is not only possible, but also desirable, because nonfarmers may be able to provide some of these goods or services at lower cost than farmers. Some provision for such payments is made in both the URAA and in the WTO's Agreement on Subsidies and Countervailing Measures.

Ensuring the viability of rural areas is also a laudable goal, but again the blunt instrument of general farm product price supports is far from optimal, particularly because agriculture is not even the dominant source of income in many rural areas, especially those close to cities. Far more appropriate are WTO-consistent, targeted, adjustment assistance (including retraining) packages, and perhaps subsidies to essential services that would otherwise be withdrawn from strategic, remote areas that are left behind.

In short, WTO rules and URAA reform commitments are not incompatible with the adoption of efficient measures for addressing nontrade concerns. There is plenty of synergy and no need for tradeoffs between domestic policy objectives and the objectives of agricultural protection reform as embodied in

WTO rules. Note, however, that some re-instrumentation of farm support measures is inevitable and is already evident as traditional measures (tariffs, export subsidies and domestic price supports) are phased down. Getting a particular measure included on the list of green box measures so that it is excluded when calculating the aggregate measure of support will be a much sought-after prize by agricultural protectionist forces during the next round of WTO negotiations. Careful scrutiny of the grounds for such inclusions is likely to be a high-payoff activity for developing-country trade negotiators.

Both exporting and import-competing countries should welcome the call for closer scrutiny of instruments used to address nontrade concerns. This is partly because once these superior instruments are identified and adopted at closer to optimal levels, greater food security and environmental protection will result. But perhaps equally important, the current blunt instruments of support to farm product prices could then be dismantled more rapidly, as there would be even less reason to maintain them. Consumers, taxpayers and exporters of nonfarm products in the countries protecting farmers, together with the world's more efficient farmers, could then join with those anxious to conserve global resources in celebrating this improvement in the management of the world's economy and environment.

CONCLUSIONS AND OPTIONS FOR DEVELOPING COUNTRIES

Several prominent EU spokespersons have already dubbed the next WTO round a development round. This is partly a response to the developing countries' disappointment in the UR, and partly a reflection of their considerably increased weight in the WTO. Developing countries now make up almost five-sixths of the WTO membership of 138, and that share will continue to rise as the 30 developing and transition economies currently in the midst of accession negotiations gradually complete that process, many before the end of the next round.

The next WTO round thus offers probably the best prospects ever for developing countries in general – and their rural communities in particular – to secure growth-enhancing reforms. In the mercantilist tradition of multilateral trade negotiations, this will necessarily take the form of requests and offers, but the so-called concessions that are offered are in fact beneficial to the economies making those reform offers: a win–win game in terms of nations' economic welfare.

The liberalization of traditional agricultural market access should be the key priority issue in the next WTO round of multilateral trade negotiations, given the enormous potential for global and developing-country welfare gains from reducing agricultural protection. Assurances are also needed that the EU and the United States will fully honour the spirit of their commitment to gradually expand market access for textiles and clothing, and not simply replace the remaining half of the QRs on trade in those products with safeguard measures. Substantial progress in freeing up more trade in both these sectors is essential if the next round is to be a genuine development round.

Such reform could boost enormously the earnings of the world's poor, the vast majority of whom are in rural households in developing countries. Rural households would benefit even in NIEs that take advantage of expanding opportunities to export textile products, for example, through some of their household members moving to new jobs in nearby clothing factories.

From an agricultural development perspective, attention should also focus on reducing protection granted to other manufacturing and service industries. Protection in those sectors still bestows a significant anti-agricultural bias in many developing countries, making benefits from the agricultural and textile trade reforms of OECD countries more difficult to achieve. These reforms can be carried out unilaterally, but the next WTO round offers an opportunity to obtain a *quid pro quo*, and can be a useful instrument for locking in such reforms domestically.

This next round will, however, be conducted in an environment in which globalization forces – including ever-faster development and international transfers of information, ideas, capital, skills and new technologies – will, by having increasingly stronger impacts on domestic markets, simultaneously trigger insulationist policy reactions. For example, further reductions in traditional measures of farm protection will meet significant resistance in numerous OECD countries, as farm groups join with food safety and environmental groups to argue for new forms of agricultural protection.

In these circumstances the mercantilist nature of trade negotiations may require that the agenda of the next WTO round include not only other sectors, but also some new trade agenda items, such as investment and competition policies, so as to provide the potential for beneficial issue linkages and tradeoffs. Such new items may cause political and administrative difficulties in some developing countries, but they may also create additional opportunities to secure domestic reforms that would boost their economies. Limited analytical and negotiating resources in developing countries make a number of them hesitant about having many new issues in the next round, but developing countries may need to agree to discuss at least some of the new trade issues if they want to ensure that agricultural (and textile) market access remains high on the WTO's agenda.

Given the apparent goodwill towards making this next WTO round a development round, and given that many developing countries have embraced major reforms unilaterally during the past decade or so (Michaelopoulos

1999), perhaps developing countries should adopt a different approach this time. For example, they might consider exchanging more MFN market access with OECD countries rather than seeking special and differential treatment and tariff preferences. Special and different treatment simply allows developing-country governments to continue to keep 'shooting their economies in the foot' by delaying beneficial reforms; and tariff preferences tend to divide developing countries into subgroups, thereby weakening their individual and collective bargaining strength.

A striking example of the latter has been exposed in the prolonged and extremely costly dispute over access to the EU market for bananas. The EU policy regime involves layers of preferences that have divided developing countries into 'we' and 'they' groups, and thereby weakened their chances of securing a better deal for all.

Another illustration of how preferential treatment has reduced the resolve of developing countries to push for OECD farm policy reform has to do with their food imports from the protectionist countries. Food export subsidies, export credits and nonemergency food aid are all by-products of OECD farm support programmes. Without these programmes, most developing countries would be better off through expanded trade opportunities, and those that would not could be compensated with expanded access to OECD markets for tropical products and/or direct financial aid, which would be a far more efficient way of transferring resources to developing countries than transferring them in kind as a way of disposing of surpluses.

With these examples in mind, would developing countries' interests be served by the new EU proposal for OECD countries to provide preferential access to exports of least developed countries? If the things that matter, such as agricultural and textile products, were to be effectively excluded from such a deal, the least developed countries would gain little of substance, yet those countries would then feel less able to join other developing countries in seeking lower MFN tariffs on products of export interest to all developing countries. Meanwhile, OECD countries could use this initiative as an excuse for not reforming as much in the key areas.

All this suggests a potentially high payoff for developing countries acting collectively to push hard for greater market access for farm and textile products, and for technical and economic assistance to aid their reform processes, in return for providing more access to developing-country markets for goods and services. The political price of the latter offer is, after all, now much lower than it used to be, because the forces of globalization are such that economies are now rewarded more, via inflows of foreign capital, for good domestic economic governance, but they are also penalized more if poor policy choices are not corrected. Two such corrections that would simultaneously help the cause of reducing agricultural protection abroad would be for developing countries to commit to not using taxes or other restraints on agricultural exports, and to reduce their often extremely high ceiling bindings on their own import tariffs on farm products.

More specific requests that agricultural-exporting developing countries might put on their wish list include the following:

- Remove tariffs on tropical, including processed agricultural products.
- Replace specific with *ad valorem* tariffs on imports of interest to developing-country exporters, because the former, which apply to 42 per cent of US and EU agricultural tariffs, discriminate against products of lower quality and ones whose international price is declining over time.
- Use the Swiss formula approach in making market access commitments, as that will reduce tariff peaks and escalation the most.
- Seek a firm phase-out date for agricultural TRQs, as was obtained for textiles and clothing in the UR, but with limits on the extent to which safeguards can replace the QRs at the end of the phase-out period.
- Seek firm commitments, preferably written into OECD countries' schedules, on the extent of economic and technical assistance that they will provide to cope with the adjustment to reforms, especially for the least developed and net food-importing developing countries.
- Support the liberalization of trade in maritime services, given the potential for the cartelized OECD firms that own most of the ships to extract much of the exporters' gain from goods trade liberalization via higher markups.

NOTES

1. This chapter draws on Anderson (1999).
2. Formed at a meeting in the Australian city that gave the group its name, the Cairns Group currently comprises 15 members: Argentina, Australia, Brazil, Canada, Chile, Colombia, Fiji, Indonesia, Malaysia, New Zealand, Paraguay, Philippines, South Africa, Thailand and Uruguay. Originally the group excluded Paraguay and South Africa but included Hungary.
3. This is increasingly likely the more their government is constrained by WTO commitments from following the earlier examples of the EU, Japan and the Republic of Korea in raising food import barriers increasingly as industrialization proceeds (Anderson and Hayami 1986). Manufacturing exporters in NIEs have a direct interest in such constraints to agricultural protection growth at home, because farm supports raise the price and reduce the quantity of mobile resources, especially low-skilled labour, available for factory work.
4. For empirical support for this proposition see, for example, Ingco (1997) with respect to the least developed countries and Anderson and Strutt (1999) with respect to Indonesia. The point is also made strongly in Martin and Winters (1996).
5. Francois and Martin (1998) demonstrate, however, that because many agricultural tariffs are specific and farm prices fluctuate from year to year for seasonal reasons, binding those tariffs does lower both the mean and variance of their *ad valorem* equivalents over time, even when the bindings are well above the applied rates.

6. Because the computational exercise involved removing all trade distortions, many of the difficulties raised in Anderson (1999, appendix) that relate to measuring the effects of partial reform of a tariff rate quota regime are absent.
7. Note that these results ignore the effect of tariff preference erosion. In so far as a developing country currently receives such preferences in OECD markets, the results slightly overstate the potential gains from reforms.
8. The importance of postfarmgate activities to farm income increases rapidly with urbanization. It is not uncommon for the costs (including normal profits) of getting a farm product from the farmgate to the retail consumer to be several times the farmer's cost of production of the unprocessed product. Also important to exporters of bulky farm products are maritime shipping costs. Shipping lines not only tend to be owned by OECD firms, but also tend to be cartelized. A recent study by Francois and Wooten (1999) estimated that, depending on the degree of collusion, shippers could absorb up to half the gains from trade liberalization in the form of higher markups.
9. Indeed, one paper has already been posted on the Internet advocating activists to argue under the Agreement on Technical Barriers to Trade for the right of WTO member governments to require compulsory labelling of products containing GMOs sold in their markets (Stillwell and Van Dyke 1999).
10. Nielsen and Anderson (2001) have made a beginning using a global, economywide model.

REFERENCES

Anderson, K. (1998), 'Domestic Agricultural Policy Objectives and Trade Liberalization: Synergies and Trade-offs', in *Proceedings of the OECD Workshop on Emerging Trade Issues in Agriculture*, Paris: OECD. See also a revised version: K. Anderson (2000), 'Agriculture's "Multifunctionality" and the WTO', *Australian Journal of Agricultural and Resource Economics*, **44** (3), 475-94.

Anderson, K. (1999), 'Agriculture, Developing Countries, and the WTO Millennium Round', paper presented at the World Bank Conference on Agriculture and the New Trade Agenda from a Development Perspective, 1-2 October, Geneva (forthcoming as Chapter 1 in M.D. Ingco and L.A. Winters (eds) (2001), *Agriculture and the New Trade Agenda From a Development Perspective*, Cambridge and New York: Cambridge University Press).

Anderson, K. and Y. Hayami (1986), *The Political Economy of Agricultural Protection*, Boston, London and Sydney: Allen and Unwin.

Anderson, K. and A. Strutt (1999), 'Impact of East Asia's Growth Interruption and Policy Responses: The Case of Indonesia', *Asian Economic Journal*, **13** (2), 205-18.

Anderson, K. and R. Tyers (1993), 'More on Welfare Gains to Developing Countries from Liberalising World Food Trade', *Journal of Agricultural Economics*, **44** (2), 189-204.

Anderson, K., B. Dimaranan, T. Hertel and W. Martin (1997), 'Economic Growth and Policy Reforms in the APEC Region: Trade and Welfare Implications by 2005', *Asia-Pacific Economic Review*, **3** (1), 1-18.

Anderson, K., B. Hoekman and A. Strutt (2001), 'Agriculture and the WTO: Next Steps', *Review of International Economics*, **9** (2), 192-214.

Elbehri, A., M. Ingco, T. Hertel and K. Pearson (1999), 'Agricultural Liberalization in the New Millennium', paper presented at the WTO/World Bank conference on Agriculture and the New Trade Agenda from a Development Perspective, 1-2 October, Geneva.

Finger, J.M. and L. Schuknecht (1999), 'Market Access Advances and Retreats: The Uruguay Round and Beyond', paper presented at the Annual World Bank Conference on Development Economics, April, Washington, DC.

Francois, J.F. (1999), 'Approaches to Agricultural Policy Model Construction', paper presented at the UNCTAD workshop on Agricultural Policy Modelling, 24–25 March, Geneva.

Francois, J.F. and W. Martin (1998), 'Commercial Policy Uncertainty, the Expected Cost of Protection, and Market Access', Discussion Paper, Erasmus University, Tinbergen Institute, Rotterdam, the Netherlands.

Francois, J.F. and I. Wooten (1999), 'Trade in International Transport Services: The Role of Competition', paper presented at the First Annual Conference of the European Trade Study Group, 24–26 September, Erasmus University, Rotterdam, the Netherlands. Available at www.etsg.org/etsg/detailedprogram.htm.

Grossman, G.M. and E. Helpman (1995), 'Trade Wars and Trade Talks', *Journal of Political Economy*, **103** (4), 675–708.

Henson, S. (1998), 'Regulating the Trade Effects of National Food Safety Standards', OECD Workshop on Emerging Trade Issues in Agriculture, 25–26 October, Paris. Available on www.oecd.org/agr/trade/.

Hertel, T.W. (ed.) (1997), *Global Trade Analysis: Modelling and Applications*, Cambridge, UK, and New York: Cambridge University Press.

Hertel, T.W. and W. Martin (1999), 'Developing Country Interests in Liberalising Manufactures Trade', paper presented at the WTO/World Bank Conference on Developing Countries in a Millennium Round, 19–20 September, Geneva.

Hillman, A.L. and P. Moser (1995), 'Trade Liberalisation as Politically Optimal Exchange of Market Access', in M. Canzoneri et al. (eds), *The New Transatlantic Economy*, Cambridge, UK: Cambridge University Press.

Ingco, M.D. (1996), 'Tariffication in the Uruguay Round: How Much Liberalization?', *World Economy*, **19** (4), 425–47.

Ingco, M.D. (1997), 'Has Agricultural Trade Liberalization Improved Welfare in the Least-Developed Countries? Yes', Policy Research Working Paper no. 1748, World Bank, Washington, DC.

James, S. and K. Anderson (1998), 'On the Need for More Economic Assessment of Quarantine Policies', *Australian Journal of Agricultural and Resource Economics*, **41** (4), 525–44.

Mahe, L.P. and F. Ortalo-Magne (1998), 'International Co-operation in the Regulation of Food Quality and Safety Attributes', in *Proceedings of the OECD Workshop on Emerging Trade Issues in Agriculture*, Paris: OECD.

Martin, W. and L.A. Winters (eds) (1996), *The Uruguay Round and the Developing Countries*, Cambridge, UK, and New York: Cambridge University Press.

Michaelopoulos, C. (1999), 'The Integration of Developing Countries into the Multilateral Trading System', World Bank and WTO Secretariat, Washington, DC and Geneva, processed.

Nielsen, C. and K. Anderson (2001), 'GMOs, Trade Policy, and Welfare in Rich and Poor Countries', in K. Maskus and J. Wilson (eds), *Quantifying the Impact of Technical Barriers to Trade: Can it Be Done?*, Ann Arbor, MI: University of Michigan Press.

Schiff, M. and A. Valdes (1992), *The Political Economy of Agricultural Pricing Policy*, vol. 4, *A Synthesis of the Economics in Developing Countries*, Baltimore, MD: The Johns Hopkins University Press.

Snape, R.H. (1987), 'The Importance of Frontier Barriers', in H. Kierzkowski (ed.), *Protection and Competition in International Trade*, Oxford, UK: Basil Blackwell.

Stillwell, M. and B. Van Dyke (1999), 'An Activist's Handbook on Genetically Modified Organisms and the WTO', Center for International Environmental Law, Washington, DC, and Geneva. Available on www.consumerscouncil/org/ccc/policyhandbk399.htm.

Tangermann, S. and T. Josling (1999), 'The Interests of Developing Countries in the Next Round of WTO Agricultural Negotiations', paper presented at the UNCTAD workshop on Developing a Proactive and Coherent Agenda for African Countries in Support of Their Participation in International Trade Negotiations, 29 June–2 July, Pretoria, South Africa.

4. Asian developing countries and the global trading system for agriculture, textiles and clothing

Prema-chandra Athukorala

The signing of the UR Agreement in 1994 and the inauguration of the WTO in 1995 have set the stage for effective participation by developing countries in a rules-based world trading system. Particularly important in this connection are the agreements relating to agriculture (URAA) and to textiles and clothing (ATC). These agreements aim to strengthen multilateral discipline in these two product areas, which are of significant export interest for developing countries.

The actual extent of liberalization to be achieved under these agreements is likely to be extremely modest. The major focus of the URAA is on the translation of nontariff barriers (NTBs) into tariffs (tariffication), but the actual reduction of protection is still to be agreed as part of a built-in agenda. The agreement included a provision to undertake further negotiations on agricultural protection in 2000, under which countries that agree to concessions will receive reciprocal concessions.[1] Unlike the URAA, the ATC contains a bound commitment by industrial countries to phase out MFA quotas. However, the ATC allows the industrial countries to delay almost all removal of MFA-sanctioned import quotas until 2005. Even then the industrial countries can use safeguard provisions of the agreement to water down promised liberalization if they choose to do so. There are also indications that the industrial countries are likely to rely increasingly on antidumping provisions as a new form of protection.

Despite these limitations, the URAA and ATC do provide for much more significant changes to protectionism in these product areas than could have been anticipated before the negotiations began. Put simply, these agreements are more important for their potential effect on future rounds of trade negotiations than for their achievements during implementation of the UR. To prepare for the task of successfully building on this foundation in future trade rounds, we must broaden our understanding of the commitments set out in the agreements, the constraints the developing countries face in their attempts to comply with the commitments and the nature of the 'unfinished' agenda. To this end this chapter provides a comparative case study of developing countries in the Asia Pacific region.

THE ROLE OF AGRICULTURE AND THE TEXTILES AND CLOTHING INDUSTRIES IN ASIAN DEVELOPING COUNTRIES

Agriculture

The relative importance of agriculture in national output and trade varies significantly among Asian developing countries, and reflects differences in the stage of economic advancement (Table 4.1). In Korea and Taiwan, the share of agriculture in GDP had declined to less than 5 per cent by the mid-1990s. Despite rapid growth over the past two decades, this sector still accounted for more than 10 per cent of GDP in Malaysia and Thailand and around 17 per cent in Indonesia. In other countries in East Asia and in all South Asian countries agriculture is still the single most important sector in terms of its contribution to GDP. In all these countries the employment share of the agriculture sector is, on average, much larger than that of other sectors. In most of the low-income countries in the region more than three-quarters of the workforce is engaged in agricultural pursuits.

On the trade front, the share of agricultural products in total exports from all countries in the region has declined significantly over the past two decades. However, these products still account for a significant share of total exports in a number of countries, particularly those lower down the development ladder.

The net food trade position (net food imports as a share of total imports) varies significantly across countries. China, India, Indonesia, Malaysia, Myanmar, Thailand and Vietnam are net food exporters, while others are net importers. Historical data for China, India, Indonesia and Vietnam show that the net food export position has largely been the outcome of import substitution in key food products rather than success in agricultural exports (Anderson 1986; Gulati 1999; Lin 1994; Srinivasan 1994). Under a more liberal agricultural trade policy regime the net export position could, therefore, erode significantly in the short to medium run until productive sectors with a comparative advantage (in particular, rice) begin to generate significant export surpluses. Malaysia and Thailand have relatively liberal food trade regimes and their export surpluses have arisen largely through export expansion.

A noteworthy recent development in agricultural exports from the region has been a rapid growth of processed food exports, despite the

Table 4.1 Agriculture in developing Asian economies, selected indicators, 1996/97 average (%)

Region/economy	Share of agriculture in GDP	Share of agricultural employment in total employment	Share of agriculture in total exports[a]	Share of food products in total exports	Share of agriculture in total exports[a]	Share of food products in total imports	Net food imports as a share of total imports
NIEs							
Hong Kong	2.5	0.3	0.6	0.2	7.3	4.0	3.8
Korea, Rep. of	3.0	11.6	3.5	2.1	12.2	4.7	2.9
Singapore	0.2	0.2	4.4	1.8	—	—	—
Taiwan	3.3	10.1	4.7	3.1	11.0	4.1	0.6
China, People's Rep.	20.5	47.8	10.3	6.7	12.1	4.1	-3.3
ASEAN							
Indonesia	16.7	44.0	18.2	7.6	17.8	9.2	0.4
Malaysia	12.7	16.4	29.7	24.0	7.4	4.6	-19.3
Philippines	20.6	41.7	9.2	6.8	11.5	7.3	3.3
Thailand	11.0	50.0	25.6	19.4	8.6	3.1	-11.9
Other Southeast Asian economies							
Cambodia	43.9	93.5	—	—	—	—	—
Lao, PDR	52.9	93.3	—	—	—	—	—
Myanmar	58.8	62.7	74.3	44.6	5.5	2.3	-18.5
Vietnam	27.8	69.3	40.4	33.4	7.7	3.7	-18.1

South Asia							
Bangladesh	24.2	44.9	13.5	11.6	18.0	15.4	6.7
India	21.5	67.0	23.8	18.3	8.8	4.5	-13.1
Nepal	41.5	95.0	13.7	9.8	13.6	6.4	3.8
Pakistan	25.2	52.5	17.6	9.4	13.2	7.4	0.4
Sri Lanka	21.9	37.1	25.9	21.1	14.7	11.2	8.8

Notes: — Not available. a Including food products.

Source: ADB (various years); World Bank (various years).

71

observed general decline in the share of agriculture in total exports (Table 4.2). The most prominent of the dynamic new items has been processed fish, whose share in total processed food exports from South Asia increased from 5.6 per cent in 1970 to 38 per cent in 1995. According to disaggregated data for individual countries, in 1995 processed fish alone accounted for 70 per cent of agricultural exports from Bangladesh, 45 per cent from India, 28 per cent from Sri Lanka, 25 per cent from Pakistan and 20 per cent from Thailand, compared with an average share of 5 per cent in the mid-1970s. The share of preserved fruit has also increased though not as spectacularly as that of processed fish. By contrast, the shares of traditional processed food items, such as sugar and molasses, animal feeds, tobacco products and vegetable oils, have either fallen or fluctuated erratically over time.

Table 4.2   *Exports of processed food as a share of total agricultural exports, selected Asian countries, two-year averages, selected years, 1980-96 (%)*

Years	Bangladesh	India	Malaysia	Pakistan	Sri Lanka	Thailand
1980–81	22.7	33.2	13.5	10.5	4.6	27.1
1985–86	44.5	32.6	20.2	14.2	9.5	30.2
1990–91	54.4	40.1	34.3	15.4	7.3	37.8
1995–96	82.7	44.8	40.1	43.0	21.5	48.6

Note: Commodities included belong to Section 3 of the International Standard Industry Classification. See Athukorala and Sen (1998) on the procedure used in separating processed food from total agricultural exports.

Source: Compiled by the author from the *Comtrade* database of the United Nations.

The emergence of processed food as a dynamic export line is not peculiar to East Asia. It is a part of a general phenomenon of globalization of processed food markets (Athukorala and Sen 1998; Henderson, Handy and Neff 1996). Powerful forces on both the demand and supply sides have underpinned this far-reaching change in world agricultural trade. On the demand side, the internationalization of food habits – the increased importance of imported, processed items in consumption patterns in the industrial countries as well as among large sections of the populace in many developing countries – appears to play a key role. Factors such as international migration, the communications revolution and international tourism have contributed to this phenomenon. This significant demand-side impetus seems to have been supported by important supply-side developments, such as improvements in food technology, refrigeration facilities and transportation that have made processed food items easily tradable across national boundaries.

The new export opportunities in processed food deserve special attention in the policy debate on global integration of countries rich in agricultural resources for a number of reasons. First, evidence indicates that the degree of income and price elasticity of demand for processed food is high. This implies that export diversification into this commodity category will result in significant terms of trade gains. Second, unlike the further processing of resources such as minerals and timber, the final stages of food processing are labour intensive. Third, in terms of net balance of payments implications, processed foods are superior to conventional manufactured goods because of their lower import intensity. Finally, the expansion of processed food exports is a powerful vehicle for linking the rural economy with the ongoing process of economic globalization.

Unfortunately, the expansion of processed food exports from developing countries has triggered a protectionist response in the industrial countries in the form of stringent SPS standards imposed on the approval of shipments. The indications are that as tariff barriers and quantitative import restrictions are progressively dismantled as part of the ongoing liberalization process, the importing countries tend to intensify the use of technical barriers to protect domestic producers' interests (Henderson, Handy and Neff 1996; Sykes 1995). Meeting SPS standards is far more complicated and costly in the case of processed food than for primary agricultural products. Thus these standards can retard trade even when they are imposed because of genuine health and safety considerations, given the unavailability of compliance resources and expertise in the developing countries.

The impact of SPS measures in industrial-country markets on processed food exports from developing countries has yet to be systematically studied. However, detention data from the US Food and Drug Administration – treated here as a proxy for the ability to meet food safety standards – seem to support the view that failure to comply with SPS standards is a far more important issue for exporters from developing countries than for their industrial-country counterparts (Table 4.3). The apparent negative relationship between the incidence of detention and the per capita income of exporting countries suggests that richer exporting countries generally tend to have a greater capacity to meet SPS standards.

Textiles and Clothing

The Asia Pacific region occupies a pivotal position in world trade in textiles

Table 4.3   US food imports and detention of shipments by the US Food and Drug Administration, by source country, May 1999–April 2000

Source country (number of countries)	Import value (%)	Detentions		Number of detentions per US$1 million of imports
		Number	%	
High-income countries (21)	31.6	1934	19.5	0.6
Mean	1.6	97.0	1.0	0.5
Range	0.37–16.0	32–399	0.3–4.0	0.1–2.7
Upper–middle-income countries (9)	27.9	2143	21.6	0.7
Mean	3.1	238	2.4	1.2
Range	0.2–3.5	311–539	0.3–15.5	0.2–1.7
Lower–middle-income countries (12)	25.8	3378	34.0	1.2
Mean	2.15	282	2.8	2.6
Range	0.2–11.1	11–765	0.2–7.7	0.8–11.0
Low-income countries (10)	10.2	1874	18.9	1.7
Mean	1.0	197	1.9	2.3
Range	0.1–4.3	14–860	0.1–8.7	0.6–8.0
Unclassified	4.4	599	6.0	1.3
Total[a] (52)	100	9875	100	0.9
Mean	1.8	179	1.8	1.7
Range	1.0–16.0	11–860	0.1–15.5	0.1–11.0

Note: The table covers only imports of fishery products, vegetables and fruit. Food imports from developing countries are predominantly concentrated in these categories. Country groupings are based on the World Bank's country classification by income levels.
a   The total number of detentions is net of shipments originating within the United States.

Source: Compiled by the author from the Comtrade database of the United Nations and US Food and Drug Administration import detention data available on http://www.fda.gov/oasis.

and clothing. By the mid-1990s, four economies in the region were among the world's ten largest exporters in this product area (China, Hong Kong, Korea and Taiwan). Exports from the region accounted for more than 80 per cent of total exports from developing countries and more than 60 per cent of total world trade in textiles and clothing.

Table 4.4 provides data on the share of textiles and clothing in total merchandise exports from the region's economies and the share of each economy in total exports from the region for 1985/86 and 1996/97.

The data point to the growing importance of this product sector for latecomers to industrialization in the region (defined broadly to cover all countries other than the four East Asian NIEs). All these countries, with the exception of Pakistan, have recorded significant increases in the share of this commodity category in total exports. Increases in the share of textiles and clothing in total merchandise exports are particularly noteworthy for Bangladesh, Cambodia, Lao People's Democratic Republic (PDR), and Sri Lanka. By the late 1990s, textiles and clothing accounted for 79 per cent of total exports from Bangladesh, 62 per cent from Sri Lanka, 62 per cent from Cambodia, and 58 per cent from Lao PDR.

The relative importance of clothing in the export composition of East Asian NIEs has declined, reflecting the erosion of their comparative advantage in this labour-intensive product line. Presumably the decline would have been much faster had it not been for the massive quota rent bestowed on these countries by the restrictive world trade regime under the MFA. Quota rent has been an effective buffer for these countries against escalating domestic cost pressure on profit margins.

Quota allocations under the MFA, coupled with mounting production costs in the NIEs, certainly played a role in the geographic spread of the garment industry within and beyond the region. However, the export success of newcomers in this product area cannot be explained in terms of this factor alone. Market-oriented policy reforms in the latter countries have also played an important role. Clear evidence shows that the export takeoff in clothing in countries like Bangladesh, Indonesia, Sri Lanka and Vietnam occurred only after these countries had embarked on market-oriented reforms (Athukorala and Rajapatirana 2000; Dowlah 1999; Hill 2000). When allowing for the size of the country, its massive labour surplus and its entrepreneurial skills, India's export record in this area does not match that of Bangladesh and Sri Lanka. However, this is not surprising given India's persistence with highly restrictive trade and foreign direct investment policy regimes relating to labour-intensive product sectors, despite significant liberalization initiatives since 1991 (Srinivasan 1998b).

Table 4.4 Textile and clothing exports from Asian developing economies, two-year averages, 1985/86 and 1996/97 (%)

Region/economy	Share in total country exports						Share in total regional exports					
	1985/86			1996/97			1985/86			1996/97		
	Textiles	Clothing	Textiles and clothing	Textiles	Clothing	Textiles and clothing	Textiles	Clothing	Textiles and clothing	Textiles	Clothing	Textiles and clothing
NIEs	6.7	14.4	21.1	6.9	4.5	13.5	48.1	64.6	58.3	49.9	25.4	36.2
Hong Kong	6.6	34.1	40.7	6.2	33.4	42.4	8.0	25.6	18.9	3.1	12.8	8.6
Korea, Rep. of	8.8	15.3	24.1	10.2	3.3	12.3	19.1	20.5	20.0	23.4	5.9	13.6
Singapore	1.7	2.7	4.4	1.0	1.2	10.2	2.6	2.5	2.5	2.3	2.0	2.2
Taiwan	7.9	11.0	18.9	9.6	2.7	11.7	18.5	16.0	16.9	21.1	4.6	11.9
China	14.0	16.0	30.0	7.8	17.0	26.0	28.3	20.0	23.2	23.4	39.7	32.6
ASEAN	2.2	4.0	6.2	2.8	5.5	14.5	6.4	7.3	7.0	10.6	16.1	13.7
Indonesia	1.6	2.6	4.2	4.9	6.4	15.4	1.8	1.8	1.8	4.6	4.6	4.6
Malaysia	1.2	2.5	3.7	1.7	3.0	12.0	1.2	1.5	1.4	2.3	3.3	2.9
Philippines	0.9	6.0	6.8	1.3	10.6	19.6	0.3	1.1	0.8	0.5	3.4	2.1
Thailand	5.9	8.8	14.7	3.1	6.0	15.0	3.1	2.9	3.0	3.1	4.7	4.0
Other Southeast Asian economies	1.3	4.2	5.4	2.1	18.9	27.9	0.1	0.1	0.1	0.4	2.5	1.5
Cambodia	1.2	2.8	4.0	0.5	52.9	61.9	0.0	0.0	0.0	0.0	0.3	0.2

Lao, PDR	1.2	0.5	1.6	0.7	49.0	58.0	0.0	0.0	0.0	0.0	0.2	0.1
Myanmar	0.2	0.9	1.1	0.2	18.5	27.5	0.0	0.0	0.0	0.0	0.3	0.2
Vietnam	2.4	7.6	10.0	2.5	16.3	25.3	0.1	0.1	0.1	0.3	1.8	1.1
South Asia	17.4	13.1	30.4	18.1	23.9	32.9	17.0	7.9	11.4	15.7	16.1	15.9
Bangladesh	32.8	20.9	53.8	9.2	69.8	78.8	2.1	0.8	1.3	0.6	3.8	2.4
India	11.4	10.8	22.2	13.3	14.5	23.5	7.1	4.2	5.3	7.8	6.7	7.2
Pakistan	37.1	12.0	49.1	50.4	25.8	34.8	7.4	1.5	3.8	6.5	2.6	4.3
Sri Lanka	1.2	25.6	26.8	4.9	52.6	61.6	0.1	1.3	0.8	0.3	2.8	1.7
Nepal	21.7	25.6	47.3	46.5	32.7	41.7	0.2	0.1	0.2	0.3	0.2	0.2
Pacific island economies	0.0	0.4	0.4	0.6	6.4	15.4	0.0	0.0	0.0	0.0	0.2	0.2
Fiji	0.0	1.9	1.9	3.2	33.7	42.7	0.0	0.0	0.0	0.0	0.2	0.2
Kiribati	0.0	0.0	0.0	0.5	0.1	9.1	0.0	0.0	0.0	0.0	0.0	0.9
Papua New Guinea	0.0	0.0	0.0	0.0	0.0	9.0	0.0	0.0	0.0	0.0	0.0	0.0
Tonga	0.0	5.4	5.4	0.2	0.4	9.4	0.0	0.0	0.0	0.0	0.0	0.0
Vanuatu	0.0	0.2	0.2	0.1	0.0	9.0	0.0	0.0	0.0	0.0	0.0	0.0
Total (%)	7.5	12.2	19.7	6.6	8.5	17.5	100	100	100	100	100	100
Total (US$ billions)	15.1	24.1	59.2	55.5	71.4	126.9	15.1	24.1	59.2	55.5	71.4	126.9

Source: Compiled by the author from the *Comtrade* database of the United Nations.

AGRICULTURAL TRADE LIBERALIZATION

Reform Agenda

The UR reform commitments in the area of agriculture are embodied in the URAA and the SPS Agreement (SPSA). The URAA contains the new rules and commitments in three key areas: market access, domestic support and export subsidies. The SPSA establishes general guidelines for human, animal and plant health regulations as they relate to international trade in agricultural products.

Market access

The market access provisions of the URAA are applicable to all WTO member countries. All members are required to convert all NTBs[2] affecting agricultural imports into bound tariffs that provide the same level of protection during the base period (1986–88).[3] Tariffs resulting from this tariffication process are to be reduced over a period of six years by an average of 26 per cent by the industrial countries and over a period of ten years by an average of 24 per cent by the developing countries. For those countries whose tariffs had not previously been bound under the GATT, there is no limit on the level of these bindings and no need to reduce ceiling bindings. The least developed countries are required only to bind their tariffs and remove NTBs; they are exempt from tariff reduction commitments. All developing countries are afforded special and differential treatment that exempts them from the commitment to liberalize trade in any agricultural product that is a predominant staple in their traditional diet.

Note that the definition of NTB adopted in the URAA does not cover state trading. Article XVII of the agreement recognizes the right of WTO members to retain state trading monopolies in export and import trade. The only related provisions are that members should ensure that such enterprises act in line with general commercial principles in a nondiscriminatory manner and provide information on their trading markups to trading partners on request. Thus there is room for a member country to subvert the market access commitment by authorizing a state trading enterprise to be the sole importer for goods previously controlled by NTBs.

Domestic support

Under domestic support provisions, the agreement attempts to distinguish between what constitutes trade-distorting support of agriculture from more general support of agriculture and rural development (the green box measures). Two criteria are used to identify nontrade-distorting (green box) support: it must be paid out of the government budget and not levied from consumers; and it must not have the effect of providing price support for the producer. Consequently, the green box lists such activities as agricultural research, extension services and pest and disease control as items that do not count as domestic support. Capital expenditures on irrigation and other production and market infrastructure are also included in the green box, but not recurrent expenditures or preferential user charges for irrigation facilities. However, developing countries may continue with the latter production support measures, provided the beneficiaries are low-income or resource-poor producers.

Export subsidies

Like market access provisions, export subsidy provisions are applicable to all WTO member countries. Export subsidies are defined to include all payments from the national budget that are contingent on export performance. Export credit and export guarantees are not included in the definition. The agreement requires industrial countries to reduce the share of exports receiving subsidies by 21 per cent and the expenditures on subsidies by 36 per cent from base period (1988–89) levels over a six-year period. The required reductions in subsidy levels and subsidy coverage for developing countries are 21 and 14 per cent, respectively, and these reductions are to be undertaken over a ten-year period. The least developed countries have no obligation to reduce export subsidies, but they are required to freeze them at the base level.

The SPSA

Promulgation of the SPSA was prompted by legitimate concern about the possibility that removing trade restrictions on imports of agricultural products has the potential to tempt countries to use SPS standards as a new form of protection.[4] The agreement aims to keep to a minimum the trade effects of government actions taken to ensure the safety of food and the protection of human, animal and plant health. Under the SPSA importing countries are required to demonstrate that their SPS measures are based on scientific grounds and are applied equally to domestic and foreign producers. It thus puts the WTO on the side of those exporters who comply with the importing country's SPS measures. The exporters now have clear grounds for challenging an import restriction provided they adhere to SPS standards as stipulated in the SPSA.

However, in practice, the agreement effectively places a heavier burden on developing than on industrial countries: the standards already in place in the industrial countries are more or less established as standards with which the developing countries must comply. For a developing country to effectively use the SPSA to defend its export rights (or to justify its import restrictions), it will have to upgrade its SPS system to international standards. It is not simply a matter of applying an existing system of standards to international trade, but a much broader matter of installing world-class systems. For the advanced countries whose standards are compatible with international standards, the WTO brings no more than an obligation to apply their domestic regulations fairly at the border.

The SPSA reaffirmed countries' rights to set their own safety and health standards, but with the proviso that such standards be based on 'sound scientific evidence' and that they adhere to international standards to the extent necessary. Unlike the URAA, the SPSA does not regulate and specify policies; rather, it establishes general guidelines for government behaviour in the area concerned. There is scope for alternative interpretation of SPS standards adopted by a given country. The effectiveness of the SPSA in achieving its objectives will therefore depend on how quickly and effectively disputes arising from different interpretations are settled. A Committee on SPS measures has been set up at the WTO for speedy settlement of disputes that arise during implementation of the SPSA.

Implementation

The URAA was concluded at a time when developing countries in Asia had already embarked on significant unilateral trade liberalization reforms. Even though substantial differences existed among countries, broadly speaking all developing countries in Asia had already embarked on unilateral trade liberalization reforms by the time the UR was concluded (Dean, Desai and Riedel 1994; Greenaway 1999; Pursell 1999). The dismantling of trade barriers erected during the early postwar decades first started in the early 1970s in East and Southeast Asian countries. Starting in Sri Lanka in the late 1970s, by the mid-1980s all the South Asian countries had embarked on a gradual process of economic liberalization, which accelerated in the 1990s. But in all countries reforms in agriculture trade generally lagged behind those in manufacturing. In this context, it is pertinent to examine how multilateral liberalization attempts can help ameliorate domestic resistance to agricultural reforms.

Market access

Practically none of the countries in the region had bound tariff rates before signing the URAA. Thus under the rules for special and differential treatment they could offer ceiling bindings rather than engaging in the tariffication of existing QRs.

As required, these countries have submitted ceiling tariff bindings for all the tariff lines relating to agricultural products covered by the agreement. In the process of converting existing barriers into tariffs and binding their levels, before applying the agreed on reductions, many countries, including some developing countries, have set their initial bound levels of tariffs high, even higher than the levels of actual applied tariffs in recent years.

Bound rates for Bangladesh, India and Pakistan are the highest among Asian countries (and also among most developing countries) (Table 4.5). Bangladesh announced a bound rate of 200 per cent for all agricultural goods defined at the six-digit level of the harmonized system of trade classification, except 13 items for which the bound rate was 50 per cent. Pakistan set bound rates in the range of 100 to 150 per cent. India submitted high bindings of 100 per cent for raw commodities, 150 per cent for processed agricultural commodities and 300 per cent for edible oils. India has zero or low (between 10 and 40 per cent) bound rates on a few import items, which pre-date the URAA. These products are imported solely by state trading enterprises. In Latin America, Colombia has the highest bound rates, but even these rates are, on average, much lower than those of Bangladesh, India and Pakistan. Sri Lanka took the unique step of binding all tariff lines at the uniform rate of 50 per cent. Only two Latin American countries, Chile and Uruguay, have lower bound rates than Sri Lanka (Valdes 1999).

The average bound rates of all East Asian WTO member countries are much lower than those of South Asian countries, ranging between 12.8 per cent in

Table 4.5   UR tariff bindings in South Asia for agricultural schedule tariff lines (%)

Tariff category	Bangladesh	India	Pakistan	Sri Lanka
Distribution of 673 harmonized system lines				
Specific tariffs	0.3	0.0	0.0	0.0
300%	3.9	0.0	0.0	0.0
200%	0.0	0.1	0.0	0.0
150%	33.1	1.2	98.1	0.0
100%	46.5	98.0	0.0	0.0
Less than 100%	16.2	0.7	1.9	100.0
Total	100.0	100.0	100.0	100.0
Simple average bound rate	114.8	199.5	197.1	50.0
Average of rates less than 100%	39.3	30.0	50.0	50.0

Note: In calculating the percentage of bound lines in Bangladesh, Pakistan and Sri Lanka we assumed that the total number of lines (both bound and nonbound) is the same as the total number in India.

Source: Pursell (1999, part 1).

Malaysia and 22 per cent in Thailand. However, the overall tariff structure in each country is characterized by a high degree of variability with some unusual tariff peaks. For instance, bound rates in Korea vary from 21 per cent for live animals to 120 per cent for edible oils. Thailand, which is the world's largest exporter of rice and is undoubtedly one of the world's most efficient rice producers, has a bound rate of 52 per cent on that commodity. Indonesia has set ceiling bindings of 180 per cent for rice and 110 per cent for sugar. Individual bound rates for more than 28 per cent of tariff lines in Indonesia are more than three times the average bound rate. In Thailand bound rates vary in the range of 0 (for agricultural raw materials) to 65 per cent, with an average rate of 38 per cent.

Sri Lanka's uniform ceiling binding of 50 per cent appears to be the best tariff binding outcome under the URAA in the region. Sri Lankan policymakers seem to have made use of the window of opportunity provided by the URAA commitments to lock in the ongoing trade reform process at low duty levels (Athukorala and Kelegama 1998). The high bound rates in other countries have rendered targeted tariff cuts under the URAA meaningless. Applied rates, which are set well below bound rates, naturally provide countries with a high degree of freedom to unilaterally change their tariffs. Of course, even extremely high ceiling bindings will truncate a recurrence of the extremes of high protection observed in the past.

Among the Asian countries, only Korea and Thailand have used tariff quotas. Korea agreed to apply tariff quotas for a group of 95 products (at the ten-digit level of the harmonized system of classification). Ceiling bindings and tariff rate quotas were applied to these products, with low within-quota tariffs and higher above-quota tariffs (IATRC 1997, table 7.1). In the case of rice, the politically most important commodity, a ten-year grace period was allowed for imports, with an initial minimum market access of 1 per cent of base period (1995) domestic consumption, which is to be increased to 4 per cent by 2004. To collect economic rent that might accrue to importers of products subject to tariff rate quotas and to return the rent to the agriculture sector, Korea is operating state trading systems for most of the products with tariff quotas. Tariff rate quotas for 21 products, including pork, poultry and milk powder, are allocated to traders through a competitive bidding system. In-tariff quotas have been introduced for 23 products, including rice, and the quotas are to be increased at 0.2 per cent a year until 2004. Various state trading organizations are the exclusive recipients of import quota allocations under these tariff quotas.

In Korea and Thailand the potential liberalization impact of tariff bindings and market access provisions under new tariff quotas under the URAA has been marginal. However, the UR has introduced a fundamental change into trade policymaking, including agricultural trade policy, through the

Understanding on the Balance of Payments Provisions included in the final UR Agreement. The balance of payments provisions (Articles XII and XVIII [B]) of the GATT permitted the use of QRs on imports by all member countries for balance of payments reasons. Developing countries often made use of these provisions to 'continue with QRs by merely citing balance of payments problems' (Srinivasan 1998a, p. 97). The URAA did not repeal these articles. However, under the agreement, all WTO members have signed an understanding in which they have pledged not to resort to the balance of payments provisions for using QRs without a serious justification for doing so. The members are also committed to announce publicly, as soon as possible, the time schedule for removing restrictive import measures taken for balance of payments purposes. Countries resorting to such exemptions will be subject to more frequent and critical surveillance (Krueger 1999; Srinivasan 1998b). This new provision, together with the new WTO dispute settlement process, seems to have put an end to the practice of justifying nontariff import restrictions on balance of payments grounds.

Before the conclusion of the UR, many countries in the region, in particular, Bangladesh, India, Pakistan and Sri Lanka, had routinely used the balance of payments exception to justify the general use of import licensing, including import licensing of agricultural products. However, in recent years their major trading partners have exerted a great deal of pressure on these countries to give up the misuse of this exception for protectionist reasons. For instance, in November 1995 the Balance of Payments Committee decided against Sri Lanka's continued reliance on Article XVIII (B) for maintaining QRs on certain agricultural products. Following this decision, in July 1996 Sri Lanka removed its QRs on four major agricultural products. In the same year, India's major trading partners challenged long-standing QRs maintained by India in the guise of balance of payments support. Finally, mutually agreed solutions were reached with Australia, Canada, Japan, New Zealand and the EU. Accordingly, India agreed to eliminate QRs on 1137 tariff lines (at the harmonized system of classification eight-digit level) from 1 April 1997 to 31 March 2000, on 1149 tariff lines from 1 April 2000 to 31 March 2002 and on 428 lines from 1 April 2002 to March 2003. The United States did not agree to this plan and requested establishment of a dispute settlement panel. In December 1998 the panel ruled in favour of the United States. In response to this ruling, India removed licensing restrictions on all imports in March 2001, retaining only a limited list of items under licensing for health and safety considerations. These outcomes indicate that by capping the use of QRs on the pretext of balance of payments difficulties, the URAA has laid a firm foundation for achieving greater transparency in world trade rules. Given the high bound tariffs in India at present, the actual trade flow effect of the WTO ruling may not be substantial, but it has certainly prompted a revolutionary change in the way future trade policy will be conducted (Panagariya 1999).

Domestic support

The URAA seems to be less demanding for Asian developing countries as concerns domestic subsidies. Except Korea, other countries have no subsidy reduction commitments. They are only required to ensure that their current aggregate measure of support values do not exceed minimum levels during the implementation period, that is, until 2004. In Korea a total aggregate measure of support of 2.18 trillion won (base period 1989–90) is to be reduced to 1.49 trillion won by 2004.

According to the estimates reported in the supporting tables provided to the WTO as part of signing the UR Agreement, the base period aggregate measure of support values of India and Pakistan are negative. This was the result of apparently negative commodity-specific support, which outweighed positive general input subsidies. In both countries noncommodity-specific subsidies were reported to add less than the allowable minimum level of 10 per cent of the value of agricultural production. India and Pakistan reported a standard list of exempted green box support measures and special and differentiated treatment measures, but neither reported blue box measures associated with production-limiting programmes.

Export subsidies

None of the Asian countries reported export subsidies on agricultural products, other than a few cases of general export incentive schemes, which are WTO-consistent. Apart from permitted subsidies for the transport and marketing of agricultural goods, they have, therefore, committed themselves not to pay any export subsidies in the future.

Among the Asian countries only India and Pakistan currently have QRs on agricultural exports in direct contravention of Article XI of the GATT. However, the mercantilist nature of the GATT process makes it unlikely that these restrictions will be challenged, because competing exporters have no motive to challenge another country that voluntarily removes itself from, or diminishes its role in, export competition. Importers are also unlikely to object unless the effect is to raise world prices or reduce availability (Pursell 1999).

The SPSA

The potential negative impact of international food safety standards on food exports has begun to attract increased attention among policy circles in Asian countries. For example, the latest issue of the major annual policy review in India emphasizes that because 'international trade in agricultural products is increasingly being dominated by concerns of quality to safeguard human health, it is very important [for India] that the agro-food-processing industry improves its functioning and pays attention to hygiene and manufacturers/ processors are made aware of the high international standards for quality' (Government of India 2000, p. 145). A recent review of Thailand's experience with the URAA has identified SPS issues as the single most important source of the country's international trade conflicts after it signed the URAA in 1994 (Poapongsakorn and Santanaprasit 2000). During this period Thailand was involved in 21 SPS disputes with its trading partners: Australia, 4 disputes; Brunei, 1 dispute; Czech Republic, 1 dispute; Japan, 2 disputes; Korea, 2 disputes; Mexico, 2 disputes; New Zealand, 1 dispute; Saudi Arabia, 1 dispute; Singapore, 1 dispute; United States, 1 dispute; and the EU, 5 disputes. The Thai government has set up an interdepartmental committee (with private sector participation) at the Ministry of Foreign Affairs to deal with trade disputes in this area.

Despite these concerns, none of the countries in the region (or developing countries elsewhere) have so far made use of the Dispute Settlement Mechanism under the agreement. While the SPSA established at the UR of trade talks was designed to minimize the likely trade-impeding impact of SPS regulations, the experience with the implementation of the SPSA over the past three years illustrates some of the main issues (WTO 1999). Many developing countries have raised concerns about their ability to participate effectively in implementation of the agreement and in the dispute settlement process. First, a key constraint in this respect is the low level of technical, scientific and legal capacity in developing countries for mounting or defending a case in the dispute settlement process. Developing countries (and other agricultural exporting countries) have also expressed concerns about the manner in which the SPSA currently operates. Second, a major complaint is that the agreement allows too much latitude in adopting SPS measures, allowing importing countries to impose measures that impede imports, no matter how unlikely or how inconsequential the risk involved. In addition, SPS standards sometimes diverge considerably across importing countries, making meeting standards costly and cumbersome for exporters. Third, critics allege that the time between the notification of new SPS measures and their application is normally too short for countries to be able to respond in an effective and appropriate manner.

PHASING OUT THE MFA

The imposition of quota restrictions on textiles and clothing imports by industrial countries began in the form of a short-term agreement in 1961 to restrain the growth of Japanese exports of cotton textiles to the United States. This agreement soon became a long-term agreement, the MFA, that encompassed trade in textiles and clothing made with other fibres, both manmade and natural. It was extended six times up to 1994, in most cases further intensifying restrictions on imports and enlarging product coverage, and affecting developing country exporters of textiles and clothing in particular (Srinivasan 1998a). By the mid-1980s almost all textile and clothing exports from the developing countries and Eastern Europe to the industrial countries (which accounted for more than 30 per cent of total world trade in textiles and clothing) had come under the cover of the MFA or other quota systems (such as non-MFA quotas on exports from Taiwan). By contrast, only about 2 per cent of trade between industrial countries, which consisted solely of Japanese exports to the United States, were quota-controlled.

Liberalization Commitments

The ATC, which came into effect on 1 January 1995, envisages the phase-out of the MFA in three stages over a period of ten years from 1 January 1995. Thus it aims to bring trade in all textiles and clothing products under WTO discipline by 2005. Products that accounted for no less than 16 per cent of total imports in 1990 (the reference year) were to be integrated into the GATT with immediate effect (stage 1). Stage 2 entailed integration of an additional 17 per cent by January 1998, stage 3 involved further integration of 18 per cent by January 2000 and stage 4 will integrate all remaining products by 1 January 2005. The agreement also set minimum limits to annual growth in import quotas on those products that are still under restraint during each stage: 16 per cent over MFA IV in stage 1 (until 1998), by no less than 25 per cent over stage 1 in stage 2 (1998–2001) and 27 per cent over stage 2 in stage 3 (2002–04).

Note that the phasing out of the MFA under the ATC is back-loaded; products accounting for as much as 49 per cent of the value of 1990 imports could still be under quota restrictions as of the end of the ten-year phase-out period (Srinivasan 1998a, p. 41). Moreover, the agreement has left the choice of products to be integrated at each stage to the discretion of individual countries. This provides importing countries with ample room to design a phase-out strategy that minimizes possible adjustment pain.

Whether the industrial countries will stick to their commitment to full and faithful implementation of the ACT has yet to be seen. So far the major importing countries have integrated mostly only those items (such as yarn) for which they had no binding quotas. At the end of stage 2 of MFA quota abolition (1 January 1998), no importing country other than Norway had eliminated more than a tiny percentage of its actual MFA quotas, as against a target rate of 33 per cent product integration by that time (Table 4.6). Observers fear that with almost five years to go before the scheduled date for complete MFA abolition, the protectionist lobby may gather enough momentum to prevent that from happening.

Table 4.6   Number of MFA quotas notified and eliminated at the end of stage 2 of the MFA phase-out, 1 January 1998

Country/region	Notified	Eliminated	
		Number	%
United States	650	8	1
EU	199	14	7
Canada	205	28	14
Norway	54	46	85

Source: Finger and Schuknecht (1999).

The industrial countries can use the agreement's safeguard provisions to water down promised liberalization if they choose to do so. The potential for this new form of protection to counterbalance MFA abolition is vividly illustrated by Reinert (2000) in an insightful account of recent EU safeguard actions under the ATC. There are also indications that the industrial countries are likely to rely increasingly on antidumping provisions as a new form of protection, as has occurred with many other manufactured good markets in recent years (Stiglitz 2000).

Impact of MFA Abolition

Assuming the industrial countries honour their undertakings under the ATC, the world textile and garment industry will undergo a dramatic reshuffle after 2005. An extremely competitive export market will emerge. Countries that cannot compete in cost as well as in quality might not be able to maintain, let alone increase, their share in growing world export markets.

Some recent studies of the impact of MFA abolition on exporting countries (for instance, Harrison, Rutherford and Tarr 1997; Kathuria, Martin and Bhardwaj 2000) predict significant long-term welfare gains to efficient exporting countries such as China, Indonesia, Malaysia, Sri Lanka and

Thailand at the expense of most countries in Eastern Europe, Latin America, the Middle East, North Africa and the former Soviet Union. The latter countries have so far locked in low-end clothing categories, thanks to quota protection under the MFA. Asian countries such as Bangladesh, the Lao PDR and Vietnam in the region may also encounter significant adjustment problems given their excessive reliance on low-end, quota-protected clothing categories. The East Asian NIEs, whose comparative advantage has already shifted to more capital- and skill-intensive sectors, may also lose market shares. Thus the abolition of quotas should stimulate further the relocation of production from NIEs to efficient producing countries in the region through both foreign direct investment and subcontracting arrangements.

How can the latecomers to industrialization in the region benefit from the post-MFA restructuring of the global textile and clothing industry? The answer seems to lie mainly in speedy trade and investment liberalization, coupled with improved basic infrastructure for export-oriented production. This will set the stage for the relocation of global production activities from high-cost sources. Concomitant trade and investment liberalization is particularly important given that international market linkages are crucial for export success in a highly competitive global market (Athukorala and Rajapatirana 2000).

Some commentators have pointed to the importance of developing domestic input linkages within the clothing industry through direct government intervention to prepare for MFA abolition (for example, Dowlah 1999). The simple underlying argument here is that ready and timely availability of inputs domestically will enhance export competitiveness. This is erroneous advice based on a misinterpretation of the experience of East Asian NIEs. While it is true that the clothing industries in these countries currently depend heavily on domestic fabrics and other inputs for export production, they reached this stage primarily by mastering the dynamics of the buyer-driven commodity chain, which required excessive reliance on high-quality imported inputs according to buyers' requests. The key asset that the exporters in these countries possessed was their close relationship with foreign clients built on the use of imported inputs to meet the clients' orders. It was only when the volume of exports had reached sufficient levels to support efficient domestic input supply industries and the buyers had become fully satisfied with the quality of such inputs that exporters began to reduce their dependence on imported inputs and turn to local supply sources. Latecomer exporters like Bangladesh or Sri Lanka have a long way to go to reach this stage. In such a context attempts to promote input linkages though direct government intervention can indeed be counterproductive (Athukorala 1998, chapter 4; Kelegama and Foley 1999).

POLICY OPTIONS

The contribution of the UR to the ongoing process of liberalization in Asian developing countries has so far been marginal. However, the new WTO regime offers opportunities for domestic reforms and effective engagement in multilateral negotiation to further the liberalization process and to keep policies from regressing to the old forms of QRs.

How can a future round of multilateral trade negotiation be built on these achievements to speed up the process of redressing disarray in agricultural trade? Our discussion on the reform process and the experience with the implementation of the WTO agenda agreed upon in the UR points to three major issues that deserve closer attention by the Asian countries in future multilateral trade talks: reducing bound tariffs; broadening reforms; and providing social safety net support.

Reducing Bound Tariffs

Perhaps the most important issue requiring immediate attention is revising bound tariffs. The intended purpose of binding tariffs was to set a benchmark against which future liberalization could be undertaken. However, the bindings eventually agreed on have turned out to be extremely high, even higher than the actual levels of protection that existed at the time of signing the agreement. Such high rates cannot serve as useful benchmarks for further tariff reduction. In addition, high tariff bounds can be counterproductive for the following reasons.

A major gain expected from a transition from QRs to tariffs is a reduction in the volatility of world market prices. However, when tariffs are bound at high levels, significant fluctuations below the bound level are possible. A country with high bound tariffs can set the operative tariff below the upper bound and vary it so as to influence domestic market prices.

Prolonged retention of high bound tariffs can harm the ongoing process of unilateral liberalization by strengthening the protectionist lobby. High bound tariffs can become a potential target for the protectionist lobby in the clamour for high protection. The Sri Lankan experience suggests that a formal international commitment in the form of relatively low bound tariffs is a great help in taming the protectionist lobby.

Cutting bound tariffs will also enhance countries' ability to participate systematically in the debate on the world trading system. As Gulati (1999, p. 17) aptly put it: 'When countries in the developing world like India ask for 300% protection, they really lose all the strength in their negotiations with the developed world.'

Negotiating with Bangladesh, India and Pakistan to bring down their present extremely high, and often prohibitive, ceiling tariff bindings for agricultural products in the next round of agricultural talks could be difficult. Sri Lanka's general rate of 50 per cent could serve as an interim target.

Broadening Reforms

In its approach to restoring orderly conditions in world agricultural trade, the URAA has gone beyond the border measures that are traditionally the targets of GATT discipline and focused on the distortionary effects of domestic support and export subsidy measures. However, it has provided countries with ample loopholes for evading implementation of the required reductions. Moreover, among the border measures, various restrictions impinging on export performance are largely ignored for all countries. Such restrictions are virtually absent in industrial countries, but are still important sources of agricultural policy in many developing countries. In South Asia export taxes have been virtually eliminated over the years, but export restrictions are still used in India and Pakistan as part of domestic price support to consumers and producers (Joshi and Little 1996; Khan 1997).

To be effective, planning for liberalization reforms in countries like India should involve simultaneous reform of import and export trade regimes and domestic subsidies. Distortionary policies in these areas are intrinsically interrelated. Trade polices support domestic (nonborder) interventions. For instance, without frontier barriers on the same product, nonfrontier policies such as production subsidies would tend to have a rather limited effect on trade flows in the long run. Maintaining low domestic prices of essential food items through government procurement and distribution schemes calls for export restrictions on these products. Thus eliminating border restrictions threatens domestic programmes. Various subsidy commitments to households and consumers also dictate the continuation of trade controls, including extensive involvement by state enterprises in foreign trade. Given these intricate links, the freeing of international trade needs to be combined with the removal of various restrictions impinging on domestic production and trade.

Paying careful attention to how state trading enterprises are used to regulate foreign trade, especially in India, is important. State trading enterprises operating as import monopolies for agricultural products could be considered to be, by their nature, QRs, and therefore illegal under the URAA. Assuming such a determination is unlikely, the distortionary impact of state trading enterprises on foreign trade could nevertheless be limited through regulatory measures to ensure that their resale margins do not exceed bound tariffs, or if they do not import at all, that the implicit protection which results is below bound tariffs.

Social Safety Net Support

Whatever the long-run benefits of freeing agriculture may be, the changes are likely to cause some large socio-economic disruptions, and a good many people might suffer, or might fear they will suffer. Dealing with these transitional problems as part of a rapid, planned move towards redressing deep-rooted disarray in domestic agriculture is important. Implementing comprehensive agricultural liberalization without considering the effects of the consequent price rises on poor people is not politically desirable.

In this context, providing financial support for implementing social safety net measures can play an important role in making these reforms politically palatable and feasible. While overloading the WTO with matters that fall beyond its purview may be counterproductive, there is certainly a case for a co-ordinated approach involving the WTO and international financial institutions, including regional development banks, in this sphere.

Some initiatives have already been taken under the UR to provide food security support for net food importers to cushion them against increases in world food prices resulting from the reduction of production support in the industrial countries. These supports are relevant for net food-importing countries like Bangladesh, Pakistan and Sri Lanka. However, providing food security support for food-deficient countries is simply an attempt to deal with the symptoms, not the cause, of the problem. These countries' long-standing, distorted, agricultural trade policy regimes are a significant factor behind their weak economic status, and makes it difficult for them to withstand reform-induced price increases. Thus safety net support should be linked to systematic policy efforts to address the root problem, not the current food deficit situation.

Institutional Support

The SPSA is particularly significant for South Asian countries given the emergence of processed foods as a dynamic export line. However, experience with implementation of the agreement in the last three years points to many practical obstacles for these countries (and many other developing countries). They have raised concerns about their ability to participate effectively in the dispute settlement process and thereby have a real influence on the implementation of the agreement. A key constraint in this respect is the low level of technical and scientific know-how in developing countries In addition, developing countries have expressed concerns about the manner in which the SPSA currently operates. In particular, they are concerned that in setting SPS standards the industrial countries do not take adequate account of the circumstances of the developing countries. The latter also allege that in many cases the time between the notification of new SPS measures and their application is too short for developing countries to respond in an effective and appropriate manner. Addressing these issues should be an important item on the future WTO agenda.

Preparing for Abolition of the MFA

Finally, despite inevitable short-run adjustment problems that may be created for some developing countries, the abolition of the MFA quota regime is important for the effective integration of developing countries into a rules-based world trading system. Thus they should make every effort through active engagement in multilateral trade negotiation to see that the industrial countries honour their commitments under the ATC. At the same time, the developing countries should prepare themselves to face competitive market conditions in the post-MFA era by speeding up domestic liberalization reforms.

The recommendation by some economists to develop domestic input linkages within the clothing industry through direct government intervention in preparation for the phase-out of the MFA is based on a misreading of the East Asian experience. Domestic input linkages within the clothing industry should come naturally as part of successful export expansion. Policy intervention to forge premature linkages can be counterproductive.

NOTES

1. At the time of finalizing this volume (April 2001), negotiations on agriculture and services were under way at WTO headquarters in Geneva.
2. In the remainder of the chapter, the terms nontariff barriers and quantitative restrictions are used interchangeably.
3. Bound tariff rates are expected to reflect the actual difference between the internal (domestic market) price and the external (border) price during the base period.
4. This agreement improves on the original Article XX of the GATT, which allowed measures against trade that are 'necessary to protect human, animal or plant life or health'.

REFERENCES

ADB (Asian Development Bank) (various years), *Key Economic Indicators*, Manila.

Anderson, Kym (1986), 'Economic Growth, Comparative Advantage and Agricultural Trade of Pacific Basin Countries', in G.E. Schuh and J.L. McCoy (eds), *Food, Agriculture and Development in the Pacific Basin*, Boulder, CO: Westview Press, pp. 89–117.

Athukorala, Prema-chandra (1998), *Trade Policy Issues in Asian Development*, London: Routledge.

Athukorala, Prema-chandra and Saman Kelegama (1998), 'The Political Economy of Agricultural Trade Policy: Sri Lanka in the Uruguay Round', *Contemporary South Asia*, **7** (1), 7–26.

Athukorala, Prema-chandra and Sarath Rajapatirana (2000), *Liberalisation and Industrial Transformation: Sri Lanka in International Perspective*, Oxford, UK, and Delhi: Oxford University Press.

Athukorala, Prema-chandra and Kunal Sen (1998), 'Processed Food Exports from Developing Countries: Patterns and Determinants', *Food Policy*, **23** (1), 41–54.

Dean, Judith M., S. Desai and James Riedel (1994), *Trade Policy Reform in Developing Countries since 1985: A Review of the Evidence*, Discussion Paper no. 267, Washington, DC: World Bank.

Dowlah, C.A.F. (1999), 'The Future of the Readymade Clothing Industry of Bangladesh in the Post-Uruguay Round World', *World Economy*, **22** (7), 933–53.

Finger, Michael J. and L. Schuknecht (1999), 'Market Access Advances and Retreats: The Uruguay Round and Beyond', paper presented at the WTO/World Bank Conference on Developing Countries in the Millennium Round, 27–29 September, Geneva.

Government of India (2000), *Economic Survey 1999–2000*, Delhi.

Greenaway, David (1999), 'Current Issues in Trade Policy and the Pacific Rim', in John Piggott and Alan Woodland (eds), *International Trade Policy and the Pacific Rim*, London: Macmillan, pp. 3–29.

Gulati, Ashok (1999), 'Agriculture and the New Trade Agenda in the WTO 2000 Negotiations: Interests and Options for India', University Enclave, Institute of Economic Growth, Delhi, processed.

Harrison, G.W., T.F. Rutherford and D.G. Tarr (1997), 'Quantifying the Uruguay Round', *Economic Journal*, **107** (September), 1405–30.

Henderson, Dennis R., Charles R. Handy and Steve A. Neff (1996), *Globalization of the Processed Food Market*, Agricultural Economic Report no. 742, Washington, DC: US Department of Agriculture.

Hill, Hal (2000), 'Export Success Against the Odds: A Vietnamese Case Study', *World Development*, **28** (2), 283–300.

IATRC (International Agricultural Trade Research Consortium) (1997) 'Implementation of the Uruguay Round Agreement and Issues for the Next Round of Agricultural Negotiation', Virginia, MD: Department of Agriculture and Applied Economics, Virginia State University (http://www.umn.edu/latrc).

Joshi, Vijay and I.M.D. Little (1996), *India's Economic Reforms 1991–2001*, Oxford, UK: Clarendon Press.

Kathuria, Sanjay, Will Martin and Anjali Bhardwaj (2000), 'Implications of MFA Abolition for South Asian Countries', paper presented at the National Council for Applied Economic Research/World Bank Conference on WTO 2000, 20–21 December, New Delhi.

Kelegama, Saman and Friz Foley (1999), 'Impediments to Promoting Backward Linkages from the Garment Industry in Sri Lanka', *World Development*, **27** (8), 1445–60.

Khan, M.H. (1997), 'Agricultural Crisis in Pakistan: Some Explanations and Policy Options', *Pakistan Development Review*, **36** (4), 419–66.

Krueger, Anne O. (1999), 'The Developing Countries and the Next Round of Multilateral Trade Negotiations', *World Economy*, **22** (6), 909–32.

Lin, Justin Yifu (1994), 'Chinese Agriculture: Institutional Changes and Performance', in T.N. Srinivasan (ed.), *Agriculture and Trade in India and China: Policies and*

Performance since 1950, San Francisco, CA: International Centre for Economic Growth, pp. 23-72.

Panagariya, Arvind (1999), 'Trade Liberalisation in South Asia: Recent Liberalisation and Future Agenda', *World Economy*, **22** (3), 353-76.

Poapongsakorn, Nipon and Panjamaporn Santanaprasit (2000), 'Experience with the Uruguay Round Agreement on Agriculture: A Case Study of Thailand', Thailand Development Research Institute, Bangkok, processed.

Pursell, Garry (1999), 'Some Aspects of the Liberalization of South Asian Agricultural Policies: How Can the WTO Help?' in Benoit Blarel, Garry Pursell and Alberto Valdes (eds), *Implications of the Uruguay Round Agreement for South Asia: The Case of Agriculture*, Washington, DC: World Bank, pp. 29-46.

Reinert, Kenneth A. (2000), 'Give Us Virtue, But Not Yet: Safeguard Actions Under the Agreement on Textiles and Clothing', *World Economy*, **23** (1), 25-55.

Srinivasan, T.N. (ed.) (1994), 'Indian Agriculture: Policies and Performance', in *Agriculture and Trade in India and China: Policies and Performance since 1950*, San Francisco, CA: International Centre for Economic Growth, pp. 155-98.

Srinivasan, T.N. (1998a), *Developing Countries and the Multilateral Trading System: From GATT to the Uruguay Round and the Future*, Delhi: Oxford University Press.

Srinivasan, T.N. (1998b), 'India's Export Performance: A Comparative Analysis', in Isher J. Ahluwalia and I.M.D. Little (eds), *India's Economic Reforms and Development: Essays for Manmohan Singh*, Delhi: Oxford University Press, pp. 197-228.

Stiglitz, Joseph E. (2000), 'Two Principles for the Next Round or, How to Bring Developing Countries in from the Cold', *World Economy*, **23** (4), 437-54.

Sykes, Alan O. (1995), *Product Standards for Internationally Integrated Goods Markets*, Washington, DC: The Brookings Institution.

Valdes, Alberto (1999), 'Overview of the Global Impact of the Uruguay Round and Lessons from Early Reforms', in Benoit Blarel, Garry Pursell and Alberto Valdes (eds), *Implications of the Uruguay Round Agreement for South Asia: The Case of Agriculture*, Washington, DC: World Bank, pp. 3-14.

World Bank (various years), *World Development Report*, New York: Oxford University Press.

WTO (World Trade Organization) (1998), *Trade Policy Review: India 1998,* Geneva.

WTO (1999), *Review of the Operation and Implementation of the Agreement on Application of Sanitary and Phytosanitary Measures*, Geneva.

5. Environmental standards and trade in agricultural products: evidence from Brazil, Germany and Indonesia*

Ulrike Grote, Claus Deblitz and Susanne Stegmann

International trade in agricultural products takes place among countries at different levels of development that have varying preferences for maintaining environmental standards. At the same time, the awareness of and emphasis on environmental problems and food safety issues have grown at the global, regional and national levels. Some of the main concerns include climate change, ozone depletion, soil degradation, vanishing biodiversity, deforestation and smoke from forest burning, mad cow disease and transgenic food products or genetically modified organisms.

This situation has led to conflicting positions between the industrial and the developing countries. The industrial countries demand the enforcement of higher environmental and food safety standards to ensure that environmental costs are internalized and the safety of agricultural products is secured. However, at the same time they fear losing international competitiveness because higher environmental standards lead to higher production costs. Developing countries, by contrast, fear that the industrial countries might use environmental standards as nontariff barriers, leading to restricted market access and the loss of competitive advantage.

In the context of WTO negotiations, this means that the industrial countries often wish to include environmental issues in the trade agenda, because the WTO offers the possibility of using trade sanctions or import bans as enforcement measures for raising environmental standards abroad, especially in developing countries. However, many developing countries perceive the entwining of environmental issues with trade policy as a threat not only to their sovereignty, but also to their open market access and competitive advantages in international trade. This dissension between different stakeholders was one of the reasons for the failure of the negotiations at the

*This is a revised and expanded version of Grote et al. (2000).

Seattle Ministerial Meeting to launch a new WTO round. While the process of general trade liberalization is in limbo for the time being and negotiations on agriculture focus on which issues the next agenda should include with little likelihood of immediate progress, research on the linkages between trade liberalization and the environment needs to proceed to better inform the on-going debate and ensure sustainable trade liberalization for the benefit of all.

This chapter reports on the findings of a comparative study of the production and processing of vegetable oils, grain and broilers (young chickens) in Brazil, Germany and Indonesia that we conducted to test the hypothesis that the costs of higher environmental standards lead to unfair competitive disadvantages among countries.

ENVIRONMENTAL STANDARDS AND COMPETITIVENESS

Several studies have tried to assess the implications of environmental standards on competitiveness in world trade. They are based on different methods and cover various countries over different time periods (Helm 1995; Nordström and Vaughan 1999).

Studies that use the cost approach generally choose a group of potentially environmentally unfriendly industries and analyse trends in the allocation of production sites and in international trade. They investigate whether increased emphasis on high environmental standards leads to a reallocation of the production sites (so-called pollution havens) or to competitive disadvantages. Results from these studies differ. Some studies found that the global export shares of industrial countries in polluting products tended to decline in relation to that of developing countries (Low and Yeats 1992; Sorsa 1994; UNCTAD 1994). Others showed that imports of heavily polluting products to Japan and the United States have increased relative to these countries' exports of these products (Kalt 1988; Lee and Roland-Holst 1994; Sorsa 1994). However, Jenkins (1999) found little evidence of a general loss of competitiveness in environmentally intensive industries in Europe, and a comprehensive empirical study of different industrial sectors in Germany failed to detect a systematic relationship between environmental costs and international competitiveness (Felke 1998).

The OECD (1997) estimated that direct environmental compliance costs make up only 1 to 5 per cent of total production costs in the industrial sector. Dean (1992) and Jaffe et al. (1995) found that for most producers, environmental costs amount to only a small part of total costs. In the United States, for example, environmental costs accounted for only 3 per cent (US$15) of the total cost of producing a ton of steel (US$513). In Mexico the total cost of production is only US$415 per ton; therefore even if the United

States did not incur environmental costs, its costs would still be higher by US$83, or about 20 per cent, compared with Mexico (OECD 1997). For primary agricultural products, Brouwer et al. (2000) demonstrated that the compliance costs of environmental standards are no more than 3 to 4 per cent of the total costs of production.

In sum, the evidence suggests that other factors such as relative wages, education level, political and economic stability, closeness to and size of markets and quality of infrastructure have much stronger effects on international competitiveness than environmental costs. The so-called innovative approach to assessing competitiveness (the Porter hypothesis) suggests that relatively higher environmental standards may actually affect producing companies' innovative power positively, leading to higher, not lower, productivity (Porter 1991). This is because the search by firms for new ways to reduce environmental pollution may act as a conduit for innovative production practices. For instance, eco-labelling, which informs consumers about the production of environmentally friendlier products, tends to fill a gap in the market, and thus conveys price advantages (Grote, Basu and Chau 1999). Alternatively, companies that, because of environmental considerations, attempt to transform their produced waste into saleable goods earn an additional income (Porter and van der Linde 1995).

Repetto (1995) carried out an extensive study of the relationship between environment standards and efficiency of production. He looked at financial and environmental data for nearly 2000 processing sites in the United States and found no general tendency for industries that attach great importance to the environment to be less profitable. Nevertheless, how long it will take until dynamic profits compensate for the static losses of increasing costs caused by higher environmental standards remains an unanswered question (Jenkins 1999).

In sum, no clear conclusions emerge about the effects of environmental standards on the competitiveness of companies or product sectors. Based on a survey of this literature, Nordström and Vaughan (1999) observe that countries' concerns about competitiveness have been highly overrated in the public debate. However, most studies to date have examined the issue at the broader industry level. More disaggregated studies that focus on individual products in different countries are needed to inform the ongoing debate.

IMPORTANCE OF SELECTED AGRICULTURAL PRODUCTS IN INTERNATIONAL TRADE

This study analyses the production and processing of oilseeds (soy oil, rapeseed and palm oil), grain (maize, barley and wheat) and broilers in Brazil,

Germany and Indonesia from a comparative perspective. All three product groups and the countries concerned play significant roles in the international market.

Brazil

The production of soybeans in Brazil increased steadily from almost 10 million tons in 1978 to more than 30 million in 1998. This increase was due mainly to a steady expansion of the production area, but also to an increase in yields, which almost doubled from 1.2 tons per hectare to 2.3 tons per hectare within the last two decades. The traditional production sites are located in southern Brazil, but recent years have seen a significant expansion in the central and northeastern states. In these latter states vast areas of dry savannah (approximately 200 million hectares) are still available for further expansion of soybean and maize production. These states are also characterized by an expanding poultry industry. However, environmental groups are increasingly voicing environmental concerns about such issues as the impact of production expansion on the natural ecosystem.

A large share of Brazil's soybean production is exported. In 1997 exports of soybeans, soymeal and soy oil totalled some 18 million tons (Figure 5.1).

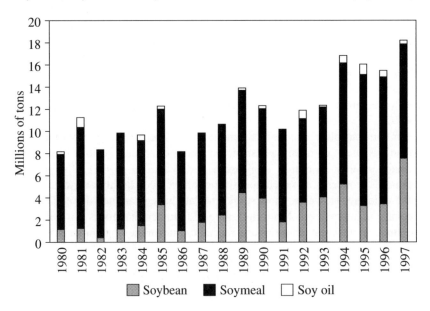

Source: FNP Consultoria and Comercio Ltda, *Agrianual*, São Paulo, Brazil, 1981–99.

Figure 5.1   Exports of soybeans, soymeal and soy oil from Brazil, 1980–97

While soybeans and soymeal are mainly exported to Europe, most soy oil exports go to Bangladesh, China, Iran and the Netherlands.

The production of maize has also increased significantly in the last two decades, but production is still predominantly for meeting domestic demand.

The domestic broiler industry is a major consumer of domestically grown maize and soybeans. Broiler production has shown a remarkable upsurge since 1970, from about 0.2 million tons to about 4.5 million tons in 1998. Export volumes of whole broilers and parts also increased significantly during this period (Figure 5.2).

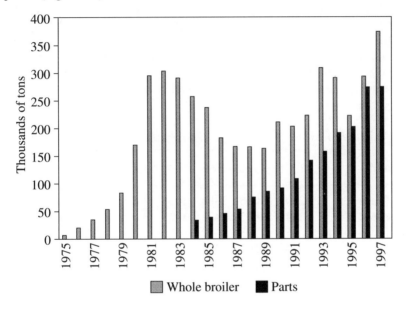

Source: *Agrianual*, Brazil, several years.

Figure 5.2   Exports of broilers from Brazil, 1975-97

Brazil is one of the world's biggest producers and exporters of soybeans and broilers. It is the third largest world exporter of broilers after the United States and France. Major export markets for Brazil are the Middle Eastern countries, such as Kuwait, Oman and especially Saudi Arabia for whole broilers, and Germany, Hong Kong, Italy and Japan for broiler parts. The only important arable product Brazil imports is wheat (OECD 1997).

Germany

Rapeseed, wheat and broilers are among Germany's key agricultural products.

Germany is Europe's second biggest producer of rapeseed. The area under subsidized rapeseed production increased rapidly during the 1980s until 1990, when it had reached some 2 million tons per year. In the 1990s, however, both the volume of production and the area under cultivation stagnated and even declined in some years.[1] The export volume of rapeseed reached 1.9 million tons in 1998, dominated by processed rapeseed products. Germany was also a big importer of around 1.6 million tons of rapeseed and its processing products, with the rapeseed playing a far bigger role in imports than its processing products.

Germany is also one of Europe's biggest oilseed processors. In 1998 Germany processed almost 4 million tons of rapeseed and soybeans (Table 5.1). While two-thirds of the rapeseed is grown domestically and one-third is imported from the EU, soybeans for processing are all imported, mainly from Brazil and the United States. In 1998 imports from these two countries amounted to 1.8 million tons and 1.3 million tons, respectively.

Table 5.1   Processing of oilseeds in Germany, 1991–98 (thousands of tons)

Oilseed	1991	1992	1993	1994	1995	1996	1997	1998
Soybeans	2703	3026	2884	3024	3494	3307	3480	3950
Rapeseed	2645	2665	2478	3023	3287	3344	3576	3957
Sunflower seed	355	393	409	435	478	415	597	436
Other[a]	304	292	315	386	421	314	324	368
Total	6007	6376	6086	6868	7680	7380	7977	8711

[a]   Includes copra, flaxseed and castor oil.

Source: Association of German Oil Mills (Berlin) data.

About 20 to 25 per cent of all agricultural land in Germany is used for wheat production. The increase in wheat production over time has resulted mainly from a rise in yields rather than an increased area for production. Wheat exports amounted to almost 1.8 million tons in 1996/97, while imports reached some 1.2 million tons that same year.

Over the past three decades broiler production has increased steadily in Germany; however, by 1998 domestic production amounted to only 68 per cent of domestic consumption. With respect to imports, the demand for broiler parts increased more than the demand for whole broilers. The major supplier of broilers and broiler parts is the Netherlands, but imports from Hungary and Thailand have been increasing rapidly in recent years. Germany exports small amounts of broilers to other EU countries and Switzerland, and to a minor extent to Russia.

Over time high livestock levels and intensive plant production have resulted in environmental problems, such as soil degradation and contamination of drinking water through overfertilization and/or intensive use of pesticides. These problems are particularly severe in highly populated areas.

Indonesia

Indonesia is one of the world's main producers and exporters of palm oil. Palm oil is produced largely for export, and competes directly with other vegetable oils. The production of palm oil increased from 1.5 million tons in 1987 to around 4.5 million tons in 1996. The plantation area more than tripled during this period, with further areas still available for expansion. The biggest increase in plantation area during the last decade was by privately owned estates, followed by smallholders and government estates. The per hectare yield of palm oil has decreased slightly since 1995, mainly because of the El Niño phenomenon. Exports of palm oil have increased steadily since the mid-1980s, reaching 3 million tons (US$1.5 billion) by 1997 (Figure 5.3).

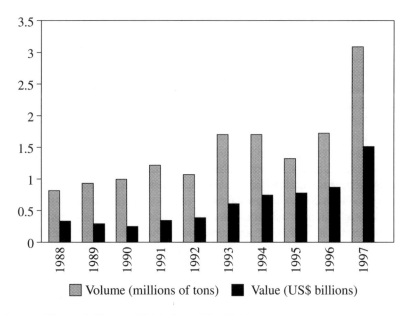

Source: Directorate General of Estate Crops (Jakarta) data.

Figure 5.3   Development of palm oil exports, volume and value, 1988-97

Major traditional destinations for palm oil exports from Indonesia are Germany, Italy and the Netherlands. Because of the government's efforts to diversify export markets, Indonesia is increasingly exporting significant amounts of palm oil to other Asian countries, especially China, India and Pakistan. The worldwide demand for vegetable oils is still high and further expansion of the plantation area is possible. However, forest land is still converted into cultivable land through fire clearance instead of mechanical land clearance methods, and the result has been forest fires of catastrophic dimensions. For example, Glover and Jessup (1999) calculated that the total economic costs (including medical costs; productivity losses; impact on timber production, agriculture and biodiversity; fire-fighting costs and the impact on tourism) of the three months of haze and fires in 1997 amounted to more than US$4 billion. Closely related to the burning issue is general concern about the protection of primary forests.

CASE STUDIES OF AGRICULTURAL PRODUCTS IN BRAZIL, GERMANY AND INDONESIA

Three case studies of agricultural products were conducted in Brazil, Germany and Indonesia to study the cost implications of environmental standards. The methodology and results are presented below.

Methodology and Data

We collected cost data and information about environmental standards for typical farms in Brazil and Germany using the International Farm Comparison Network, which permits analysis of agricultural production systems worldwide.[2] We set up panels, with each panel consisting of four or five farmers, one adviser and one scientist. These panels defined the farms typical of a region in terms of size and crops grown or livestock system and technology used. For each typical farm we obtained a comprehensive physical and economic data set. Given a standardized procedure and identical definition of costs, the International Farm Comparison Network allows comparison of international data. Lists of environmental standards from input through processing were established for each product group, and then related to the individual costs.

For the study of cultivation practices we defined three typical farms in Brazil (1000 hectares in Goias, 500 hectares in Minais Gerais and 290 hectares in São Paulo) and four typical farms in Germany (700 hectares in Mecklenburg-Vorpommern, 560 and 1300 hectares in Saxony-Anhalt and 100 hectares in Lower Saxony). For broiler production, we used two enterprises with capacities of 24 000 and 15 000 broilers respectively in São Paulo, Brazil, and one enterprise in Lower Saxony, Germany, with a capacity of 28 000 broilers as typical enterprises.

Data on costs and environmental information about the production of oil palm trees and palm oil, respectively, were collected from two oil palm plantations in Indonesia (10 000 hectares in Sumatra and 4250 hectares in west Java). The processing of fruit from palm oil trees is undertaken at the same plantations because the fresh fruit needs to be processed within a few hours after harvest.

At the processing level, the oilseed and broiler sectors in Brazil and Germany are extremely competitive, hence obtaining data from the companies was difficult and the figures have to be interpreted as rough orders of magnitude only. While balance sheets were partly available, other costs and environmental information had to be collected through interviews with experts.

Empirical Results for Oilseeds, Fruit and Grain

For plant production, we calculated production and processing costs and identified relevant environmental standards in the three countries. The results are summarized in the following paragraphs.

Production costs
At the production level, cost differences between typical farms in Brazil and Germany are considerable. The total costs of rapeseed production on the three typical German farms vary between US$29 and US$31 per 100 kilograms, while the total costs of soybean production on the three typical Brazilian farms range between US$14 and US$21 per 100 kilograms. Thus, on average, Brazil's production costs are about 50 to 70 per cent of Germany's production costs (Figure 5.4).

Because of Germany's higher yields (3.9 to 4 tons per hectare) compared with Brazil's (2.4 to 3.2 tons per hectare), the cost differences per hectare are even bigger than the cost differences per 100 kilograms. Palm oil production in Indonesia has a significant cost advantage compared with soybeans from Brazil, mainly because of the relatively high average yield per hectare (4.5 tons). While the total costs for 100 kilograms of crude palm oil from the 10 000-hectare plantation in Indonesia are 40 per cent below the cost for 100 kilograms of soybeans of the lowest-cost farm in Brazil, the costs of smaller palm oil plantations in Indonesia are only slightly above the costs of the Brazilian soybean farm. Similarly, total costs for the typical Brazilian farm producing grains are 30 to 67 per cent of the cost of German grain-producing farms. Why are production costs on the typical Brazilian farms so much lower

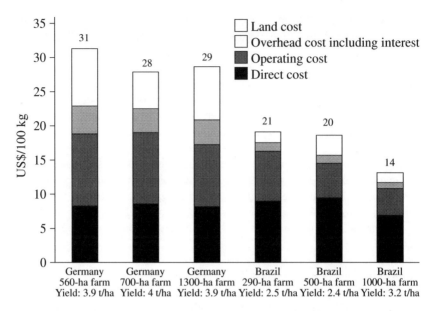

t/ha = tons per hectare.

Note: To reflect the different oil and protein content of rapeseed and soybean, the cost of
          soybean production was adjusted to rapeseed equivalents. The exchange rate used was
          R$1.4 to the Deutschmark and DM1.8 to the US dollar.

Source: International Farm Comparison Network data.

*Figure 5.4   Total cost of rapeseed production in Germany and soybean
             production in Brazil, 1998/99*

than on the typical German farms? The detailed cost structure shows that
direct costs, which consist mainly of the costs of fertilizer and herbicide, are
comparable, even slightly higher in Brazil. The share of direct costs in total
costs is around one-third in Germany and half in Brazil. A cost comparison
among the Brazilian farms shows differences with respect to herbicide costs
because of different cropping systems. The herbicide costs for the small farm
with a conventional cropping system (Brazil, 290 hectares) are one-third of the
cost for the two other farms (Brazil, 500 hectares; Brazil, 1000 hectares),
where production is based on the no-tillage system, which requires higher
herbicide inputs because of the absence of mechanical weed treatment.

There are considerable differences between Brazil and Germany with
respect to operating costs. In Germany, operating costs for grain production
are between two and six times higher than in Brazil. Furthermore, farms in
both countries can realize relatively high economies of scale with increasing

farm size. The major causes of international cost differences relate to the depreciation of machinery and labour cost.

Overhead costs include the costs of maintenance and depreciation of buildings, land improvement investments, energy and water, advisory services, accounting, farm insurance, taxes and duties and phone and office expenses and are about seven times higher for the German farms than for the Brazilian farms. This is mainly because in Brazil, depreciation for buildings is low and insurance, taxes and duties are nonexistent or negligibly low.

We calculated land costs by adding up the expenses for rented land and the opportunity cost of owned land by applying the current regional rental price. Based on these calculations, land costs in Germany are almost five times higher than in Brazil.

Environmental standards and their cost implications

Germany's fertilizer regulation incorporates European regulations on the use of mineral and organic nitrogen fertilizers. The regulation specifies, for example, that annual nitrogen balance statements have to be produced for farms of more than 10 hectares. The cost of the required soil sampling amounts to about US$0.03 per 100 kilograms for grain and US$0.06 per 100 kilograms for rapeseed, which in both cases is less than 1 per cent of the total cost of production. For oil palm cultivation in Indonesia, fertilizer requirements are normally tested by means of leaf analysis, but costs have not been calculated. While this regulation creates minor costs, nutrient records may also lead to cost reductions through a more efficient adjustment of fertilizer levels to soil conditions and the plants' needs.

As regards plant protection, some pesticides that are either completely banned or for which approval has expired in Germany are widely used in Brazil and Indonesia. To quantify the costs of such restrictions, we calculated the additional costs of using more expensive substitutes in Germany. For instance, German grain producers have to incur an additional cost of US$0.4 per 100 kilograms by substituting another pesticide in place of Simazin, which is banned for grain production. We have taken these costs into account in the total cost calculation.

With respect to costs related to the approval of pesticides, we found that costs charged by the relevant authorities are negligible with regard to the costs of developing new plant protection substances. Nevertheless, they have an implicit effect on development costs, and thus on final product prices. Such costs cannot be estimated because of differences in the pricing and marketing strategies of pesticide producers and because of insufficient data. Furthermore, there is evidence that disposing of pesticide packages is problematic for many farmers in Brazil. In Germany the chemical industry has established a system that allows farmers to return empty packages after use and collection is free of charge. We assume that the costs of disposal are added to the product price; however, we were not able to quantify this additional cost.

There is no indication that environmental standards have any impact on differences in the design and technical fittings of farm machinery in the three countries; however, there are differences in safety standards. For instance, the standards for work safety are higher in Germany than in Brazil or Indonesia. However, these costs are mostly included in the prices of buildings or equipment and could not be isolated.

We found, isolated and analysed higher environmental standards in some technical security areas with respect to their cost implications. For example, we found that the typical farm has to cover additional costs because of technical security standards for pesticide sprayers in Germany, but these costs are negligible, merely US$0.002 or less per 100 kilograms of wheat. German farms also incur higher costs from the requirement to have a special area designated for cleaning machines and equipment. Farmers have to construct a paved area with an oil separator, and sometimes even a sewage treatment plant for the disposal of, for example, liquid manure from cleaning slurry spreaders. Also to have gas fuelling facilities, farmers must cover the costs of technical supervision, building permission and the fuel tank must be surrounded by a basin in case the fuel tank leaks. For the typical German farm, these additional costs amounted to US$0.04 to US$0.06 per 100 kilograms of rapeseed and between US$0.006 and US$0.03 per 100 kilograms of grain.

We found no evidence to suggest that in Germany the regulatory framework has a strong influence on fuel prices, nor any indication of different environmental standards leading to a significant difference in fuel prices between Germany and Brazil and Indonesia. We found the same with respect to water and wastewater, electricity and energy prices. While electricity prices in Brazil are about half German prices, we found no correlation between environmental standards and electricity prices. The typical German farms obtain water mainly from public water pipes at a cost of US$1.1 to US$2.2 per cubic metre, and no longer from private pipes from their own wells or nearby public lakes. The total cost for fresh water amounts to about US$1.7 to US$3.3 per hectare. The fee for wastewater disposal amounts to about US$1.7 to US$2.2 per cubic metre. In Brazil water costs are difficult to quantify, because farmers draw water from their own wells and wastewater disposal is currently free of charge. The Brazilian government has, however, announced that it will introduce fees for wastewater disposal.

Further costs due to environmental standards that are often neglected because they are even harder to identify and to quantify (Chapman, Agras and Suri 1995) include labour costs resulting from additional environmental activities, such as the time spent writing environmental reports or testing pesticide sprayers and the costs to transport and load and unload empty pesticide packages at the nearest disposal location. However, these additional expenses might be compensated for by the benefits of, for instance, spraying pesticides more effectively. Sometimes costs are incurred because of long approval periods and delays for such activities as setting up new broiler units.

In Brazil, the most important environmental regulation imposed on the typical farm since 1965 is law number 4.771/65. It has two main parts that affect land use and land costs. The first mandates that all farmers permanently set aside at least 20 per cent of their land to maintain or replant local species, mainly trees. The second obligates farmers to permanently set aside strips along rivers, lakes and waterways for nature conservation. However, because of insufficient enforcement, in most cases these standards do not add to farmers' costs. If the laws were strictly enforced, Brazilian soybean farmers would, in extreme cases, face 15 to 23 per cent higher production costs.

Similarly, the production costs of palm oil producers in Indonesia are likely to increase if the Zero Burning Law that bans the use of fire for forest conversion were to be strictly imposed. The additional costs of mechanical land clearing methods are roughly 20 to 25 per cent of a plantation's establishment costs.

Processing costs

We estimated the total cost of processing oilseeds at US$26 to US$39 per ton of crude oil for rapeseed processors in Germany, US$20 to US$36 per ton for soybean processing enterprises in Brazil and US$31 to US$33 per ton of crude oil for Indonesian palm oil producers. Compared with the Brazilian processors, the costs for energy, taxes, insurance and especially depreciation are significantly higher in Germany. The cost of depreciation is lower in Brazil and Indonesia because, unlike in Germany, processing is undertaken in open facilities, and therefore expensive investments in equipment for explosion protection, which is essential in closed buildings, are not needed.

In a comparison of processing mills of different sizes we observed significant scale effects. In Germany, a medium oil mill with a processing capacity of 300 000 tons of crude oil per year has a total cost of US$39 per ton of crude oil. By contrast, a large oil mill with a processing capacity of 1 million tons of crude oil per year has total costs of US$29 per ton of crude oil, and a very large oil mill with a processing capacity of 2.5 million tons of crude oil per year has total costs of US$26 per ton of crude oil.

Rapeseed processing mills in Germany incur higher costs than soybean processing mills in Brazil and palm oil mills in Indonesia because of higher environment standards and more stringent environmental regulations. In Germany these additional costs amount to US$1.3 to US$2 per ton of crude oil, or about 5 per cent of processing costs. The corresponding figures are US$

0.2 to US$0.3 per ton of soy oil (0.5 to 1 per cent of processing costs) in Brazil and US$0.1 to US$0.4 per ton of palm oil (0.4 to 1.1 per cent of processing costs) in Indonesia.

Considerable differences exist among the three countries with respect to the cost of setting up new processing mills that relate to explosion protection, air pollution control and wastewater disposal. These differences pertain not only to investments needed to meet environmental standards, but also to operating costs.

EMPIRICAL RESULTS FOR BROILERS

For broilers, we calculated the production and processing costs and estimated the impact of environmental standards on total costs.

Production Costs

Total production costs were comparable for the two Brazilian broiler farms and amounted to about US$0.6 per kilogram live weight. Total costs for the German farm amounted to US$0.8 per kilogram live weight. The corresponding estimates per broiler produced were US$1.3 for the small Brazilian farm (15 000 broilers), US$1.4 per broiler for the larger Brazilian farm (24 000 broilers) and US$1.6 per broiler for the German farm (28 000 broilers).

Direct costs include feed and other direct costs, with the latter representing the costs of broiler chicks, veterinary care and medicine, bedding, cleaning and disinfection and electricity, water and gas. In Brazil the total direct costs amounted to about 90 per cent of the total production costs, compared with 85 per cent in Germany.

Feed costs are by far the most important component of total costs of production in both countries. They amounted to US$0.43 per kilogram live weight (50 per cent of total costs) in Germany and US$0.37 per kilogram live weight (63 per cent of total costs) in Brazil. The differences in feed costs between the two countries arose from differences in feed prices (US$0.19 per kilogram in Brazil, US$0.23 per kilogram in Germany) and from feed conversion rates (approximately 1:1.8 in Germany and 1:2.0 in Brazil).

Other direct costs ranged between US$0.27 per kilogram live weight in Germany (one-third of total costs) and US$0.15 per kilogram live weight in Brazil (one-quarter of total costs). The most important of these cost items in both countries was the purchase of broiler chicks, which varied between US$0.11 per kilogram live weight in Brazil to US$0.18 per kilogram live weight in Germany. The second most important cost component in Germany was electricity, water and gas (US$0.03 per kilogram live weight), followed by expenses for veterinary care and medicine (US$0.02 per kilogram live weight). The costs for veterinary care and medicine were slightly lower in Brazil than in Germany, but still ranked as the second most important cost item.

Depreciation (US$0.06 per kilogram live weight) and maintenance (US$0.02 per kilogram live weight) costs for buildings and equipment were four to five times higher in Germany than in Brazil. This is not surprising considering the differences in investment costs. Capital investment in buildings ranged from US$37 200 to US$65 600 for the two farms in Brazil, compared with US$229 000 for the German farm. The respective values for equipment were US$77 200 to US$36 100 for the Brazilian farms and US$84 400 for the German farm. This large difference arose mainly because the Brazil farms use relatively old technology and manual feeding. The percentage share of depreciation and maintenance in total costs varied between 3 and 4 per cent for the Brazilian farms and amounted to 6 per cent for the German farm.

Labour costs include both wages and salaries, as well as the opportunity cost for the farmer's household labour input. They ranged between US$0.03 per kilogram live weight for the small Brazilian farm and US$0.02 per kilogram live weight for the larger Brazilian farm. For the German farm, labour costs amounted to US$0.03 per kilogram live weight. The labour share in total cost amounted to 3 per cent in Brazil and 4 per cent in Germany. Finally, other overhead costs, including interest payments, amounted to about 3 per cent of the total cost for both Brazilian and German farms.

Environmental Standards for Broiler Production

We found that the cost disadvantages emanating from environmental standards are significant only with respect to the German farm's buildings and equipment.[3] Such costs simply did not exist in Brazil. The German regulations in this connection include standards for the following:

- Environmental protection according to the Federal Emission Control Act requires floors of concrete with a certain reinforcement and thickness, a platform for dung and development costs for water and electricity connections because of distances to villages.
- Animal welfare protection mandates a certain number of windows (3 per cent of the floor space), a certain number of feed and drinking troughs and nipples, roof ridge ventilation, a cooling system, an alarm system for climate regulation and power supply and an emergency generator.

- The conservation of landscape regulations require buildings to be painted on the outside.
- Work safety is mandated by means of automatic trough winding systems.

The additional costs for the German broiler farm arising from these environmental and animal welfare protection standards amounted to 2.7 per cent of total costs. However, some of these measures might have been implemented by the firm under study even in the absence of any regulations. In particular, cooling and alarm systems can prevent the deaths of animals; thus they are not only relevant from the perspective of animal welfare protection, but also from an economic point of view.

Note that this additional cost could be significant for a broiler producer with low profit margins. Furthermore, farmers can incur control and planning costs, for example, the time spent meeting safety officers or producing environmental reports. Approval costs and opportunity costs caused by delays (up to a few years for the establishment of broiler facilities in Germany) can be significant market entry barriers.

Processing Costs

A difference of up to US$15 per 100 kilogram live weight was found between slaughtering costs in Brazil and Germany. While experts estimate that costs of slaughtering broilers are some US$14 per 100 kilogram live weight in a Brazilian processing plant, the cost in a German processing plant amounts to US$29 per 100 kilogram live weight. To a large extent, these differences emanated from environmental standards that exist in Germany, but not in Brazil. Especially with respect to wastewater disposal and process quality control, the German processing plant incurred significantly higher expenses than the Brazilian plants.

Brazilian plants derive a considerable relative cost advantage from the sale of waste products arising from processing. By contrast, waste products do not have any market value in Germany, and also incur disposal costs.

The largest share of the additional cost in Germany results from the use of the air-cooling system, compared with the less expensive water-cooling system used in Brazil. However, the use of air-cooling systems improves the quality of the final product. Thus the incentive for German plants to shift from water- to air-cooling systems was based on the expectation of higher prices due to better quality, but the necessary change in the carcass classification system has not yet been introduced.

Representatives of the German broiler processing industry stated that German environmental standards were extremely high by international standards. For the German plant, we estimated that total costs resulting from environmental standards amounted to US$4.8 per kilogram live weight, or 17 per cent of total processing costs. For Brazil we estimated that these additional costs amounted to only US$0.55 per 100 kilogram live weight, or 4 per cent of total costs.

In addition, the administration of environmental standards and the related delays can involve significant costs, but we did not consider these costs in this study.

TRANSFERABILITY OF ENVIRONMENTAL STANDARDS TO OTHER COUNTRIES

In addition to analysing the cost-effectiveness of environmental standards, this study has attempted to answer two related questions. Does it make sense to transfer environmental standards from one country to another? Is there a need to harmonize product-specific standards internationally? We can address these questions by comparing production systems and environmental conditions in the three countries.

With respect to cultivation practices, Brazil and Indonesia use pesticides (Atrazin and Simazin in Brazil and Sevin in Indonesia) that are no longer approved in Germany. However, all three pesticides are approved in other EU countries and in the United States. In Brazil and EU countries other than Germany an insecticide with the active substance triflumuron is also allowed. This insecticide is no longer approved in Germany, but only because the domestic market for the product was too small. Carbaryl, an active substance in Sevin, which is used in Indonesia, was forbidden in Germany on the basis of bee protection. The substance was considered hazardous to bees, especially the European honey bee. Not only does the European honey bee not exist in Indonesia, but more important, palm oil trees are neither pollinated nor used as a food source by domestic bees. Therefore, one must consider environmental factors when analysing the transferability of standards to other countries.

The intensity of production and the level of yields in Brazilian oilseed farms and in grain production are lower than in Germany. Thus the need for fertilizer per hectare is lower in Brazil than in Germany. Taking yields into account, rapeseed in Germany is more nutrient-efficient than soybeans in Brazil. Nitrogen efficiency seems to be higher for maize in Brazil than for wheat and barley in Germany. However, no inferences about the need for internationally harmonized environmental standards for fertilizer can be drawn from these figures, for example, to protect groundwater, because required fertilization depends on regional soil and climatic conditions.

The analysis of environmental standards at the processing level shows that the need for and the nature of standards are primarily determined by differences in processing methods and local conditions. For example, the regulations for oilseed processing plants with respect to explosion and emission protection are irrelevant to Brazil, because there soybean processing takes place in open facilities where there is no danger of explosion from accumulating hexane gas. Similarly, palm oil in Indonesia is processed through pressing in open buildings rather than through extraction under closed factory conditions.

For broiler production and processing, the environmental and animal welfare protection standards are higher in Germany than in Brazil, but again, many of these regulations refer to buildings that are not relevant for Brazil, where broilers are normally kept in open Louisiana-type facilities.

There are significant international differences with respect to the stocking rate for poultry. The typical farms in Brazil have about 12 to 16 broilers per square metre, compared with about 23 on the German farms. However, the health of the broilers is determined not only by the stocking rate, but also depends on the temperature and ventilation. Some Brazilian farms have tried higher stocking rates, but they found that the broilers competed too much for food and water, which resulted in skin damage, which makes the broilers unpalatable to consumers. Thus different factor price relationships and consumer preferences have led to the choice of lower stocking rates in Brazil.

In general, regulations relating to air emissions of odours and the landscape are relatively strict in Germany. The introduction and implementation of these regulations is mainly due to Germany's higher population density and society's preferences for a high environmental quality, compared with the other two countries. In Brazil, these kinds of regulations play only a minor role because the broiler producers are mostly located far away from residential areas. Considering the relatively low population density in some remote production areas, whether the introduction of environmental standards similar to those in Germany would be appropriate for Brazil and Indonesia is debatable.

CONCLUSION

The case studies of selected agricultural products in Brazil, Germany and Indonesia have shown that the impact of environmental standards on production costs is relatively small in the case of the typical farms considered. In Germany environmental standards account for 0.3 to 4.4 per cent of total production costs for rapeseed, grain and broilers on the typical farm. These standards refer mainly to the use of fertilizers, pesticides and technical safety. In Brazil and Indonesia environmental laws are poorly enforced, resulting in significant gains for producers. However, such cost advantages are of minor significance in determining international competitiveness compared with the huge cost differences resulting in particular from differences in wage levels and in the prices of machinery, buildings and equipment. Even if the environmental standards were fully enforced, the total costs of the two soybean farms in Brazil would be still 10 to 45 per cent less than the costs of the German rapeseed farms. Likewise, in the case of grain production, the total production costs of the Brazilian farms would be still 20 to 50 per cent below those of the German farms.

At the processing level, the results are ambiguous. The costs of meeting environmental standards in the German oil mills account for about 5 per cent of total processing costs. For the soybean processing firms, the corresponding figure is a mere 0.5 to 1 per cent for their Brazilian counterparts and 0.4 to 1.1 per cent for their Indonesian counterparts.

Major product-specific differences exist in the three countries with respect to the establishment of new processing mills for explosion protection (only necessary in Germany), air pollution control and wastewater disposal.

The costs of meeting environmental standards for processing broilers in Germany was estimated at 17 per cent of total processing costs, compared with 4 per cent in Brazil. Standards relating to wastewater disposal and process quality control were found to be the most cost-intensive in Germany. However, the total costs of broiler production in Germany were almost double those in Brazil. Thus in determining Brazil's international competitiveness in relation to Germany for this product, environmental standards are important only at the margin.

The evidence also indicates that environmental standards are not easily transferable from one country to another, given the differences in climate and population density and the scarcity of environmental goods. This is especially relevant to standards relating to buildings (number of windows in broiler facilities, explosion control in oilseed processing and so on) and to the use of certain pesticides. Environmental standards need to be carefully designed and adapted to suit the environment in different countries and regions. However, enforcement needs to be improved to avoid possibly significant adverse environmental externalities (such as overextended land use in Brazil and forest burning in Indonesia) as part of the move towards greater liberalization of trade in agricultural products. This recommendation is particularly valid for the expansion of export-oriented soybean production in Brazil and palm oil production in Indonesia.

NOTES

1. In 1991 the reported area peaked at almost 3 million.
2. For further information on the International Farm Comparison Network see the following web site: http://www.fal.de/bal/ifcn.html
3. For the purposes of this study, we interpret animal welfare protection standards as environmental standards.

REFERENCES

Brouwer, F., D. Baldock, C. Carpentier, J. Dwyer, D. Ervin, G. Fox, A. Meister and R. Stringer (2000), *Comparison of Environmental and Health-Related Standards Influencing the Relative Competitiveness of EU Agriculture vis-à-vis Main Competitors in the World Market*, The Hague, Netherlands: Agricultural Economics Research Institute.

Chapman, D., J. Agras and V. Suri (1995), 'International Law, Industrial Location and Pollution', *Indiana Journal of Global Legal Studies*, **3** (5).

Dean, J.M. (1992), 'Trade and Environment: A Survey of the Literature', in P. Low (ed.), *International Trade and the Environment*, Washington, DC: World Bank, pp. 15–28.

Felke, R. (1998), *European Environmental Regulations and International Competitiveness*, Baden-Baden, Germany: Nomos.

Glover, D. and T. Jessup (1999), *Indonesia's Fires and Haze. The Cost of Catastrophe*, Singapore and Ottawa: Institute for East Asian Studies and International Institute for Sustainable Development.

Grote, U., A.K. Basu and N.H. Chau (1999), 'The International Debate and Economic Consequences of Eco-Labelling', Discussion Papers on Development Policy no. 18, Centre for Development Research, Bonn, Germany.

Grote, U., C. Deblitz, T. Reichert and S. Stegmann (2000), 'Umweltstandards und internationale Wettbewerbsfähigkeit: Analyse und Bedeutung: insbesondere im Rahmen der WTO', Centre for Development Research, Bonn, Germany.

Helm, C. (1995), *Sind Freihandel und Umweltschutz vereinbar?*, Berlin, Germany: Edition Sigma.

Jaffe, A.B., S.R. Peterson, P.R. Portney and R.N. Stavins (1995), 'Environmental Regulation and the Competitiveness of US Manufacturing: What Does the Evidence Tell Us?', *Journal of Economic Literature*, **33** (S), 132–63.

Jenkins, R. (1999), 'Environmental Regulation and International Competitiveness: A Framework for Analysis', paper presented at the conference on Environmental Regulation, Globalization of Production and Technological Change, 1–2 July, University of East Anglia, Norwich, UK.

Kalt, J. (1988), 'The Impact of Domestic Environmental Regulatory Policies on US International Competitiveness', in M. Spence and H. Hazard (eds), *International Competitiveness*, Cambridge, MA: Harper and Row, Ballinger, pp. 221–62.

Lee, H. and D. Roland-Holst (1994), 'International Trade and the Transfer of Environment Cost and Benefits', in J. Francois and K. Reinerts (eds), *Applied Trade Policy Modelling*, Cambridge, UK: Cambridge University Press.

Low, P. and A. Yeats (1992), 'Do "Dirty" Industries Migrate?', in P. Low (ed.), *International Trade and the Environment*, Discussion Paper no. 159, Washington, DC: World Bank, pp. 89–104.

Nordström, H. and S. Vaughan (1999), *Trade and Environment*, Geneva: WTO.

OECD (Organization for Economic Co-operation and Development) (1997), 'Brazilian Agriculture: Recent Policy Changes and Trade Prospects', Working Papers vol. V, no. 55, Paris.

Porter, M. (1991), 'America's Green Strategy', *Scientific American*, April, p. 68.

Porter, M. and C. van der Linde (1995), 'Green and Competitive', *Harvard Business Review* (September–October), 120–34.

Repetto, R. (1995), *Jobs, Competitiveness, and Environmental Regulation*, Washington, DC: World Resources Institute.

Sorsa, P. (1994), *Competitiveness and Environmental Standards: Some Explanatory Results*, Policy Research Paper no. 1249, Washington, DC: World Bank.

UNCTAD (United Nations Conference on Trade and Development) (1994), *Sustainable Development. Trade and Environment: The Impact of Environment-Related Policies on Export Competitiveness and Market Access*, TD/B/41 (1)/4, Geneva.

6. Labour standards, social labels and the WTO

Arnab K. Basu, Nancy H. Chau and Ulrike Grote

The collapse of trade negotiations in Seattle in December 1999 has brought social dimensions to the forefront of post-UR multilateral trade talks. While the anti-globalization lobbies in the industrial countries have intensified their demands for including minimum labour standards relating to working hours, workplace safety and employment of women and children in WTO trade rules, the developing countries strongly oppose these demands and condemn the clamour for labour standards as disguised protectionism. Developing countries claim that labour-related issues are best left under the auspices of the ILO, which has been attempting to protect the rights and safety of workers in general, and of children in particular, through United Nations conventions.

This chapter reviews the broader issues related to the demand for including minimum labour standards in the form of a social clause in the WTO Agreement. It also analyses whether social labelling – attaching labels or certificates to products that have been produced under 'acceptable' working conditions – offers an alternative to the direct imposition of labour standards. The discussion on social labelling focuses on three key issues. First, do the developing countries have an incentive to advocate or initiate social labelling, particularly if the industrial countries continue to threaten to impose sanctions against unlabelled products? Second, who should bear the cost of monitoring social labelling – the industrial countries where major consumer markets are located, or the developing countries where most of the production is carried out? Third, would workers in developing countries be better off under a social labelling regime as compared with one with an institutionally imposed minimum labour standard?

LABOUR STANDARDS AND INTERNATIONAL TRADE POLICY

The literature on the merits and demerits of linking labour standards with trade policy is vast, and the broader issue that has emerged in recent years seems to revolve around whether the rights of workers in the developing countries are best served through the ILO's current methods of monitoring and persuasion or through binding trade agreements that allow the use of trade policies as a punishment mechanism for countries that fail to elevate their standards. In this context, the following sections briefly discuss key issues related to labour standards and international trade policy.

The Basic Conflict in Relation to Trade and Labour Standards

The debate about appropriate policies for raising labour standards in developing countries has ranged from the demand to include a social clause in the WTO that attempts to solicit compliance with a core set of minimum labour standards, to calls for legislation that bans imports that fail to meet existing minimum standards in the industrial countries. As Kahn (2000) points out, labour interests and human rights activists in the industrial countries argue that market access for developing-country goods in the industrial countries should be conditioned on raising labour standards in the developing countries. They fear that unhindered imports of cheap, labour-intensive imports from the developing countries will rapidly erode their own higher labour standards, leading to a global 'race to the bottom' in wages and benefits. In addition, industrial countries are often concerned about losing international competitiveness because of higher production costs created by higher labour standards in their own countries, while the developing countries are able to increase their production (and market share) at the expense of the well-being of developing-country workers and children (Srinivasan 1996). Finally, as highlighted by the recent version of the Child Labor Deterrence Act (Harkin's Bill) in the United States, the institution of trade sanctions against countries that continue to employ children in their export sectors stems from a moral concern for the well-being of children in developing countries. In sum, lobby groups in the industrial countries perceive trade policy as a useful and effective instrument for enforcing labour standards in their developing-country trading partners.

Meanwhile the developing countries view the idea of a social clause as disguised protectionism that would impair their international competitiveness and market access for their products. They are fighting vigorously against industrial-country initiatives to give the WTO a role in the area of labour standards and thereby intertwine social policy with trade policy. Instead they stress that any concerns about labour standards or any other social dimension of international trade policy should be dealt with through the ILO.

The ILO, founded in 1919, is the main international organization concerned with labour standards, and so far more than 180 ILO conventions have become binding obligations for WTO member states (Wiemann 1999). These conventions cover many issues, including a number of core labour standards, for instance, freedom of association, the right to organize and bargain collectively, the prohibition of forced labour and a minimum age for employing children. Except for a few notable exceptions, especially the United States, almost all countries have signed and ratified a set of covenants that recognize diverse labour rights that go beyond the core ILO standards (Srinivasan 1996). The ILO's enforcement mechanisms are, however, considered less effective than the proposed social clause under the WTO that allows for direct action through trade sanctions. To encourage compliance the ILO has to rely on international pressure, persuasion, advice and monitoring. Countries that do not ratify or do not comply with ILO conventions may face moral pressure, but there are no explicit sanctions, such as import bans for traded goods, as is possible under the WTO.

Implications of Higher Labour Standards

Let us assume that higher labour standards are successfully enforced in the developing countries. How would these higher standards actually affect efficiency and equity? The literature provides no clear answer, hence no generalization is possible.

High labour standards imposed on developing countries might achieve some positive results (Brown, Deardorff and Stern 1996). First, developing-country governments that are unable to enact legislation on their own because of domestic political pressures can take such initiatives under the cover provided by international legislation. Second, guaranteeing such standards as the right to organize may help promote the development of democratic institutions. For instance, as Freeman (1993) and Marshall (1994) argue, setting the stage for effective collective bargaining could promote the functioning of the labour market. The efficiency wage theory suggests, for instance, that producers will set minimum standards to ensure productivity and maximize profits (Figueroa 1997). Piore (1994) assumes that labour standards could lead to more efficient production strategies. Summarizing the theoretical literature, Krueger (1997) states that labour standards could enhance labour market efficiency and contribute to better income distribution in some situations.

However, there might be situations where labour standards could prove counterproductive to efficiency and equity. Higher labour standards that are imposed on export-oriented companies in developing countries often worsen the situation of workers, as firms' incentives might lead them to increase layoffs to guarantee higher standards for the remaining workforce. For developing countries that already have high unemployment rates, this has the potential of pushing workers from poverty into destitution. One of the core labour standards the ILO promotes is workers' freedom to form labour unions and bargain collectively. However, in many developing countries most poor workers are self-employed in agriculture or in the informal urban sector, so labour standards are irrelevant to them (Srinivasan 1998). In addition, labour unions in developing countries often constitute a small elite that uses its power to improve the conditions for a few at the expense of others. Thus, even minimum labour standards like the freedom to bargain need to be adapted to country-specific socio-economic situations.

The Race to the Bottom Debate

A vast analytical literature deals with the 'labour standard competition' between the industrial countries (the North) and the developing countries (the South) (for example, Bagwell and Staiger 2000; Maskus 1997; Panagariya 1999; Rodrik 1996; Srinivasan 1998). On the welfare and trade implications of raising labour standards in the South, Krugman (1997) and Krueger (1997) argue that the gains from trade may be diminished as the South begins to adopt labour standards that are similar to those of the North. Indeed, diversity in labour standards can be perfectly legitimate for countries that differ in terms of preferences, technologies and factor endowments (Bhagwati 1996; Srinivasan 1996). Standards are unlikely to improve workers' economic conditions unless such standards are appropriate to the level of development in the given country. When standards are too high, employers are likely to ignore or abuse them (Krueger 1997).

When domestic distributional and political concerns guide countries to deviate from economic efficiency, a concerted effort to harmonize labour standards, coupled with internationally acknowledged checks and balances, may ultimately benefit all (Brown, Deardorff and Stern 1996; Rodrik 1996). Despite the possibility of joint North and South welfare gains, the likelihood of simultaneous, endogenous adoption of high labour standards depends crucially on the nature of the competition between North and South. In their discussion of the incentives underlying the adoption of high labour standards in the North and South, Brown, Deardorff and Stern (1996) point out that for small countries as price-takers in the world market, the question of strategic interaction simply does not arise, and as a result, a race to the bottom is unlikely. This may not be the case, however, when the importing North and the exporting South countries are both large and their choice of labour standards affects the terms of trade. The importing country's welfare is adversely affected because costly labour standards could raise the price of imports. In contrast, exporting countries will adopt labour standards that are too high compared with the Pareto-optimal or Pareto-efficient level, as long as the costs of higher labour standards are translated into an increase in the final price of exports. Here a race to the top takes place when high labour standards are adopted in the name of terms of trade gains. Strategic interaction between North and South may, however, actually imply asymmetric labour standards across the North and South if the North overestimates and the South underestimates the true gains from higher standards.

Srinivasan (1996) provides numerical examples that illustrate yet another possibility: a case where both North and South have low labour standards. In that case a race to the bottom in labour standards would be synonymous with the 'prisoner's dilemma'. The underlying model of the economy that governs the incentives of the two countries in adopting high labour standards is central to whether low labour standards in the North and the South can be interpreted as a prisoner's dilemma. Freeman (1993) and Ehrenberg (1994), for instance, take the different labour standards adopted in various US states as a case in point, and argue that in the context of international trade and labour standards competition, a race to the bottom does not necessarily take place.

Chau and Kanbur (2000) complement this North–South perspective with an examination of the possibility of a South–South race to the bottom in labour standards. The analysis focuses on the interdependencies among incentives to improve labour standards in the face of export competition among developing countries. They show that the nature of import demand is key to determining whether improved labour standards in one developing country encourage or hamper incentives for other developing countries to improve their standards. Simply put, a loss of market share caused by export competition is not, by itself, sufficient for a downward spiral in labour standards. Rather, whether a race to the bottom is inevitable is a function of the extent to which export competition achieved through low labour standards affects changes in market shares.

Openness to trade: a cause of low labour standards?
Given that under some circumstances trade competition may exacerbate failure on the part of exporting countries to improve labour standards, is openness to trade the culprit in bringing about low labour standards and can import restrictions prevent the race to the bottom?

Indeed, international trade liberalization is no longer only about reducing existing border measures. As noted earlier, in sharp contrast to trade liberalization efforts in the last four decades, some industrial countries have proposed including a social clause in the WTO Agreement that would permit the imposition of trade restrictions on imports that are not in compliance with a core set of labour standards. The Harkins Bill in the United States proposes trade measures to protect adult wages against the unfair advantage of imports that are known to have involved child labour. Section 307 of the US's Tariff Act of 1930 takes the denial of labour rights (prison labour, forced or indentured child labour) as a violation of US trade law, and the US has applied retaliatory trade measures against China and Mexico. A common theme that characterizes these proposals and measures is that trade partners' willingness to abide by the principle of free trade has become conditional on the harmonization of national labour standards that affect world trade, so that global competition is conducted on a level playing field.

The idea that trade protection can promote improved labour standards in developing countries is attractive to many, but it is also an idea that fails to withstand economic analysis. Consider a small import tariff levied by the industrial countries on the exports of developing countries. By undermining market share rivalry among exporters, trade restrictions can prevent a race to the bottom in labour standards (see Chau and Kanbur 2000 for details). As may be expected, this tariff lowers the price exporters receive and has an initial effect of harming workers and employers in the export sectors of low-income countries. Ironically, the lower terms of trade can actually improve incentives to adopt higher labour standards in exporting countries, because the higher the import tariff, the smaller the extent of export revenue gains that can be achieved by expanding exports by means of low standards. However, once the window of conditioning trade policies on labour standards is open, the small tariff argument suffers from a credibility problem. Indeed, proposals to hand over authority on import tariffs to the importing country can be counterproductive, because exporting countries rationally expect any terms of trade improvement via high labour standards to be offset by corresponding changes in import tariffs. More specifically, allowing the importing nation to impose its optimal tariffs conditional on labour standard choices in exporting nations simply serves to eliminate the terms of trade motive underlying the adoption of high labour standards.

Another indirect trade implication of labour standards refers to their impact on international competitiveness. Many industrial countries are concerned about losing international competitiveness through high labour standards, which they assume create higher production costs. After controlling for international differences in labour productivity, Rodrik (1996) shows that the relationship between comparative advantage in labour-intensive sectors such as textiles and clothing and labour standards is not statistically significant. Instead, relative differences in the abundance of factors of production and technology and cost differences reflecting countries' different endowments of skilled and unskilled labour, capital, technology and natural resources determine the international competitiveness of low-income countries (Gans 2000; Wiemann 1999). The industrial countries would be acting against their own interests, as well as those of the developing countries, if they were to push for a levelling process of international cost differences and remove the basis for specialization that is advantageous to all countries (Siebke and Rolf 1998).

However, among countries there are, of course, winners and losers in relation to international trade. Based on an input–output model for the economy of the former Federal Republic of Germany in the 1970s, Schumacher (1981) found that trade liberalization created more than 4 per cent of new jobs, mainly in the processing sector, while close to 2 per cent of jobs were lost; thus the net job effect was positive. Therefore, we can conclude that trade-induced structural changes put some economic sectors under pressure, while others gain international competitiveness. This also implies that, in the industrial countries, trade policies directed at harmonization to protect certain weak sectors (for example, the textile sector) in which the developing countries have comparative cost advantages would be counterproductive, and would even weaken the competitiveness of other sectors in the industrial countries. Therefore for the industrial countries the effective and efficient economic solution to labour market problems is to strive to improve their economies' internal capacity for adjustment, not an international harmonization of social standards (Gans 2000).

SOCIAL LABELS: AN ALTERNATIVE TO LABOUR STANDARDS?

So far we have focused on North–South and South–South race to the bottom arguments, with an emphasis on how sanctions or tariffs by industrial importing countries help to alter the incentives of developing exporting countries to adopt high labour standards. In this section we focus on social labelling, an alternative market-based mechanism to raise labour standards in the developing countries.

Trend Towards Social Labelling

Social labelling – the provision of information via product labels regarding the use of acceptable labour standards in the production process – has gained currency in recent years as a voluntary, industry-based initiative to combat the prevalence of low labour standards in the developing countries. The origins of social labelling can be traced back to the 'white label', sponsored and monitored by the US National Consumers League as early as 1899, which assured consumers that women's and children's stitched cotton underwear was manufactured under decent working conditions and without the use of child labour, and draws on the success of more recent 'green label' initiatives that promote environmentally friendly production methods (Hilowitz 1997). The first modern social label, RUGMARK, was instituted in 1994 to guarantee to German and US consumers that hand-knotted carpets made in India and Nepal had not been produced using child labour.

Since 1994 many different labels have been developed. While many of them focus on child labour (Basu, Chau and Grote 2000), the number of labels focusing on more general working conditions in developing countries is increasing. One example is fair trade labelling in the international flower trade: the Max Havelaar Foundation in Switzerland has designed its own label for flowers. The flowers are purchased directly from small farmer organizations or from plantations that participate in the labelling programme. To guarantee the farmers a minimum of social security, a minimum price has been established. In addition, participating farmers enjoy rights like freedom to belong to a trade union, freedom from discrimination and a guarantee of equal pay, no forced labour or child labour and safe working conditions. The Max Havelaar flower labelling programme, which was initiated in 1996 as a co-operative initiative by traders, labour unions and NGOs, is an example of how to enforce higher labour standards on exports from developing countries. There are also some export associations in developing countries, like the Flower Council in Kenya or the Florverde programme in Colombia, which have developed codes of conduct to promote labour standards (Grote 1999).

The Effects of Social Labelling

Can social labels that certify that certain products are being produced under acceptable labour conditions induce voluntary participation by producers in the developing countries, and thereby provide an alternative to the imposition of minimum labour standards across countries?

The attractiveness of social labelling is derived from its market-based approach to enticing producers to improve their workers' wages and benefits with little or no government support. In addition, levies collected by the label foundations, either nonprofit or government, from participating businesses constitute a potential, alternative source of income that the foundation or agencies can use to encourage improved work conditions and human capital acquisitions in the production process.

Another benefit of social labelling is its informational role, in that it helps increase public awareness in both the industrial and the developing economies about labour conditions, and allows producers to internalize consumers' willingness to pay a higher price for products that have higher labour standards.

Despite these advantages of social labelling as an alternative to the imposition of standards, economic analysis has yet to keep pace with policy recommendations in regard to the effectiveness of social labelling. What seems puzzling to the casual observer is that social labelling initiatives originate largely from major consumer markets, rather than from the developing economies, which are presumed to gain through an increase in producer revenues for labelled products. This raises an interesting question. If the gains from social labelling accrue solely to the developing countries, then why are these countries reluctant to institute labelling schemes and take advantage of the terms of trade effect? The only social label instituted by a developing country so far is the Indian government's KALEEN label, which aims at eliminating child labour. However, the KALEEN label does not subject producers to on-site monitoring and inspection.

Even if social labelling programmes were credibly enforced, they might not translate into improved welfare for workers. In particular, wage increases that result from social labelling schemes lead to a decline in the demand for labour. Thus in developing countries that already have high unemployment rates, social labelling could push workers from poverty to destitution. Moreover, explicit labelling renders unlabelled products vulnerable to allegations of unfair trade practices and provides a means for interest groups in the industrial countries to advocate restrictions to market access.

In what follows we synthesize the foregoing insights by identifying three groups of stakeholders and examining the links that social labelling creates between them. These three groups are: (a) consumers in the developed North whose preferences are characterized by a desire to boycott products that are produced with low labour standards; (b) producers in the developing South whose labour standard choices depend on the tradeoff between cost increases and revenue gains associated with higher standards; and (c) producers in the North who compete with producers in the South for market share.

To understand the mechanism whereby social labelling can improve labour standards, note that consumers have to regard the labelled products as private goods, in the sense that an individual consumer's willingness to pay a higher price for a labelled product does not depend on other consumers' willingness to pay. Otherwise, the free-rider problem may not generate any price premium for labelled products. In the absence of social labels, consumers cannot differentiate between products produced under different labour standards, and as such pay a uniform price. However, there might be circumstances in the absence of social labels where consumers pay different prices for the same product originating in different countries if they believe that certain countries have lower standards relative to others. As an example, consumers might be unwilling to pay the same price for a shirt made in India as for an identical shirt made in Bangladesh if they believe that labour standards are lower in Bangladesh than in India. This example illustrates that consumers may still discriminate among products based on the country of origin label because they do not have perfect information about labour standards in a particular country.

Once social labelling is instituted, a homogeneous product bearing the same country of origin label is now transformed into a differentiated product. Consider identical white shirts made in Bangladesh. These are now of two types: those that have been labelled as manufactured under higher labour standards and those that are unlabelled, signifying low labour standards. If Northern consumers value higher labour standards and are willing to pay a price premium for labelled products that exceed or equal the cost of raising standards, for instance the higher wages that need to be paid, then a market-based incentive for Southern producers to improve standards is created. However, the same process that generates a price premium for labelled products also provides an incentive for producers to practise false labelling.

Monitoring social labels thus becomes critical. This issue is not just confined to the extent of monitoring or the credibility of the monitors, but also extends to the questions of who, the North or the South, has higher incentives to monitor, and who bears the cost of monitoring. However, before discussing the problems associated with monitoring and the effect of false labels on consumers' willingness to pay for labelled products, we need to understand how labelling works under ideal circumstances, that is, with perfect monitoring and without any false labels.

We have argued that if consumers are willing to pay a premium that equals or exceeds the cost of raising standards, then a market-based incentive is created for producers to choose higher labour standards. If all producers were homogeneous in terms of their production costs, or, more important, had access to a production technology that permits improving labour standards, then in an extreme result either all producers would choose higher standards in the presence of labelling or no producers would voluntarily raise standards. In reality, even if monitoring were perfect, we would still find the co-existence of both labelled and unlabelled products originating from the same country. A classic example is Indian hand-knotted carpets sold in the United States and Western Europe: some are labelled as 'child-labour free' while others are unlabelled. This implies heterogeneity among producers in terms of their access to technology that can improve labour standards. In other words, the more cost-effective producers will choose to label, while the high-cost producers will continue to employ low standards of production, thereby guaranteeing a segmented market for the same product. The degree of heterogeneity among producers plays a crucial role in determining the South's incentive to monitor social labels.

Under perfect monitoring, social labelling does offer an incentive for some producers to raise their labour standards. The flip side of this is that producers who choose to employ higher production standards and incur the full cost of improvements could well end up with no compensation for their efforts, simply because consumers cannot distinguish between goods produced via high or low labour standards. Thus the ability of social labels to provide a market-based solution to the problem of low labour standards becomes diluted when monitoring is imperfect. The weaker the monitoring intensity and the lower the fine associated with being discovered, the more it benefits producers to apply false labels by employing lower standards and engaging in free-riding and benefiting from the true labellers by capturing their price premium.

This prevalence of false labelling has an adverse effect on the price premium. On the one hand, consumers rationally expect a certain fraction of labelled products to be false, which lowers their willingness to pay a premium. This, in turn, encourages the marginal producer, who would otherwise have chosen higher standards, to opt for false labelling. In sum, imperfect monitoring lowers both the price premium and the number of producers who choose to employ higher standards.

Thus social labelling should be presented as a corrective policy that targets the lack of complete information for consumers who cannot otherwise reveal their preferences regarding labour standards in the production process. Likewise, the choice of monitoring intensity in the context of social labelling (as opposed to the enforcement of acceptable labour standards) should be viewed as a corrective policy that resolves the free-rider problem associated with the incentive to apply false labels. Thus whether the by-product of such a consumer- and producer-oriented corrective policy can produce welfare benefits for labour in the developing countries depends critically on whether significant diseconomies are associated with higher standards.

Who Initiates Labelling Programmes?

We can now turn to the incentives of Southern governments to initiate credible social labelling programmes. Note that social labelling explicitly exposes products that are produced under lower standards, thereby enabling the North to impose trade restrictions on unlabelled products. If the North does impose restrictions, then the price of unlabelled products rises for Northern consumers who, as a consequence, shift demand away from unlabelled to labelled products, leading to an increase in the price premium for labelled products. Southern producers can avoid being subject to the restrictions by either raising standards or practising false labelling. In a situation where most Southern producers do not have access to superior production technology, the only option is false labelling. As the number of products with false labels increases, consumers lower their willingness to pay the premium and the price of labelled products falls.

The above reasoning is contingent on the fact that monitoring intensity does not increase as a result of trade restrictions to ensure that the higher price premium is preserved. If the gains from social labelling accrue to the developing countries, then why are Southern governments not actively engaged in initiating and promoting social labelling? More important, even if social labelling is initiated, would it make sense for the South to make any effort to increase monitoring intensity if the North imposes trade restrictions on unlabelled products? The answer is that in most developing countries few producers have access to technologies that can improve work conditions and raise labour standards. In this scenario, the difference between the increase in the price premium and the increase in the costs of enforcement may well be negative. By contrast, in the absence of increased monitoring, trade restrictions simply dissipate the price premium with no potential gains for the South.

Furthermore, from the welfare point of view, in its choice to initiate and choose the level of monitoring intensity, the South has to account not just for the higher price premium that labelled products command and the higher wages for the workers who are employed by producers of validly labelled products, but also for the lower revenue from unlabelled products, the loss of jobs resulting from higher wages paid by producers of true labels (a high elasticity of demand for labour by producers of true labels would have a significant negative effect on employment) and for any diseconomies of scale associated with increased unemployment within the economy. If the adverse effects of labelling outweigh the gains, then a developing country has no incentive to initiate or monitor social labels.

If social labelling is not in the South's interest, does the North have anything to gain from such policy? Surely Northern consumers who are willing to pay a price premium derive a higher utility from purchasing products. If Northern governments care about their consumers' welfare, then why are the industrial countries not eager to incur the cost of monitoring labelling in the South? The answer seems to be that initiating social labelling on Southern products adversely affects the market share, and hence the profits, of Northern firms. The argument originating from consumer markets that social labels be applied and monitored to eliminate Southern producers' unfair competitive edge by conferring damage to producers in the South and benefits to producers in the North is false. In the absence of social labelling of Southern products, Northern producers face no competition and are able to capture the entire market for products with high labour standards. As social labelling is instituted in the South, labelled Southern products become competitors of Northern products (even with the incidence of false labels), and cut into the market share for Northern producers. A Northern government that puts a higher weight on the welfare of Northern producers than of consumers will never find it in its interests to advocate social labelling of Southern products. Worse still, if the North pays for enforcing Southern labels, the market share of Northern producers falls further as the decline in false labels makes Southern products more competitive.

CONCLUSIONS

Do higher labour standards promote labour market efficiency and equity in developing countries? As this chapter has shown, the literature provides no clear answer. In some situations labour standards could enhance the efficiency of the labour market, increase the productivity of workers and contribute to better income distribution. However, in many other cases labour standards could also prove counterproductive in terms of labour market efficiency and equity.

Including a social clause in the WTO that would allow countries to restrict imports of products originating from countries not complying with a specified set of minimum standards is likely to make developing countries worse off. Instead, diverse labour standards should reflect the differences in preferences, technologies and factor endowments among countries, which generates greater welfare gains from international production and trade.

Social labelling might provide a better solution to the problem of low labour standards. It gives consumers information about production methods, and hence generates a market-based solution by enabling the provision of products that have been produced according to acceptable labour standards, for which the producers deserve a price premium. Thus under systematic monitoring, social labelling does offer a higher incentive for some producers to raise labour standards. However, the price premium for labelled products raises incentives for false labelling in the presence of imperfect monitoring and may render social labelling efforts futile. In this case the effect is to lower the price premium and reduce the number of producers who choose to employ higher standards. Thus social labelling is more a corrective policy that targets the lack of information on the part of consumers regarding the prevalence of true labour conditions in the developing countries.

However, if properly enforced, social labelling schemes may reduce the demand for labour, with a resultant adverse impact on workers' welfare. In developing countries with high unemployment rates, it could push workers from poverty into destitution. Another danger is that labelling may render unlabelled products more vulnerable to allegations of unfair practice, resulting in restricted market access for such products from developing countries. If the industrial countries were to impose trade restrictions on unlabelled products from the developing countries without setting up an effective monitoring system, producers in the latter countries would have an incentive to increase the number of falsely labelled products. For developing countries, initiating a labelling scheme only makes sense if monitoring costs and the various negative effects of labelling do not outweigh the price premium paid for the labelled product.

REFERENCES

Bagwell, K. and R.W. Staiger (2000), 'The Simple Economics of Labor Standards and the GATT', in A.V. Deardorff and R.M. Stern (eds), *Social Dimensions of U.S. Trade Policies*, Ann Arbor, MI: University of Michigan Press, pp. 195–231.

Basu, A.K., N.H. Chau and U. Grote (2000), 'Guaranteed Manufactured Without Child Labor', Working paper series no. 2000-04, Cornell University, Department of Applied Economics and Management, Ithaca, New York.

Bhagwati, J. (1996), 'The Demands to Reduce Domestic Diversity Among Trading Nations', in J. Bhagwati and R. Hudec (eds), *Fair Trade and Harmonization: Prerequisites for Free Trade?*, vol. 1, Cambridge, MA: MIT Press, pp. 9–40.

Brown, D.K., A.V. Deardorff and R.M. Stern (1996), 'International Labor Standards and Trade: A Theoretical Analysis', in J. Bhagwati and R. Hudec (eds), *Fair Trade and Harmonization: Prerequisites for Free Trade?*, vol. 1, Cambridge, MA: MIT Press, pp. 227–80.

Chau, N.H. and R. Kanbur (2000), 'The Race to the Bottom, from the Bottom', Working paper series no. 2000-28, Cornell University, Department of Applied Economics and Management, Ithaca, New York.

Ehrenberg, R. (1994), *Labor Markets and Integrating National Economies*, Washington, DC: The Brookings Institution.

Figueroa, A. (1997), 'Comments on International Labor Standards and Trade by Alan B. Krueger', in *Proceedings of the World Bank Annual Conference on Development Economics, 1996*, Washington, DC: World Bank, pp. 303–6.

Freeman, R. (1993), 'Labor Market Institutions and Policies: Help or Hindrance to Economic Development?', in *Proceedings of the World Bank Annual Conference on Development Economics, 1992*, Washington, DC: World Bank, pp. 118–44.

Gans, O. (2000), 'Umwelt- und Sozialstandards: Eine offene Flanke der Welthandelsordnung?', in E. Scholing (ed.), *Währung und wirtschaftliche Entwicklung, Volkswirtschaftliche Schriften*, no. 505, Berlin: Duncker and Humblot, pp. 157–77.

Grote, U. (1999), 'Sustainable Development in the Flower Sector with Eco-Labels?', in K.J. Peters (ed.), *TSAF – Proceedings of Deutschen Tropentag*, Berlin: Humboldt University Berlin.

Hilowitz, J. (1997), 'Social Labelling to Combat Child Labour: Some Considerations', *International Labour Review*, **136** (2), 215–32.

Kahn, J. (2000), 'Multinationals Sign UN Pact on Rights and Environment', *New York Times*, 27 July.

Krueger, A. (1997), 'International Labor Standards and Trade', in *Proceedings of the World Bank Annual Conference on Development Economics, 1996*, Washington, DC: World Bank, pp. 281–302.

Krugman, P.R. (1997), 'What Should Trade Negotiators Negotiate About?', *Journal of Economic Literature*, (35), 113–20.

Marshall, R. (1994), 'The Importance of International Labour Standards in a More Competitive Global Economy', in W. Sengenberger and D. Campbell (eds), *International Labour Standards and Economic Interdependence*, Geneva: International Institute for Labour Studies, pp. 65–78.

Maskus, K. (1997), 'Should Core Labor Standards be Imposed Through International Trade Policy?', Policy Research Working Paper no. 1817, World Bank, Washington, DC.

Panagariya, A. (1999), 'Trade Openness: Consequences for the Elasticity of Demand for Labor and Wage Outcomes', University of Maryland – College Park, Maryland, processed.

Piore, M. (1994), 'International Labor Standards and Business Strategies', in *International Labor Standards and Global Economic Integration: Proceedings of a Symposium*, Washington, DC: US Department of Labor, Bureau of International Labor Affairs.

Rodrik, D. (1996), 'Labor Standards in International Trade: Do They Matter and What Do We Do About Them?', in R.Z. Lawrence, D. Rodrik and J. Whalley (eds), *Emerging Agenda for Global Trade: High Stakes for Developing Countries*, Overseas Development Council Essay no. 20, Baltimore, MD: The Johns Hopkins University Press.

Schumacher, D. (1981), *Handel mit Entwicklungsländern und Beschäftigung in der Europäischen Gemeinschaft*, Berlin: German Institute for Economics.

Siebke, J. and U. Rolf (1998), 'Was ist fairer international Handel?', in *Volkswirtschaftliche Korrespondenz der Adolf-Weber-Stiftung*, no. 7, Munich: Adolf-Weber Foundation.

Srinivasan, T.N. (1996), 'Trade and Human Rights', in A.V. Deardorff and R.M. Stern (eds), *Constituent Interests and U.S. Trade Policies*, Ann Arbor, MI: University of Michigan Press, pp. 225–53.

Srinivasan, T.N (1998), *Developing Countries and the Multilateral Trading System*, Oxford, UK: Oxford University Press.

Wiemann, J. (1999), 'Umwelt- und Sozialstandards in der WTO', in *Entwicklung und ländlicher Raum*, Frankfurt: DLG-Publisher, pp. 17–21.

7. Competition policy, the Pacific Economic Cooperation Council and the WTO

Kerrin M. Vautier

The Competition policy (CP) has become an increasingly prominent topic on international agendas and is currently the subject of serious discussion at all levels: national, bilateral, regional and multilateral. Over the years it has given rise to national competition laws; bilateral co-operation agreements; formal competition provisions in regional trading arrangements; nonbinding agreements and recommendations in the GATT, the United Nations and the OECD; the Pacific Economic Cooperation Council's (PECC's) competition principles for guiding the development of a competition-driven policy framework for Asia Pacific Economic Cooperation (APEC) economies; and the derivative APEC principles to enhance competition and regulatory reform. At the multilateral level, a WTO Working Group was established to study issues relating to the interaction between trade and competition policy, including anticompetitive practices, and at the time of writing is in its fourth year of deliberations.

All these initiatives reflect growing interest in the role of competition in market processes and economic policy, in what is meant by a competition culture and in the policy and institutional implications of promoting competition in globalizing markets. An important product of these initiatives has been the sharing of policy perspectives and experiences and learning where CP fits in international discussions on trade and investment liberalization.

To date, CP discussions in international forums have focused principally on the perceived risk to international trade posed by restrictive and anticompetitive business practices and by powerful firms or groups of firms. Competition law has featured prominently as the primary policy instrument for responding to this perceived risk.

Various multinational (that is, intergovernmental) responses to the international dimensions of CP have been documented (see, for example, Lloyd and Vautier 1999). While some of these transnational responses are narrowly focused (certain regional trading arrangements, for example); generically limited (bilateral competition co-operation agreements, for example); or discriminatory (EU treatment of cartels, for example), there is much to support in these multinational approaches. However, Lloyd and Vautier (1999) conclude that there is little, if any, prospect of a single, workable approach to transnational competition issues, let alone any prospect of multilateral competition rules and supranational enforcement in the WTO, even assuming these were desirable. After some initial enthusiasm in some quarters for such a multilateral approach, this is now being met with considerable caution, if not outright rejection. The complex issues surrounding the interaction between trade and competition policy are being exposed.

The 1996 Singapore Declaration, which gave the WTO Working Group on the interaction between trade and competition policy its mandate, was clear that any CP negotiations would proceed only after WTO members had reached consensus to do so. The role of the WTO Working Group was deliberately limited to reporting, not recommending, to the WTO's General Council, although areas of convergence and divergence of views can be identified. Of particular significance is the fundamental divergence of views among the three major players, the EU, Japan and the United States, relating to the WTO's role and where antidumping fits, if at all, in international discussions on CP. At the same time, the major players do agree on the importance of domestic competition law and its enforcement, based on common objectives, including for developing countries.

The EU considers that the time is right for WTO-level negotiations to commence on 'a basic framework of binding principles and rules on competition law and policy' (WTO 1999a). According to the EU, these rules should relate to 'the adoption and enforcement of a domestic competition law and provisions on co-operation among WTO Members', having regard to those few business practices that have a significant international dimension. Japan also considers that 'an effective multilateral framework' that would give priority to the application of a competition perspective to trade measures is important, and should cover antidumping and hard-core cartels 'that clearly restrict trade' (WTO 1999b).[1] In contrast to Japan, the United States is extremely opposed to CP covering antidumping. It is opposed to the idea of negotiating multilateral competition rules, which could well subordinate and dilute its own antitrust laws, and instead favours a network of national competition laws and bilateral co-operation agreements with positive comity provisions.

The purpose of this chapter is to broaden understanding about the issues surrounding the current international debate on CP, in particular the role of PECC's and APEC's competition principles and their relevance for the WTO.

CONCEPTUAL ISSUES

The following section addresses the principal conceptual issues that arise from positioning CP in an international context.

Meaning and Scope of CP

CP has come onto the international stage without a formal definition, although there is still a general tendency, including among policymakers and advisers, to see it as synonymous with competition law. This primarily reflects the US stance that CP is and should be confined to antitrust matters, and is therefore properly directed only at business mergers and takeovers and the conduct of private firms. At the official level the United States treats trade policy as a separate area that is governed by different objectives; that is directed at government measures; and that lends itself to multilateral negotiations, rules, enforcement and dispute resolution whereas antitrust matters do not.

This issue of the scope of CP has been discussed extensively in the specialist working groups of both APEC and the WTO. While these groups have paid much attention to the harm to competition that certain business practices can cause and to the role of competition law in addressing the causes of such harm, a much broader approach to CP has been finding favour. This is because it is generally recognized that both government and business actions can raise market entry barriers and distort the competitive process. This means that competition law is only one of many policy instruments that are relevant to the promotion or defence of the competitive process. These instruments relate, for example, to tariffs, trade remedies, foreign direct investment and intellectual property. It is this broad conception of competition issues, and an appreciation of the various policies and instruments that are needed to deal with them, that are essential for more open and growing markets. This leads to proposition 1:

Promoting or defending competition in markets cannot be achieved by competition law alone and requires a broader policy approach, which deals with both government and business actions that unduly interfere with the competitive process.

Role and Objectives of Competition Law

While competition law and the business activities it is designed to address have received much prominence in international discussions, there is far from universal acceptance that a general competition law is a 'good thing' for all countries. This is not a case of a simple division of views between the industrial and the developing economies. Industrial economies, notably Hong Kong and Singapore, have preferred to rely on a broad-ranging approach to the promotion of competition, and therefore do not regard a general competition law as necessary (although they do not rule out targeted, industry-specific regulation). Developing economies, particularly relatively small developing economies, share concerns about the sequencing of any introduction of a general competition law. They could well have priorities that are more urgent than designing and enforcing such law and meeting the capacity-building requirements. Debate on the advantages and disadvantages of competition laws for developing economies continues (see, for example, APEC CTI 1999).

More broadly, there is the paradox that growing official interest in competition law comes at a time when competitive discipline is increasing as a result of lower border barriers, new technology and wider regulatory reforms. Many consider as overstated the argument that private regulation will substitute for various market deregulation initiatives by governments. Indeed, they point to the risks of re-regulation via international interventions and of welfare reduction if these interventions have the effect of compromising rather than enhancing efficient competition.

Nevertheless, APEC is clearly contemplating the continuing risks of anticompetitive business conduct, even though its 21 diverse member economies have not reached consensus on the need for domestic competition laws. As a result, the 'APEC Principles to Enhance Competition and Regulatory Reform' (APEC Leaders 1999) make no explicit reference to competition law. This would be a disappointment to those countries and representative agencies such as the OECD that strongly favour the introduction of domestic competition laws for all and view the number of new national laws introduced in recent years as a measure of international progress on CP.

The number of statutes in place is, however, an unsatisfactory measure of progress. Far more important are the stated and applied objectives and the extent to which these actually focus on the role of competition in enhancing economic efficiency. If the pursuit of competition pays insufficient regard to efficiency objectives, then the law is likely to compromise economic welfare rather than promote it. If a country uses competition law to pursue multiple and conflicting objectives, then its ability to promote competition, efficiency and welfare effectively will be severely curtailed. The WTO (1997, p. 49) considers that the observed, significant degree of convergence in goals toward promoting economic efficiency and consumer welfare is 'an important development that helps to ensure an overall degree of consistency in approaches to competition policy as it is practised in many countries'.

There is no denying that in pursuing development, a country will face the political reality of multiple objectives. The issue here is about choosing the most appropriate policy instrument(s) for pursuing each of those objectives as efficiently as possible. This leads to proposition 2:

Any domestic competition law should be clearly focused on the objective of promoting and safeguarding the competitive process in all markets as a means of enhancing efficiency and economic welfare.

Irrespective of a country's stage of economic development, the objective of competition law should not be construed as being against business; or against big business, mergers or market concentration; or against joint ventures or other co-operative alliances. Note that ease of exit is relevant to the consideration of market entry. Thus if merger law, for example, is too restrictive, in that it is perceived as a barrier to exit, then entry itself may be inhibited.

Only some firms, alliances and market concentrations will warrant scrutiny under clearly focused competition law, in accordance with the agreed social constraints reflected in that law. Its overall thrust should favour competitive business, whether large or small, and promote competition on the basis of merit rather than on the basis of special government-provided protections and privileges. Merit-based competition also bears on the question of fairness for international suppliers and consumers. Rather than being a casualty of competitive and efficient markets, fairness will accompany the growth of opportunities for both suppliers and consumers to participate more freely in economic activity and market processes. This leads to proposition 3:

Promoting competitive business is a means of harnessing the private sector to the broader social and economic goals of governments.

A New Trade-related Issue?

The current positioning of CP on various international agendas is largely a response to its description as a new trade-related area. To a large extent this description is a carry-over from the UR negotiations on trade-related intellectual property rights and trade-related investment measures, where the trade-related qualification served to confine the negotiations in these relatively new areas. Even so, this characterization is not surprising, as the lowering of border barriers to foreign trade gives more exposure to other policies and actions, which may discriminate against foreign supplies or discriminate in favour of domestically owned or operated production. As governments have moved to reduce border barriers, they and their advisers are giving special attention to how businesses might undermine negotiated trade concessions and market access gains through their conduct. This focus on the risk that business practices might impede freer international trade has supported the equating of CP with competition law. Furthermore, it has lent support for the view that the importance of CP lies in its potential to increase international trade or to protect the gains from this trade.

A trade perspective tends to emphasize the traditional indicators of market access, fairness and the promotion and/or protection of a particular country's trade flows, exporters and producers. A trade-related framework for CP thus suggests that the focus should be on traditional trade policy concerns and negotiated market access. From this perspective, CP is a mechanism both for supporting trade liberalization and traditional country access objectives and for preventing the impairment or nullification of negotiated trade concessions.

By contrast, a competition perspective tends to emphasize all those conditions that are relevant to an effective competitive process and to protect that process (as distinct from individual competitors) in the interests of more efficient markets. International support for this perspective and for the relevant mix of policies is important not to maximize the benefits of free trade, but to achieve better functioning, globalizing markets. These markets are not only supplied from international trade, but also from other sources, including foreign direct investment. From a competition perspective, all modes of supply and related policies influence how markets function.

In summary, the description of CP as a new trade-related area is not entirely appropriate. Especially in so far as it is seen as synonymous with competition law, the area is not new, but even more important, neither is CP simply, or even primarily, a trade-related issue (for a full discussion see Vautier and Lloyd 1997). A dual risk is associated with such a description: first, it ignores any lessons from past attempts at internationalizing business competition problems and solutions; and second, trade and competition objectives become confused. In theory, both competition and trade policies are directed at global efficiency and welfare goals, but in practice, real conflicts between trade and competition purposes can arise. However, an advantage in explicitly linking trade and competition policies on international agendas is widening the trade agenda to encourage the application of competition perspectives to trade policies and measures.

As far as trade is concerned, a competition perspective emphasizes competitive trade and not simply fair trade. The significance of the distinction is that the notion of fairness in competition, as with fairness in trade, risks being interpreted as a means of promoting the interests of particular traders or competitors rather than promoting efficiency in the overall process of trade and competition.

These important differences between trade and competition perspectives lead to proposition 4:

Competition-driven policies are about welfare maximization in the interests of all consumers, and not about trade maximization in the interests of particular exporters or producers.

A Shift in Competition Thinking

This reference to competition-driven policies in proposition 4 is deliberate, and reflects a shift in competition thinking. The historically narrow view of CP as being limited to competition law and harmonization issues is shifting to a broader view that encompasses all government policies that affect competition in national and globalizing markets. This is a shift in competition thinking that is coming to terms with the concept of a competition-driven policy framework that takes a comprehensive approach to promoting competition in all markets. This approach recognizes that both government and private actions can work against the competitive process, that both government and private actions need to be addressed if conditions conducive to efficient business competition are to prevail and that a range of policies and policy instruments are relevant for stimulating and reinforcing these conditions. Taking a stance in favour of competition in such areas as deregulation, privatization, trade and foreign direct investment is vitally linked to the objective of more open, competitive and workable markets and to the achievement of growth and development aspirations.

Experience with competition analysis and competition law enforcement under different market circumstances indicates that assessing ex post whether or not particular business transactions or conduct warrant intervention is more difficult than determining ex ante the contribution to competition and efficiency of policy measures in areas such as deregulation and trade and investment liberalization. Why is this? The latter can draw on a vast economic literature on economies' experiences with removing border and other barriers to competitive endeavour and with shifting commercial activities from the government to the private sector. The general intent and effect of these widespread and market-oriented policy reforms have been to create market conditions that are more conducive to competitive and efficient business, and hence to international competitiveness and economic growth.

A large literature is also available on the types of business conduct that can raise barriers to competition by, in effect, re-regulating the marketplace. In individual cases, however, the effects of such conduct are seldom clear-cut, and may result in both procompetitive and anticompetitive effects. It is because of this ambiguity that few business practices lend themselves to a *per se* rule, that is, an outright prohibition, and that most practices should be subject to a rule-of-reason or case-by-case competition and efficiency analysis. Competition law and enforcement can provide an ultimate safeguard, but a comprehensive approach to promoting competition is necessary for setting the scene.

The way in which competition thinking bears on international trade policy and the use of trade instruments by individual countries is clearly a key issue flowing out of this framework. Policies and instruments relating to anti-dumping, export cartels and parallel importing, for example, are all directly trade related, are potentially trade distorting and can have important implications for the competitive process in transnational markets. Such trade-related practices and policies need to be viewed within a competition-driven policy framework, along with any transnational trade disputes that also have a competition dimension. Competition analyses and welfare assessments are particularly important in these circumstances.

If this shift in competition thinking at a conceptual level is to make a difference at a practical level, it will need to be accompanied by appropriate responses and co-operation at an institutional level, both within governments working nationally and between governments working internationally. This gives rise to proposition 5:

A directional shift in competition thinking that centres on competition-driven policies, together with intergovernmental co-operation to that end, are necessary to promote and protect the competitive process in all markets.

Important capacity-building requirements at each of the conceptual, practical and institutional levels follow from this proposition.

What is Competition?

The appeal of this last proposition is that everybody knows the meaning of competition and the competitive process. Or perhaps they do not. The terms cannot be defined easily and competition issues are not clear-cut. Such uncertainty demonstrates why competition rules are difficult to make and why a bottom-up approach, which allows flexibility in the approach for individual economies, is preferable to a top-down and prescriptive approach.

Attempts to define competition for application in a real-world policy context may not be particularly helpful. For example, New Zealand's definition for competition law purposes is workable or effective competition. This tells us more about what competition is not than about what competition is: it is not the theoretical construct of pure or perfect competition. Competition in real-world markets is imperfect, and effective competition in these markets does not need to be structured around numerous firms selling identical products at prices over which no single firm has any influence. However, as the WTO has stated (WTO 1997, p. 48): 'There is no all-encompassing model of imperfect competition that can guide the actions of competition authorities in all circumstances. And even when theory can identify common principles, the lessons may be difficult to implement because they depend on market characteristics that are intrinsically difficult to observe.'

Viewing CP as an instrument of trade policy and trade maximization, that is, the trade-related approach, would have policymakers targeting every perceived trade restraint, impediment or distortion. Properly directed competition analysis is focused on any material harm to competition and efficiency arising from particular practices. It is the outcome of this analysis that should determine whether or not interventions by policymakers or competition law enforcers is warranted. This involves constraints analysis, that is, an assessment of the extent to which the actions and reactions of other domestic or foreign suppliers and the choices available to intermediate or final customers constrain particular suppliers of goods and services. Competition analysis should also carefully assess market entry conditions to distinguish between artificial entry barriers of possible significance in competition terms, for example, quantitative import restrictions or industry licensing; legitimate barriers that might be required to protect property rights; and entry conditions such as capital requirements and economies of scale that might restrict the entry of some businesses, but not undermine effective competition unduly.

Competition is probably best described as a continual process of discovery by existing and potential suppliers of what customers want and what prices they are prepared to pay, taking product and service quality into account. Competition-driven policies should therefore be directed at creating and maintaining those market conditions that are conducive to this process of discovery, responsiveness and innovation. Encouraging competitive business is about fostering opportunities for businesses to compete on their merits. Inevitably this will require governments to understand and be prepared to use the range of policy instruments that determine business operating conditions and hence firms' ability to participate in economic processes. It is merit-based competition that provides the impetus for firms to be responsive, both to what other firms are doing and to what consumers are saying.

In return for marketplace opportunities, firms will have to manage marketplace risks by constantly bearing in mind efficient business practices and consumer preferences. This leads us to a view of efficiency that focuses on increasing overall economic capacity (domestically and internationally) to supply goods and services at competitive prices for both intermediate and final customers in all markets. This welfare-enhancing role is the responsibility of both governments and business, and as markets enlarge beyond their traditional country boundaries, the need for government co-operation in promoting business competition in these globalizing markets increases.

The economic argument for preferring an effective competitive process as the means for generally allocating the use of resources is sound. The emphasis here is on 'means'. When trade, regulatory or other decisions are being contemplated in a pro-competition policy framework, a review of efficiency is still necessary to ensure that markets, in practice, do serve as the best guide for the quantity, quality and composition of goods and services to be produced and consumed. This brings us to proposition 6:

Efficiency is a necessary link between competition and economic welfare and should therefore be a primary consideration in any competition analysis.

THE PECC COMPETITION PRINCIPLES

The following section explores the substance and role of the PECC and APEC competition principles.

Origins

In 1999 PECC published its competition principles (PECC 1999).[2] These followed its conclusion two years previously that a conceptual framework was required to address complex competition issues in international markets. PECC's comprehensive approach to competition issues and its competition-driven policy framework for APEC economies originated from its recognition of the importance of addressing both government actions and private conduct from a competition perspective. The extensive process of consultation, debate and consensus building that led the PECC Standing Committee to endorse the principles is described in the publication (see also Vautier 1999), as is the strategic rationale for the principles and their relevance for policy development within APEC economies and for sustainable recovery after the 1997 Asian crisis.

The principles approach responded to the requirement of APEC's Collective Action Plan to 'consider developing non-binding Principles on Competition Policy and/or laws', and it fitted well with the APEC model of 'concerted unilateralism'.[3] The approach also played to APEC's comparative advantage, namely, its potential to build consensus on an inclusive strategic and policy framework for guiding decentralized policy decisions by individual member economies. This advantage combines top-down leadership with bottom-up policymaking.

The APEC Principles

During the period from inception to completion of the PECC competition principles project (mid-1997 to mid-1999), PECC made five formal presentations to APEC officials. These presentations undoubtedly helped build understanding and consensus among APEC economies, culminating in the adoption by APEC Leaders of a set of principles to enhance competition and regulatory reform (APEC Leaders 1999). The Leaders endorsed these principles as 'a core part of the framework for strengthening markets'. They reflect a directional shift in thinking in favour of greater coherence in policymaking. As PECC stated at APEC's Competition Policy and Deregulation Workshop (Vautier 2000), they also signal a willingness to pursue an economic approach to integration in the Region

- that is oriented to competition and consumer welfare and not just trade
- that draws from economic knowledge
- that harnesses competitive business to the growth and development goals of APEC members; and
- that does not rely on top-down one-size-fits-all legal rules.

The PECC Principles Package

The PECC competition principles package comprises four core principles and a number of key requirements for upholding these in practice. The core elements on their own would not have provided a sufficient guide for applying competition principles in practice. PECC saw the more detailed or layered approach as particularly valuable for those economies where the balance between the market and the state is changing rapidly; for those economies undertaking regulatory reform; and for those thinking generally about the ingredients for better functioning markets, especially since the Asian financial crisis. Indeed, the crisis focused attention on the functioning of markets as a central issue. According to PECC (1999, p. 4):

> Because the PECC Competition Principles directly address the conditions for well-functioning markets, they are seen as an integral part of an effective response to the crisis and, in particular, a central part of promoting coherent policy responses to it. Adoption of the PECC Competition Principles, coupled with institutional capacity-building, provide a framework in which to address some of the critical issues that have arisen in financial and other markets.

Core Principles

First and foremost (principles 1–6) the PECC principles urge APEC economies to

- foster greater reliance upon well-functioning markets and the role of competition based on economic merit for allocating resources and for consumer and economic benefits;
- employ a competition-driven approach to a broad range of policy areas that affect market conditions (the competition framework);
- minimize exceptions from reliance upon well-functioning market mechanisms;
- make any government intervention that is deemed necessary conditional upon minimal distortion to the competitive process and upon clear and explicit net welfare gains;
- ensure competitive neutrality by nondiscriminatory application of the same competition principles to the different modes of goods and services supply;
- bring transparency to the basis and application of policies, rules and legal, administrative and regulatory procedures.

The core principles or central themes that emerge are as follows:

- *Comprehensiveness*: all policymaking that affects globalizing markets should have a competition dimension, and this framework should apply to all goods and services.
- *Nondiscrimination*: once an economy has completed a particular transition, it should apply the enduring principles in a non-discriminatory manner so as to ensure competitive neutrality in respect of the different modes of domestic and international supply.
- *Transparency*: the substantive principles on which policies are based and the processes by which they are applied should be clear to all stakeholders.
- *Accountability*: those responsible for applying the competition principles should be accountable for any departures from those principles.

Regulatory Framework

The PECC competition principles are at the heart of the regulatory framework for APEC economies (Vautier 1999). They help inform decisions about the type and extent of any rules or regulations with market effects. Their emphasis is more on the quality of regulation than on the amount of regulation, and they take for granted that competition will be fettered to some extent by appropriate social constraints relating, for example, to business conduct, corporate governance, safety standards and prudential requirements in the financial sector. Specifically, principles 7–9 urge economies to:

- review existing and new government interventions with a view to identifying distortions to the competitive process;
- eliminate progressively regulatory barriers and other interventions that reduce efficiency; and
- minimize the risk of anticompetitive business conduct.

Business Conduct

The consensus reached within PECC was that the principles should provide for selective or general discipline on business conduct, both of which should include the following characteristics:

- a sole and clear objective, namely, promoting competition and efficiency;
- a reliance on relevant analytical tools;
- the transparency of substantive provisions, procedures and decision-making.

Where competition law is considered appropriate, this should include:

- minimum exemptions and exceptions;
- outright prohibitions of specific business practices only where these are unambiguously harmful to efficiency and welfare;
- a rule-of-reason approach;
- effective and accountable enforcement for serving public, not private, interests and total economic welfare;
- access by complainants to relevant authorities.

Implementation and Capacity Building

The PECC principles acknowledge the challenge of linking implementation issues with different stages of economic development. Given the Asia Pacific region's diversity, they have special regard for transition periods and the need for flexibility, in terms of both timing and policy mix, while at the same time stressing that the flexibility provision is not intended as an opt-out provision. The principles also stress the importance of a focused, practical and deliverable agenda for institutional capacity building and individual competency building. APEC clearly accepted that the region's diversity was not a barrier to governments adopting a set of competition principles, and it is now progressing with work on how its agreed principles can be reflected in APEC's individual and collective plans and how they can be supported by APEC's capacity-building agenda. The theme for the next stage of PECC's competition work is also competition principles in practice, with special regard to capacity building and technical assistance.

COMPETITION PRINCIPLES AND THE WTO

The section below considers the relevance of the PECC and APEC competition principles for the WTO (see also Lloyd and Vautier 1999; Vautier, Lloyd and Tsai forthcoming).

The WTO's Mandate and Role

Compared with APEC, the WTO is a very different intergovernmental mechanism. Its mandate is multilateral trade liberalization based on specific and mainly binding concessions via rules-based negotiations. APEC's mandate goes beyond trade liberalization to welfare maximization. It is not rules based nor are its declarations binding, and reciprocity, in the form of general concessions over time, is embodied in the notion of concerted unilateralism. The co-operation that has given rise to the competition principles might stimulate interest in having some rules at the regional or multilateral level, but essentially, APEC's approach to economic integration is not about swapping concessions and the creation of rules, but about accommodating the different approaches of its diverse members within agreed strategic and principled policy frameworks.

Looking at the WTO from a CP perspective reveals no formal objective relating to the promotion of competition, no substantial rules explicitly relating to competition and no national competition law obligation imposed on its members. While some specific competition provisions have been agreed, they rely on intergovernmental consultation and co-operation, and members are not obliged to take competition law actions (which is hardly surprising given that most members do not have general competition laws). Certainly, these provisions do not demonstrate the principle of comprehensiveness. For example, they apply to some services, not at all to goods and essentially to government measures. The concern with the trade effects of dumping and subsidized goods and state traders and the lack of action against trade cartels clearly demonstrate that the GATT's international trade law was not addressing competition issues. However, the WTO's focus on trade issues as distinct from competition issues is not surprising, given that organization's constitution and mandate.

None the less, as evidenced from the widespread participation in and substantive communications to the WTO Working Group, there is considerable interest among participants in the outcome of discussions on any potential role for the WTO in respect of CP. The WTO Working Group's initial two-year work programme focused on the relationship between the objectives, principles, concepts, scope and instruments of trade and CP. It included stocktaking and analysis of national competition policies and laws as they related to trade and the impact on international trade of anticompetitive practices, state monopolies, exclusive rights and regulatory policies. The renewal of the Working Group's mandate at the end of 1998 has enabled it to focus on the relevance of fundamental WTO principles of national treatment, transparency and MFN treatment to CP and vice versa, and there has been some discussion as to what might be included in a basic multilateral framework.

The WTO and CP: a Cautious Response

Currently the WTO has no negotiating mandate in relation to CP.[4] The EU's wish that the WTO commence negotiations on a basic framework of binding principles and rules on competition law and policy seems to have raised the spectre of supranational scrutiny, enforcement measures and dispute resolution. Whatever its initial aims, the EU has moved to allay such fears by saying that it does not envisage that the WTO would be empowered with an investigative role, nor that individual decisions would be subject to dispute settlement review, although it has also said that dispute settlement modalities will need to be considered further so that they are well adapted to the specifics of competition law (WTO 1999a).

The spectre of negotiating supranational competition obligations is especially unwelcome for those developing economies with limited understanding of the debates on competition rules and their enforcement in other countries, and with little or no direct experience of their own. For them CP is indeed a new issue, and therefore the prospect of multilateral negotiations is somewhat daunting.

In its communications to the WTO Working Group, Japan has been focusing on those areas where trade policy and CP can be contradictory and is encouraging relevant WTO agreements (which would inevitably include antidumping) to be reviewed from a competition perspective. The United States is opposed to any multilateral antitrust rules, and is clearly resistant to any prospect of trade remedies being subject to explicit competition considerations.

The positions being taken by the EU, Japan and the United States, coupled with the conceptual issues raised earlier, indicate the practical difficulties of importing competition law into a multilateral, rules-based, trade liberalization body and into a reciprocity-centred negotiating framework that is mainly focused on government measures. The complexities of competition law at the national level cannot be avoided at the multilateral level; for example, which, if any, business conduct should be subject to *per se* rules? Even a *per se* prohibition on so-called hard-core cartels raises definitional (and enforcement) questions. In any event, measures for dealing with anticompetitive business conduct in globalizing markets will never be easily integrated into the WTO's trade and country access model.

As a result of the EU's position in particular, and of general uncertainty as to the shape and implications of a basic framework, any prospect of multilateral disciplines, particularly as they might apply to private sector conduct, is appropriately being met with caution.

Trade Measures and Competition

Lloyd and Vautier (1999), among others, have argued that perhaps the most important contributions the WTO can make to foster competition are to continue removing border measures that restrict goods and services trade and to continue enforcing nondiscrimination in that trade via the MFN principle. Opening up opportunities for actual or potential imports provides an important source of competition discipline, particularly in countries concerned about high domestic levels of industry concentration. However, if the WTO is to have credibility as a body that is actively promoting competition (and consumers' interests) and not just trade (and exporters' interests), then it needs to reflect an explicit competition dimension in its own rules and instruments, as well as in their applications by member countries. For a start, it needs to acknowledge that some multilateral trade rules and instruments can themselves be harmful to the competitive process and economic welfare, and that, logically, the WTO is the most appropriate mechanism for dealing with those trade issues that are of significance in competition terms and that arise from government-condoned measures, such as antidumping, export cartels, parallel importing restrictions and subsidized trade. These issues affect the interests of both industrial and developing countries.

It is difficult to avoid the conclusion that trade measures, and consideration of their competition impacts on globalizing markets, need to be brought within any multilateral competition framework based on efficiency and welfare aims. This conclusion is consistent with the WTO Working Group's mandate to study the interaction between trade and CP to identify any areas that may merit further consideration in the WTO framework. Any argument that international scrutiny of competition issues be confined to anticompetitive business practices, and hence to antitrust policy, should be rejected for what it is, namely, an inappropriately narrow approach and one that risks leaving government measures, including trade measures, off competition agendas. Furthermore, nothing in the mandate of the WTO Working Group suggests that either the reference to CP or to anticompetitive practices is confined to anticompetitive business conduct.

While the lowering of border barriers and the exposure of trade measures to competition criteria are necessary conditions for stimulating procompetitive business conduct, they are unlikely to be sufficient. Any progress in supporting the competitive process at the multilateral level will need to be reinforced by unilateral policy responses at the national level in accordance with the competition principles.

Competition Principles versus WTO Principles

Let us now turn to the next proposition, proposition 7:

A principles-based approach to international competition issues and policies is preferable to prescriptive rules and the risk of inflexible re-regulation.

The PECC competition principles, and the competition-driven policy framework that they promote, are just as relevant at the multilateral level as they are at the regional, bilateral and national levels. They are especially important in the context of interest in subregional trading arrangements following the 1999 Seattle WTO meeting. They are intended as an aid to competition thinking in both industrial and developing economies. They are unequivocal on the necessary ingredients for well-functioning markets and for the generation of welfare-enhancing outcomes, and serve as a reference point for assessing policies and policy instruments, conflicts and tradeoffs and for informing and guiding any rule making.

One of the four core principles in the PECC competition framework is nondiscrimination (in the sense of competitive neutrality). The notion of contestable international markets is underpinned by competitive neutrality between all modes and sources of supply, which supports trade and investment liberalization. The principle embodies national treatment in two respects: first, treatment that is no less favourable than that accorded producers in the home country (as defined in the GATT and some other agreements); and second, treatment that does not discriminate in favour of foreign investors over domestic investors. Competitive neutrality also supports the notion of fairness.

In international trade law the principle of nondiscrimination (in the sense of MFN treatment) is directed at geographic discrimination in goods and services trade and is restricted to nondiscrimination among foreign nations. Exceptions such as discriminatory regional trading arrangements, do exist. Non-discrimination in the MFN sense is much narrower in concept than nondiscrimination in the sense of competitive neutrality.

A second core PECC principle is comprehensiveness. This principle is clearly not adhered to in the WTO's current treatment of competition issues. One has only to note the absence of goods-related competition provisions and the differential treatment of service sectors. Also, certain competition issues of international significance that flow from trade-related measures are not encompassed by the present multilateral approach, and business conduct is largely untouched. The WTO Working Group has identified some form of cartel activity in each of three categories of anticompetitive business practices for analytical purposes. While this suggests that cartel activity is a priority area for competition discipline, and an area of particular interest for developing countries, the prospect of a formal and binding cartel rule is not imminent, as evidenced by the competition laws of the EU, Japan and the United States, all of which legally permit export cartels for their producers.

Transparency is the third core element of the PECC competition principles and is particularly relevant for the sharing of information about the state of competition and regulatory regimes in various markets. As earlier indicated, the WTO Working Group has been exploring the relevance of fundamental WTO principles of transparency, national treatment and MFN treatment to competition policy and vice versa. The focus on these fundamental international trade principles is encouraging, given their relevance for nondiscrimination and transparency in globalizing markets. However, as the basis for a multilateral competition framework, national treatment and MFN are limited by definition and do not adequately capture the essence of either of the core PECC principles of nondiscrimination and comprehensiveness.

Inevitably, in practice, pragmatism will often win over principle, but the principles themselves must not become subordinated to special and conflicting interests. If pragmatism had been built into the actual PECC principles, this would have devalued their role as a robust and coherent guide for competition-driven policy development at the multilateral, regional and national levels.

Finally, capacity building is highly relevant for deepening understanding of the PECC competition principles and the APEC principles. Investment in the tools for competition analyses and in the groundwork for applying the principles in welfare-enhancing ways is also of paramount importance.

NOTES

1. In 1998 the OECD promulgated the Recommendations Concerning Effective Action Against Hard Core Cartels and defined a hard-core cartel, national or international, as: 'An anticompetitive agreement, anticompetitive concerted practice, or anticompetitive arrangement by competitors to fix prices, make rigged bids (collusive tenders), establish output restrictions or quotas, or share or divide markets by allocating customers, suppliers, territories, or lines of commerce'.
2. PECC (see http://www.pecc.net) is a tripartite voluntary organization that comprises researchers, business people and officials (acting in their private capacity).

3. 'Concerted' is an important qualifier, because it embodies the notion of generalized reciprocity over time through continuous unilateral decisionmaking in line with APEC's agreed strategic direction.
4. Any negotiating mandate, and any agenda relating to competition law in particular, would need to be clear on what might appropriately be addressed; for example, principles, substantive rules, enforcement obligations, enforcement procedures, interagency co-operation, supranational dispute settlement.

REFERENCES

APEC CTI (Asia Pacific Economic Cooperation Committee on Trade and Investment) (1999), *Competition Law for Developing Economies*, Singapore: PriceWaterhouseCoopers.

APEC (Asia Pacific Economic Cooperation) Leaders (1999), 'The Auckland Challenge', Auckland, New Zealand, 13 September.

Lloyd, P.J. and Kerrin M. Vautier (1999), *Promoting Competition in Global Markets: A Multi-National Approach*, Cheltenham, UK, and Northampton, MA: Edward Elgar.

PECC (Pacific Economic Cooperation Council) (1999), *PECC Principles for Guiding the Development of a Competition-Driven Policy Framework for APEC Economies*, Auckland, New Zealand.

Vautier, K.M. (1999), 'The PECC Competition Principles', presentation to the PECC Trade Policy Forum, 3 June, Auckland, New Zealand.

Vautier, K.M. (2000), 'Comments as PECC Observer at APEC's Competition Policy and Deregulation Workshop', 27 May, Bandar Seri Begawan, Brunei Darussalam.

Vautier, K.M. and P.J. Lloyd (1997), *International Trade and Competition Policy: CER, APEC and the WTO*, Wellington, New Zealand: Institute of Policy Studies.

Vautier, K.M., P.J. Lloyd and I.W. Tsai (forthcoming), 'Competition Policy, Developing Countries and the WTO', in Will Martin and Mari Pangestu (eds), *Options for Global Trade Reform: A View from the Asia-Pacific*.

WTO (World Trade Organization) (1997), *Annual Report*, vol. 1, *Special Topic: Trade and Competition Policy*, Geneva.

WTO (1999a), 'Preparations for the 1999 Ministerial Conference, EC Approach to Trade and Competition', Communication from the European Community, Geneva, 28 May.

WTO (1999b), 'Communication from Japan', Geneva, 15 July.

8. Export competition in Asia and the role of China

Yongzheng Yang

Policymakers have become increasingly concerned about export competition among Asian developing countries since the 1997 Asian financial crisis. Those engaged in analysing the causes of the crisis have often cited export competition among the developing Asian economies and the resultant export slowdown as a main source of the vulnerability of the crisis-affected countries. In particular, they view China's strong competitive position in labour-intensive manufactured goods as an important negative shock to other Asian economies. Some even predict that the emergence of other large developing countries, such as India, as competitors in export markets could also lead to further competition in labour-intensive goods and result in crisis in the region (Choi 2000).

The issue of export competition among Asian developing countries is also at the heart of current concerns about economic recovery in the crisis-affected countries. Export expansion has a key role to play in the recovery, because these countries have to repay their larger foreign debt following the collapse of their pegged exchange rates. If competition among Asian developing countries is a zero-sum game, then the recovery will not be sustainable, at least in some countries. Indeed, if China decides to devalue the renminbi (the Chinese national currency) as it tries to boost aggregate domestic demand, the possibility of another crisis cannot be ruled out. Should smaller Asian economies be worried about China's growth and rapid export expansion? In general, do developing countries face a 'fallacy of composition trap', that is, will attempts by many countries to pursue export-oriented growth at the same time ultimately be self-defeating? How likely is China to devalue the renminbi? How much would this affect other Asian developing economies? This chapter examines these issues based on recent empirical research.

THE FALLACY OF COMPOSITION DEBATE

The success of several NIEs in Asia, namely, Hong Kong, the Republic of

Korea (henceforth referred to as Korea), Singapore and Taiwan, in promoting growth through export-oriented strategies has not convinced the export pessimists. They argue that while a few small developing countries have succeeded in export expansion, their experience cannot be generalized because the exports of similar products by a large number of developing countries will drive down export prices and/or trigger increased protection in the industrial countries (Cline 1982). Based on the exports to GDP ratios achieved by these Asian economies adjusted for country size, Cline simulates the rate of market penetration in industrial countries if more developing countries were to follow the development path of the Asian NIEs. Using the threshold of 15 per cent of market penetration as a trigger that elicits a protectionist response from the industrial countries, Cline concludes that the industrial countries cannot accommodate export expansion by a large number of developing countries.

A number of subsequent studies (for example, Bhagwati 1990; Ranis 1985) criticized Cline's findings. Three criticisms stand out. First, both Bhagwati and Ranis emphasize the divergence of developing countries in their endowments and policies, and hence in the timing and size of their export surges. For all developing countries to begin to increase their exports to the same extent, at the same time or with the same commodity composition is unlikely. Thus a 'flying geese' (Akamatsu 1962) pattern of growth and trade will alleviate the pressure on export markets. Second, trade among the developing countries has been increasing, and this should mitigate the impact of developing-country exports on industrial-country markets. Indeed, trade among developing countries, especially among Asian developing economies, has grown rapidly with trade liberalization and improved diplomatic relationships. In this context the most noticeable trade growth has been the explosive expansion of trade between China and Korea and Taiwan. Third, the share of developing countries in industrial-country markets is still small, and these markets will not become saturated for some time. Thus Hughes and Waelbroeck (1981) predicted that developing-country exports of manufactures could keep growing in the 1980s (and they did – very rapidly) despite increased protection in the industrial countries.

Other researchers have also questioned Cline's 15 per cent threshold. While Ranis (1985) disputes its arbitrary nature, several others (Balassa 1989; Baldwin 1985; Hughes and Krueger 1984) argue that the effects of protection in industrial countries on developing-country exports have been exaggerated, because developing countries are often able to find ways to circumvent import restrictions. They further argue that it is the policies of the exporting countries that largely determine their export performance, not those of the importing countries.

By contrast, Faini, Clavijo and Senhadji (1992) find that both demand and supply factors are important in determining developing countries' export performance. Based on their econometric models of export demand, they argue that some East Asian economies have succeeded in export expansion at least partly because other developing countries have failed to do so. They further claim that for a representative developing country, a large share (almost 80 per cent) of the benefits of a devaluation on export revenue vanishes when other developing-country competitors adopt similar policies.

The issue of the fallacy of composition is best suited to general equilibrium analysis. Several studies have used computable general equilibrium models to examine the issue. Hughes et al. (1990) use a multiregional general equilibrium model to evaluate the impact of China's growth on other Asian developing economies. The study concludes that China's emergence will not have a severe impact on other Asian developing countries as long as these countries also pursue policies that increase their productivity.

Martin (1993) employs a simple general equilibrium model to address the issue of the fallacy of composition. He tests whether simultaneous trade liberalization and productivity improvements in developing countries reduce their welfare. Martin finds that simultaneous trade liberalization tends to make developing countries worse off than unilateral trade liberalization, while simultaneous productivity improvements enhance the welfare gains of productivity improvements in individual countries. Martin's first result is somewhat surprising (probably due to the relatively small elasticities of export demand implied in this model), because computable general equilibrium models frequently find that concerted trade liberalization tends to be more beneficial to individual countries than unilateral trade liberalization.

In an attempt to investigate the causes of the 1997 Asian crisis, Diwan and Hoekman (1998) examine export competition among Asian developing economies. Through a series of correlation analyses, they find that China tends to compete with other developing countries while Japan tends to complement Asian developing countries. Japan, however, does compete with more advanced developing countries in at least some products. Thus China's competition from the bottom and Japan's slowdown from the top have a 'sandwich' effect on other Asian economies. The difficulty with Diwan and Hoekman's approach is that one cannot establish causal relationships between China's growth and Japan's slowdown on the one hand, and the Asian crisis on the other. The results are at best suggestive.

Yang and Vines (2000) use a global general equilibrium model of the Global Trade Analysis Project (for details of the model and its database see Hertel 1997 and McDougall, Elbehri and Truong 1998) to re-visit the fallacy of composition debate. Unlike previous studies using general equilibrium models (such as Hughes et al. 1990; Mai 1994; Martin 1993), Yang and Vines (2000) attempt to simulate the impact of their actual growth on developing countries instead of the effects of hypothetical trade liberalization and marginal productivity improvements. They argue that the latter approach cannot adequately represent the growth process of developing countries in the past, and hence fails to prove whether growth in developing countries involves a fallacy of composition. With such a modelling approach, the fallacy of composition is unlikely to occur, because multilateral trade liberalization tends to offset the negative terms of trade effects for all liberalizing countries, unless losses from competition in third country markets outweigh the benefits of an increased demand for exports. As for productivity experiments, the approach is even less likely to show the existence of the fallacy of composition. Typically, exports account for considerably less than 50 per cent of GDP. Even if productivity improvements lead to the loss of export revenue because of falling export prices, this can be more than compensated for by the gains from reduced costs in the production of domestic goods. In theory, productivity improvements in the presence of distortions can lead to immiserizing growth, but as Johnson (1967) has shown, that only happens when the productivity improvements are small and when they occur in a distorted industry.

Examining the fallacy of composition hypothesis using a general equilibrium model requires capturing the important characteristics of the actual growth process. These include the growth of various industries and commodities and their trade over time. This in turn requires proper consideration of historical changes in factor accumulation, technological change and trade policies in simulations. After taking these factors into account, Yang and Vines ask the following question: how different would the terms of trade and welfare levels of developing countries have been had they not grown (in terms of output and factor cumulation) or liberalized (in terms of openness to trade) relative to industrial countries since 1975? In other words, how have relative growth and liberalization of developing countries affected their terms of trade and welfare?

Table 8.1 presents their simulation results. The table shows clearly that more rapid growth relative to industrial countries has indeed led to a deterioration in the terms of trade facing developing regions. The NIEs experience the largest decline in the terms of trade as they are collectively the largest exporter among the developing regions. As expected, a fall in the price of exports dominates the overall terms of trade effects, but import prices decline simultaneously, which helps mitigate the effect of falling export prices. This suggests that while developing countries may compete with each other when they expand their exports, these expanding exports also help reduce their import costs. One would expect that the more intensive the trade among developing countries, the greater the reduction in import prices.

Table 8.1   The effects of accelerated growth in selected developing regions and China, 1995 (%)

	NIEs	ASEAN	China	South Asia	Latin America
Terms of trade	−14.2	−7.3	−11.6	−8.4	−4.9
of which:					
Contribution of					
World prices	−0.6	0.0	−0.2	−0.5	0.3
Export prices	−14.0	−8.1	−13.0	−8.3	−5.6
Import prices	−0.4	−0.8	−1.8	−0.4	−0.4
Utility index	207.7	132.0	244.8	76.1	19.9
Terms of trade effect as a percentage of welfare gain	5.0	3.3	2.7	1.6	3.3

Source: Yang and Vines (2000).

Significant as the adverse terms of trade effects may be, their welfare impact is relatively limited. The welfare losses resulting from the terms of trade effects are no more than 5 per cent of the gains from growth relative to industrial countries. Thus there is no immiserizing growth. One needs to bear in mind that these results are comparatively static, and they represent deviations from the state of the world economy in 1995 if all developing countries had only grown and liberalized at the same pace as the industrial countries during 1975–95.

Note that such adverse terms of trade effects are not unique to developing countries. Any large region that expands faster than the rest of the world will tend to experience a decline in the terms of trade as it grows. This is simply because a region that is expanding more rapidly than other regions tends to supply its goods at a pace that is faster than the rest of the world can absorb without a decline in the price of these goods. Therefore, the declining terms of trade do not imply a fallacy of composition in developing-country growth; the fallacy of composition exists only when one country's expansion is at the expense of other countries' expansion. Whether this occurs or not depends on a number of factors, as will be discussed in the context of China's role in this process in the following section.

THE ROLE OF CHINA

Although much has been said about the possibly negative impact of China's growth on other developing countries, few rigorous studies have examined this issue. Hughes et al. (1990) tackle the issue using a multiregion general equilibrium model, but do not simulate China's impact by characterizing China's actual growth process in the past. China's economy has grown enormously since the mid-1980s, which is the period that the study examines. To evaluate the impact of China's growth, one needs more than just an examination of marginal changes.

Choi (2000) constructs a two-good, three-region general equilibrium model to examine the fallacy of composition in the context of China's entry into the world market. The three regions are China, a labour-abundant country; the rest of Asia, which is also abundant in labour; and the North, which is capital abundant. The two homogeneous goods identified are exportables, which are assumed to be labour intensive, and importables, which are assumed to be capital intensive. With this standard Heckscher–Ohlin framework, Choi finds that China's trade liberalization would worsen the terms of trade and welfare for the rest of Asia. He then concludes that 'sudden economic growth of a low-income, labour-abundant country can cause a crisis in other labour-abundant countries in the South and benefits the capital-abundant industrial countries in the North' (pp. 17–18).

As Yang and Vines (2000) point out, Choi's finding is predictable given his analytical framework. As China competes with the rest of Asia in both goods markets, its liberalization will necessarily increase import prices for the rest of Asia and reduce the prices of its exports, leading to terms of trade and welfare losses. Had Choi considered two-way trade between China and the rest of Asia, the results might have been quite different. Given that substantial two-way trade between China and the rest of Asia does indeed exist, Choi's results almost certainly exaggerate the negative impact of China's growth on the rest of Asia.

Yang and Vines (2000) examine how China's growth has affected other developing countries by considering a counterfactual scenario in which China had grown only at the same pace as the industrial countries during 1975–95. Comparisons between this and actual 1995 equilibria reveal the impact of China's growth (Table 8.2). As expected, China's growth relative to that of the industrial countries worsens its own terms of trade. However, all the other developing regions experience a terms of trade gain, albeit only marginally.

These terms of trade gains occur predominantly through improved export prices. Import prices actually contribute negatively to the terms of trade facing other developing regions. This suggests that in net terms, China's growth tends to increase import costs for other developing countries while

Table 8.2   The effects of China's accelerated growth on selected regions and China, 1995 (%)

	NIEs	ASEAN	China	South Asia	Latin America
Terms of trade	1.0	0.2	–17.0	0.1	0.2
of which:					
Contribution of					
World prices	–0.1	–0.1	–0.1	–0.3	0.1
Export prices	1.0	0.4	–16.5	0.4	0.2
Import prices	–0.1	0.2	0.4	0.0	0.0
Utility index	0.6	0.0	238.8	0.1	0.1

Source: Yang and Vines (2000).

simultaneously improving their export prices. Overall, the production or welfare impact on developing regions is minimal.

To explain these results, Yang and Vine decompose the changes in the exports of other developing regions into the effect in the Chinese market (the complementary effect) and that in third-country markets (the competitive effect). Because industrial country markets are important for both China and other developing countries, one would expect China to compete with other developing countries in these markets. At the same time, China's growth should increase the demand for exports from other developing regions. The net effect of China's growth on other developing countries thus depends on the relative strengths of these two effects. As Table 8.3 shows, most developing regions suffer a small decline in their overall exports as a result of China's growth; that is, much of the loss in exports in third-country markets is compensated for by increased exports to China. For the NIEs, increased exports to China more than compensate for their lost exports to third-country markets, so they actually increase their overall exports as a result of China's expansion. This is why the NIEs experience a welfare gain from China's growth, as shown in Table 8.2. Note that none of the other developing regions suffers any welfare loss, even though their exports are adversely affected. The improvement in their terms of trade fully compensates for the welfare loss resulting from reduced exports.

The impact of China's growth on the exports of other developing countries in third markets is surprisingly small (Table 8.3). This is because China's export expansion in third markets generates some second-round effects. When imports from China increase in third markets, they do not simply replace

Table 8.3   The impact of China's growth on the exports of China and selected regions, 1995

Region or country	China market %	China market US$ billions	Third-country markets %	Third-country markets US$ billions	Total %	Total US$ billions
China	0.0	0.0	571.1	181.5	571.1	181.5
NIEs	740.3	49.0	–8.5	–38.6	2.4	10.4
ASEAN	545.2	6.6	–3.4	–8.0	–0.4	–1.5
South Asia	870.9	1.0	–2.4	–1.5	–0.8	–0.5
Latin America	481.4	3.2	–1.3	–3.5	0.0	–0.3
Japan	713.0	27.9	–5.6	–21.0	1.5	6.9
Other industrial countries	525.0	41.6	–1.2	–41.4	0.1	0.2
Rest of the world	619.4	9.2	–1.6	–8.6	0.3	0.6
World	629.9	138.5	1.1	58.9	3.6	197.4

Source: Yang and Vines (2000).

imports from other developing countries. Lower import prices resulting from China's expansion induce greater total imports from developing countries, which in turn leads to increases in exports from these countries in the long run. Overall trade expansion in third-country markets induces global trade expansion, including increased exports to China and countries in other developing regions. As Table 8.3 shows, China's accelerated growth has made world exports US$16 billion (US$197.4 billion minus US$181.5 billion) larger than they would otherwise have been.

SHORT-RUN VERSUS LONG-RUN ISSUES

Clearly China's emergence, and for that matter the emergence of any large country, is unlikely to result in large welfare losses to other developing countries, even though export growth may be adversely affected to some extent. In the short run, however, China's emergence and changes in its macroeconomic policies may have more disruptive effects on other developing countries. Nevertheless, one should put the shocks from China in a global and regional perspective. Even though many estimates have ranked China's economy among that of the world largest countries, China's trade is much smaller than that of the EU, Japan and the United States. As far as Asian developing economies are concerned, shocks originating in these economies are likely to be much larger than those originating from China. A depreciation of the US dollar or Japanese yen, for example, will probably have a far greater impact on exports from developing countries than a similar devaluation of the renminbi. Of course, greater product similarities between China and other developing countries may make shocks originating from China greater than the size of its economy suggests, but these greater similarities are probably unable to compensate for the smaller size of the Chinese economy compared with the EU, Japan and the United States.

What is the likelihood of a devaluation of the renminbi? In the immediate aftermath of the Asian crisis a substantial devaluation of the renminbi appeared to be inevitable if China was to restore its competitiveness following substantial devaluations in the crisis countries. Remarkably, the short-run impact of the crisis on China's exports was limited, and China's exports continued to grow strongly until late 1998. This mild impact was partly the result of short-run supply constraints on exports from the crisis economies, where widespread insolvencies and credit crunches following the crisis had made the supply of exports somewhat inelastic. The timing of China's macroeconomic cycle was also helpful. In the mid-1990s China had begun tightening its monetary policy to control high inflation. By 1997, when the Asian crisis struck, domestic inflation was low and under control. The decision to maintain nominal parity with the US dollar after the crisis meant that China had to continue its pursuit of a tight monetary policy. This has resulted in deflation, which was −0.8 per cent in 1998 according to official statistics. Anecdotal evidence and modelling results suggest that the extent of deflation is likely to be much more severe than official estimates show (Yang and Tyers 2000).

Downward rigidities in nominal wages have raised real wages in the presence of deflation and the growth of domestic production and employment has slowed considerably (Yang and Tyers 2001). The official estimate of GDP growth in 1998 was 7.8 per cent, but most independent estimates indicate that the true growth rate was considerably lower, and perhaps as low as 5 per cent (Fernald and Babson 1999; Wu 1999).

An important internal shock to the Chinese economy has been a remarkable increase in domestic savings at the expense of consumption. This seems partly to be a result of increased real interest rates arising from the tight monetary policy, but the main reason seems to be ongoing economic reforms. Liberalization of the housing market and retrenchments in state-owned enterprises have meant that urban workers have greater incentives to own their houses, to counter the increased uncertainty about employment and to meet the need for risk insurance (Wu 1999).

Increases in perceived risks to investment in China appear to have led to large capital outflows, which were only partly offset by the deceleration of growth of official reserves. In 1998 net outflows amounted to US$30 billion, or 3 per cent of GDP. Yang and Tyers (2001) estimate that this shock is far more important in explaining the slowdown of growth in China than falling export prices caused by the Asian crisis. Given massive capital outflows, domestic private investment remains weak, even though the expansion of public investment has prevented a decline in total investment.

The short-run supply constraints in the crisis countries gave China a breathing space for adjustment. Now the domestic price level has fallen so much, the real effective exchange rate of the renminbi may have depreciated, even though it has appreciated against the currencies of the crisis countries in real terms. If China can continue to improve its productivity through the reform of state-owned enterprises, together with moderate growth, or even declines, in real wages, particularly in the nonstate sectors, the pressure for devaluation will be eased substantially, and a devaluation may not be necessary. The first half of 2000 saw a strong recovery of export growth. Whether this can be sustained remains to be seen.

The renminbi exchange rate in the black market has depreciated considerably since the peaks reached in 1998. In recent months the interbank exchange rate has broken through both its lower and upper bands, suggesting the absence of pressure to devalue (for details of these recent developments see *Oxford Analytica Asia Pacific Daily Brief*, 1 June). However, this may change in the process of China's accession to the WTO. If imports do expand substantially as a result of trade liberalization, then downward pressure on the renminbi will begin to mount again. As the implementation of WTO commitments will be phased in over the next five years, the impact may not be large enough to warrant devaluation in the short run. Indeed, it is even possible that the renminbi will face pressure for revaluation if inward foreign investment increases substantially as a result of WTO accession.

China has a long-term goal of making the renminbi fully convertible so as to attract more foreign portfolio investment. To achieve this China must ease control over the capital account: greater capital mobility is better managed with a more flexible exchange rate regime. Given wage and other nominal rigidities, China would be in a much better position to manage domestic price levels and aggregate demand with a more flexible exchange rate. Thus China may have an incentive to take the opportunity to float the renminbi should economic growth continue to be sluggish in the next few years. However, this is more likely to be a medium- to long-term policy change, as China faces significant constraints to making such changes immediately.

Perhaps the most critical constraint is the poor state of China's financial sector. The heavily indebted state banks must be cleared of huge bad debts and reformed to operate on a commercial basis. This, however, is unlikely to happen unless the state-owned enterprises are restructured and stop putting more burdens on the banks. Furthermore, deepening the reform of state-owned enterprises is difficult without overhauling China's social security system and social institutions. This restructuring is necessary to maintain social stability, which is imperative for the Communist Party.

A floating renminbi also has associated risks. For example, China's competitors could devalue their currencies in retaliation if the floating of the renminbi results in its depreciation. Competitive devaluations could then increase uncertainties in trade and financial transactions, which would be detrimental to all countries involved. From China's perspective, a floating renminbi means the loss of a nominal anchor, which seems to have helped control inflation in the past. Clearly China needs to balance the benefits and costs of a floating exchange rate regime. As far as other developing countries are concerned, they must be prepared for a floating renminbi in the long run and learn how to deal with it, as they do with other major floating currencies.

IMPLICATIONS OF CHINA'S WTO ACCESSION

China will probably accede to the WTO in 2001. This will have significant implications for other developing countries as well as for China. China's objectives in acceding to the WTO can be summarized as follows:

●   to secure more predictable market access for its exports in the rest of the world;
●   to anchor domestic economic reform;
●   to reduce domestic distortions and increase domestic competition in order to achieve efficiency gains;
●   to attract more foreign investment from abroad.

What are the implications for other developing countries of China's WTO accession if China succeeds in all these objectives? In the long run, China's WTO accession will have impacts on other developing countries similar to those discussed earlier, that is, it is likely to have positive effects on other developing countries, especially those that have more intensive trade and investment links with China. In the short run, the outcomes will depend on what happens to China's capital account and trade account. If the market perceives improved growth potential in China, which also hinges on China's implementation of its WTO commitments, capital inflows into China will accelerate. While this may raise the cost of foreign investment for other developing countries, it is likely to increase the opportunities for other developing countries to increase their exports to China, as China's real exchange rate will tend to appreciate and foreign direct investment will induce more import demand in China.

If China fails to attract more foreign investment, other developing countries may find it easier to raise funds in the world capital market. However, with extensive liberalization across virtually all sectors of the economy but without increased capital inflow, imports into China are likely to increase, and China will probably face pressure to devalue its currency in order to boost its exports. The consequence will be increased export competition from China in the third-country market and weaker import demand in the Chinese market. This is hardly a superior outcome for other developing countries compared with increased capital inflow to China, and hence greater export opportunities there.

How individual developing countries are affected by China's WTO accession depends to a large extent on their current and future economic relations with China. Countries that already have large foreign direct investment in China and have the potential to invest more are likely to benefit more from China's WTO accession. These tend to be the relatively advanced developing countries in Asia, which also export extensively to China and whose products are less competitive with Chinese exports. Less advanced developing countries that have less extensive trade and investment links with China will probably be unable to gain as much, if anything. If, however, these countries have a complementary trade structure with China, such as a large potential to export primary commodities, the benefit from China's liberalization will increase. Countries that are likely to do least well are those that are heavily reliant on food and energy imports. China's WTO accession is expected to raise the demand for these commodities in the world market, and this could have a negative terms of trade effect on food- and energy-dependent countries.

Current quota premiums indicate that China probably faces the most stringent restrictions on clothing exports in the US and EU markets. China is therefore expected to increase its share in the world clothing market once MFA quotas and other restrictions on its exports are removed after its WTO accession. However, the prolonged restrictions (until 2008) on China's textile and clothing exports as part of China's WTO accession package could potentially benefit some developing countries in the short to medium term. In the longer term, China's expansion of clothing exports should also benefit textile and fibre producers in other developing countries. How much China will continue to rely on textile and clothing exports beyond 2008 is not clear, as antidumping measures and the special safeguard mechanisms could then replace current quota restrictions and lead to increasing export diversification in China. Some developing countries may be able to gain sufficient competitiveness in the meantime to maintain their export growth in the longer term.

Leaving aside specific commodities, China's WTO accession should have a longer-term benefit as far as short-run economic management is concerned. Increases in trade and investment links between China and other developing countries, especially those in Asia, will provide, together with Japan, a third-pillar market around the world. As long as China's business cycles are not synchronized with those of North America and Europe, China can be an important stabilizer for global demand.

CONCLUSION

The fallacy of composition argument has attracted increased attention in recent years because of rising competition among developing countries in the exports of labour-intensive manufactures, now the backbone of developing-country exports. The emergence of China and other large countries as significant exporters of manufactured goods has made the argument more appealing than before as a source of export pessimism. However, growing evidence suggests that this new export pessimism is unwarranted. The traditional arguments against this pessimism are increasingly being validated and understood. This chapter shows that rapidly growing trade among developing countries plays a critical role in mitigating the terms of trade effects of export expansion by developing countries. Further growth in this type of trade will make the fallacy of composition even less relevant. The multiplier effect of trade expansion by any country or countries means that trade is not a zero-sum, one-off economic activity, and this also mitigates the competitive effect of initial trade expansion. For this reason, the emergence of China, or of any large developing country, is unlikely to undermine the growth of other developing countries or to cause an international crisis.

The existence of large and increasing trade among developing countries suggests that the standard Heckscher–Ohlin framework is unsuitable for analysing the fallacy of composition in manufactures trade. The theoretical possibility of immiserizing growth arising from the fallacy of composition has little relevance in reality. In a world of differentiated products, developing countries both complement each other and compete with each other. The net effect on any particular country depends on the intensity of its trade with its competitors and partners and the extent of competition in third-country markets.

In the short run, competition among developing countries is more likely to involve a fallacy of composition. Export competition via macroeconomic instruments, especially the exchange rate, can cause external and internal imbalances without the benefits of overall trade expansion. With great capital mobility, competitive devaluations can lead to major disruptions to the economies involved.

For this reason Asian developing countries have been rightly concerned about China's exchange rate policy. However, China is still a much smaller economy than the EU, Japan and the United States, and its impact on other developing countries should be viewed in a global perspective. Nevertheless, with the deepening of economic reform, China's exchange rate setting is likely to become more flexible. Given the various constraints on China's move towards a more flexible exchange rate regime, this will be a gradual process. The primary driving force for a more flexible renminbi is China's desire to attract more portfolio investment with less control over the capital account. A more flexible renminbi exchange rate will give China's central bank greater autonomy in managing aggregate domestic demand, even though it increases the risk of rekindling inflation. How to deal with a more flexible renminbi is therefore an important issue for China as well as for other Asian developing countries.

REFERENCES

Akamatsu, K. (1962), 'A Historical Pattern of Economic Growth in Developing Countries', *Developing Economies*, **1** (1), 17–31.

Balassa, B. (1989), 'The Adding up Problem', *Banca Nazionale del Lavoro Quarterly Review* (March), No. 168, 47–72.

Baldwin, R. (1985), 'Ineffectiveness of Protection in Promoting Social Goals', *World Economy*, **8** (2), 109–18.

Bhagwati, J.N. (1990), 'Export-Promoting Trade Strategy: Issues and Evidence', in C. Milner (ed.), *Export Promotion Strategies*, Hemel Hempstead, UK: Harvester Wheatsheaf.

Choi, E.K. (2000), 'The Asian Crisis: Growth That Immiserizes the South and Benefits the North', paper presented at the international conference on The Asian Crisis II, 4–5 January, University of Washington, Seattle, Washington.

Cline, W.R. (1982), 'Can the East Asian Model of Development Be Generalized?', *World Development*, **10** (2), 81–90.

Diwan, I. and B. Hoekman (1998), 'Competition, Complementarity and Contagion in East Asia', paper presented at the Centre for Economic Policy Research/World Bank Institute conference on Financial Crises: Contagion and Market Volatility, 8–9 May, London.

Faini, R., F. Clavijo and A.S. Senhadji (1992), 'The Fallacy of Composition: Is it Relevant for LDCs' Manufactures Exports?', *European Economic Review*, **36** (4), 865–82.

Fernald, J.G. and O.D. Babson (1999), 'Why Has China Survived the Asian Crisis so Well? What Risks Remain?', International Finance Discussion Papers no. 633, Board of Governors of the Federal Reserve System, Washington, DC. Available at http://www.federalreserve.gov/pubs/workingpapers.htm.

Hertel, T.W. (ed.) (1997), *Global Trade Analysis Using the GTAP Model*, New York: Cambridge University Press.

Hughes, H. and A.O. Krueger (1984), 'Effect of Protection in Developed Countries on Developing Countries' Exports of Manufactures', in R.E. Baldwin (ed.), *The Structure and Evolution of Recent US Trade Policy*, Chicago: University of Chicago Press, pp. 389–423.

Hughes, H. and J. Waelbroeck (1981), 'Can Developing Country Exports Keep Growing in the 1980s?', *World Economy*, **4** (2), 127–47.

Hughes, H., Philippa Dee, Frank Jarrett, David Pearce, David Vincent and Maree Tait (1990), 'Asian Interdependence: The Impact of Chinese Exports on Other Asian Economies', report prepared for the Asian Development Bank, Australian National University, National Centre for Development Studies, Canberra.

Johnson, H.G. (1967), 'The Possibility of Income Losses from Increased Efficiency or Factor Accumulation in the Presence of Tariffs', *Economic Journal*, **77**, 151–54.

Mai, Y.H. (1994), 'The Role of Industrial Upgrading in the Asian NIEs', unpublished PhD dissertation, Australian National University, Canberra.

Martin, W.J. (1993), 'The Fallacy of Composition and Developing Country Exports of Manufactures', *World Economy*, **16** (2), 159–72.

McDougall, R.A., A. Elbehri and T.P. Truong (eds) (1998), *Global Trade, Assistance and Protection: The GTAP 4 Database*, West Lafayette, IN: Purdue University, Center for Global Trade Analysis.

Ranis, G. (1985), 'Can the East Asian Model of Development Be Generalized? A Comment', *World Development*, **13** (4), 543–45.

Wu, H.X. (1999), 'Has China's Actual Growth Been Exaggerated by Official Claims?', *Association for Chinese Economic Studies Newsletter* (August). Available on http://ajrcnet.anu.edu.au/acesa.htm.

Yang, Y. and R. Tyers (2000), 'GTAP-Based Comparative Static Macroeconomics: An Application to China's Policy Options', Working Papers in Economics and Econometrics no. 384, Australian National University, Canberra.

Yang, Y. and R. Tyers (2001) 'The Crisis and Economic Change in China', *The Japanese Economic Review*, **52** (4), 492–511.

Yang, Y. and D. Vines (2000), 'The Fallacy of Composition and the Terms of Trade of Newly Industrialising Countries', paper presented at a seminar in the Department of Economics, Oxford University, 9 November.

9. The enlargement of ASEAN and its impact on regional integration

Jayant Menon

Regional trading arrangements (RTAs) are currently popular, and have been proliferating. From 34 RTAs in 1992, the number now stands at more than 200. The demand to form or join RTAs on political grounds is strong. As Bhagwati (1997, p. 282) put it: 'No politician is happy unless he has put his signature on at least one of them.' Apparently there is also a strong compulsion to avoid being an outsider on economic grounds. As far back as 1964, Mundell demonstrated how trading partners who do not join a preferential trading arrangement might be made worse off through terms of trade effects even when global welfare is enhanced. (This occurs when the preferential arrangement is large enough to affect world prices, and outsiders as a whole are harmed because their terms of trade deteriorate as a result of trade diversion.) Even without terms of trade effects, that is, even if the RTA is small, the fact that an outsider's competitors may have negotiated preferential access to its major markets suggests that the costs of not joining could be high. Thus the threat of trade and investment diversion is viewed as a compelling reason to seek membership in RTAs.

On the supply side, RTA members are usually quite receptive to expanding their membership for both political and economic reasons. Size matters in politics. Political clout in international negotiations is often a function of size, and size can only be increased by increasing the number of members in the club. In economic terms, the addition of new members can create greater opportunities for regional division of labour and specialization, and an enlarged duty-free market is attractive to firms in member countries. Thus if the last two decades have been characterized by growth in the number of RTAs, then more recent years reflect a period during which these RTAs have been widening their membership.

The most popular type of RTA continues to be the free trade area (FTA). FTAs are the least restrictive type of RTA, requiring member countries to remove only trade barriers among themselves, and allowing each member country to set its own barriers to trade with nonmembers. Lawrence (1996) has described the removal of trade barriers alone as a 'relatively shallow form of integration'. FTAs (as well as other forms of RTA) have been extending their agendas beyond just the removal of barriers to trade. In other words, they have been deepening. Perhaps the strongest motivation to pursue deepening is the desire to promote international investment and the operations of multinational enterprises as much as the desire to promote trade. In addition to pursuing regional agreements aimed at promoting international investment, FTAs are negotiating agreements that facilitate trade in services, the harmonization of standards, the protection of intellectual property rights and so on. In some cases the agenda on these issues is more ambitious in terms of scope, depth and/or speed of implementation than that now being considered by the WTO.

This chapter examines the impact of widening and assesses the progress of deepening in AFTA. AFTA began in 1992 with the six ASEAN members (the ASEAN-6): Brunei, Indonesia, Malaysia, the Philippines, Singapore and Thailand. ASEAN adopted Vietnam as its seventh member in 1995, and in 1997 Lao PDR and Myanmar increased the membership to nine. With Cambodia's accession to full membership in 1999, ASEAN had finally achieved its objective of incorporating all Southeast Asian nations in ASEAN's membership.

THE WIDENING OF AFTA

The decision to establish AFTA was taken at the Summit Meeting of the ASEAN Heads of State in 1992. All six members were envisioned to participate in AFTA. From the outset, the ASEAN-6 countries agreed to a deadline of 2008 for reducing the common effective preferential tariff (CEPT) rates to 0 to 5 per cent. This deadline was moved to 2005 at the Fifth ASEAN Summit Meeting held in Bangkok, Thailand, in December 1995, and was later moved to 2003, then to 2002. In addition, the participants agreed that each ASEAN-6 country would have a minimum of 85 per cent of their tariff lines in the inclusion list with tariffs of 0 to 5 per cent by 2000. Thereafter, this would be increased to a minimum of 90 per cent of the inclusion list in the 0 to 5 per cent tariff range by 2001.

The first step in widening AFTA took place at the Fifth ASEAN Summit Meeting, when Vietnam acceded to the CEPT agreement and agreed to the following provisions: (a) to extend, on a reciprocal basis, MFN and national treatment to ASEAN member countries; (b) to prepare a list for tariff reduction and start tariff reduction on 1 January 1996, ending at the 0 to 5 per cent tariff rate by 1 January 2006; (c) to phase in products that were temporarily excluded in five equal instalments beginning on 1 January 1999 and ending on 1 January 2003; (d) to phase in agricultural products that were temporarily excluded beginning on 1 January 2000 and ending on 1 January 2006; and (e) to provide information on its trade regime whenever requested. Thus Vietnam, like the ASEAN-6, was given ten years to reduce its tariffs to 0 to 5 per cent.

The second stage in the widening of AFTA took place at the Seventh ASEAN Summit Meeting in Kuala Lumpur, Malaysia, in 1997, when Lao PDR and Myanmar acceded to the CEPT agreement. The provisions were identical to those for Vietnam, except for the time frame. While both countries would also have ten years to satisfy AFTA obligations, they were to begin their programme on 1 January 1998 and conclude it on 1 January 2008. Cambodia was to join Lao PDR and Myanmar in formally acceding to ASEAN on 23 July 1997. However, following the rupture of the coalition between Prime Minister Hun Sen and Prince Ranaridh in June 1997, ASEAN decided to postpone Cambodia's membership. Cambodia finally moved from observer status to full membership on 30 April 1999, and its membership completed the widening of AFTA to include all ten Southeast Asian nations.

Two other recent and important developments have occurred in the region. The first is the 'ASEAN+3' idea, which refers to China, Japan and Korea. The country composition is exactly that proposed by Prime Minister Mahathir as part of the East Asian Economic Caucus more than a decade ago. Although the exact nature of the relationship between ASEAN and the three is still unclear, it does hold out the potential for a significant enlargement. At present, the likelihood of such a formal arrangement among these economies is low in the face of likely opposition from the United States and other countries in the region, particularly Australia and New Zealand.

ASEAN+3 has announced a regionwide system of currency swaps to help members deal with future crises, and the Asian Monetary Fund idea, which was rejected just three years ago, may soon be revived in a watered-down form. At the 2000 IMF–World Bank annual meetings in Prague, for the first time Fund Managing Director Horst Koehler indicated support, in principle, for an Asian Monetary Fund type of institution if it could complement the role of the IMF. Bergsten (2000) claims that the machinery of ASEAN+3 is already more sophisticated than that of the North American Free Trade Area, and that it is more active than any other grouping outside Europe. Attempts to further widen ASEAN in this way, however, are a recognition of its internal weakness, and that even with its new members, ASEAN is somewhat barren without its major trading partners in the region. Such attempts also implicitly recognize the need to involve these three countries if ASEAN is to pursue intensified regional co-operation in any worthwhile or meaningful way.

The second important development is the growth in bilateralism in the region. Within ASEAN, Singapore has been active in pursuing such arrangements, having already concluded one with Australia. Currently Singapore is negotiating a bilateral free trade agreement with New Zealand and with Japan. Singapore also has plans for bilateral agreements with Canada and Mexico. These agreements are intended to go beyond what is prescribed by the WTO. Within ASEAN+3, Japan and Korea are negotiating a bilateral free trade agreement, but each has been active in pursuing bilateral arrangements with countries outside the region. Japan is pursuing bilateral agreements with Canada and Mexico, while Korea is negotiating with Chile and New Zealand.

Impact of AFTA Widening on New Members

Trade

Apart from Myanmar, the other new ASEAN members are not WTO members. The significance of this is that WTO nonmembers do not have legal rights to MFN or national treatment for exports to member countries. However, AFTA will provide these countries with such legal rights for exports to the ASEAN market. Because most of the trade of the new member countries is with other ASEAN countries, MFN and national treatment in ASEAN markets will be significant. Take, for instance, the case of Lao PDR. Currently it has a catalogue of claims with respect to unfair treatment and restricted market access in its trade with Thailand. In agriculture in particular, Lao PDR authorities claim that Thailand operates a system of implicit and variable quotas on its agricultural exports (mainly livestock such as cattle and pigs, and coffee and wood products). With the conferment of legal rights to fair treatment and access to dispute settlement procedures, ASEAN should provide Lao PDR with an effective forum to negotiate market access issues with Thailand.

As the new members of ASEAN already conduct most of their trade with other ASEAN countries, the potential for trade diversion associated with AFTA is low. Reduced tariffs on goods already sourced from ASEAN will be welfare enhancing if reductions in the prices of these goods lead to increased consumption, or, if they are inputs to production, lead to increased exports. The main problem in the Southeast Asian transition economies (SEATEs) of Cambodia, Lao PDR, Myanmar and Vietnam relates to the wide range of nontariff barriers (NTBs) that restrict trade. AFTA stipulates that all NTBs on tariff lines in the Inclusion List will have to be phased out within five years of participating in AFTA, with quantitative restrictions abolished immediately. Eventually, NTBs on all products will have to be phased out as part of AFTA obligations. Thus AFTA will provide the SEATEs with the opportunity to deal with, and eventually to dismantle, the many NTBs that currently restrict trade. As long as ASEAN is serious about its members complying with this obligation and monitors the process closely, then the dismantling of NTBs in the SEATEs could be trade creating. Because only a small share of domestic demand for nonagricultural goods is currently met by domestic production in these countries, however, the potential for trade creation associated with AFTA is low.

Foreign investment

How is membership of AFTA likely to affect foreign direct investment flows to the SEATEs? Although AFTA is unlikely to significantly alter the composition of foreign direct investment flows to these countries in the short to medium term, both the volume and quality of foreign direct investment could change. Perhaps the most significant constraint to foreign direct investment flows to these countries is the perceived risk associated with investing there, which derives from the absence of a strong legal and regulatory environment. In such an environment investors will require a higher minimum return on their investment to compensate for the higher level of perceived risk. This has implications for both the level and nature of foreign investment flows. First, the total amount of foreign investment in any industry is likely to be lower than it would be if this risk could be reduced or eliminated. Second, the higher levels of return required usually result in a large share of investments that are short term in nature. Apart from these effects, the weak legal and regulatory environment may result in foreign investors trying to protect their investments through *ad hoc* arrangements with local officials and partners. In this instance corruption occurs not as a means to bypass government regulations, but rather as a substitute for their absence. Such arrangements provide opportunities for rent-seeking activities that can impose costs on the domestic economy and distort the local investment climate. Most rent-seeking activities also run counter to national interests.

Membership in AFTA could signal to foreign investors that administrative, legal and bureaucratic systems would have to change to satisfy the obligations of membership, that is, the transition to a fully fledged market economy would be certain and more rapid than it would be otherwise.[1] These sorts of perceptions are likely to be important to potential investors in assessing the risk of expropriation, especially when they are aware that international contracts are practically impossible to enforce.

Revenue effects

The most significant perceived cost of AFTA membership relates to the potential loss in revenues from trade taxes associated with tariff reductions. Revenue from trade taxes constitutes a significant share of total government revenue in the SEATEs, for example, in Lao PDR trade taxes contributed about 30 per cent of total government revenue in 1995. While the contribution of trade taxes to total government revenue is likely to fall, particularly in the short term, a number of factors suggest that the size of the fall will be moderate.

First, the reduction in tariffs and other economic reforms will, over time, increase economic growth, which will stimulate imports. Thus while less tariff revenue will be collected on each imported good, the increase in the volume of imports will mitigate the fall in revenue in the aggregate (assuming that the new tariff is greater than zero).

Second, a significant share of tariff revenue in the SEATEs is collected on goods such as alcoholic beverages and cigarettes. These goods will be quarantined from tariff reductions as they are on the general exceptions list.

Third, the reduction in tariffs and other trade barriers is likely to reduce the incentive to engage in informal cross-border trade (smuggling). The volume of informal trade is suspected to be quite high in all the SEATEs. In Lao PDR, for instance, informal or unrecorded trade is suspected to be at least 30 per cent of recorded trade, but could be as high as 50 per cent (Menon 1999). Unrecorded trade among the Greater Mekong subregion economies (Cambodia, Lao PDR, Myanmar, Thailand, Vietnam and China's Yunnan province) is estimated at double that of recorded trade among these countries (Than 1997). If smuggling does indeed fall in response to a lowering of barriers, then the share of trade that can be assessed for tariffs will increase.[2]

The overall impact on revenue from trade taxes (in the absence of significant trade diversion) will depend on (a) the size of the tariff reduction; (b) the extent of the switch from unrecorded to recorded trade; and (c) the growth in recorded imports as a result of tariff cuts, and indirectly through the increase in economic activity associated with trade liberalization (see Menon 1999 for a formal analysis of the impact of reducing barriers to trade on smuggling activity). As tariffs are already generally low and effective tariffs in the SEATEs are even lower (with the various duty exemption schemes), the increase in the share of recorded trade or the extent of the growth in recorded imports need not be high to offset significantly the reduction in revenue associated with preferential tariff cuts. If tariff revenue loss is still a concern, however, then the SEATEs could replace the lost revenue by raising domestic taxes by means of a value added or sales tax. Such taxes are also less likely to distort domestic resource allocation if applied equally and independently of the supply source. In this way AFTA accession would provide the impetus for important, complementary, domestic tax reform. All in all, concerns about revenue losses associated with AFTA-related tariff cuts should not be a stumbling block.

Impact of Widening on AFTA as a Group

Economic effects

What are the welfare effects associated with the widening of AFTA? Could they be superior to those of the original AFTA? Furthermore, could the welfare effects of a widened AFTA be superior to those of nondiscriminatory or unilateral liberalization? In answering both these questions, we should note first that RTAs, irrespective of their size, are generally second-best in nature, in that they are generally an inferior option to nondiscriminatory or unilateral liberalization. As far back as 1965, Cooper and Massell showed that nondiscriminatory tariff reductions would enable a country to enjoy trade creation without any trade diversion.

The only case where the formation or expansion of an RTA is superior, in welfare terms, to unilateral liberalization is where the formation or expansion of the RTA results in substantial terms of trade gains. This is where the size of the RTA might matter. (By contrast, unilateral liberalization would unambiguously lead to a deterioration in a country's terms of trade.) If the RTA is large enough, this could lead to an improvement in the RTA's collective terms of trade by reducing its imports from and supply of exports to the rest of the world. Such an outcome would imply a substantial amount of trade diversion. In this scenario the welfare gain from the terms of trade improvement is large enough to offset the welfare loss associated with increased trade diversion. As noted earlier, the fact that most new ASEAN members conduct a substantial portion of their trade with other ASEAN countries suggests that the potential for trade diversion is low. Furthermore, given that the expansion in AFTA is small, any trade diversion and associated terms of trade improvement that might occur is also likely to be small.

Thus the welfare effects of an expanded AFTA are unlikely to be any better than those associated with the original AFTA, and, by implication, nondiscriminatory liberalization remains a superior option compared with either the expanded or the original AFTA. If the expansion of AFTA results in a substantial amount of trade creation, then this could lead to a deterioration in the terms of trade, because part of the resultant increase in real incomes is likely to spill over into greater demand for imports from the rest of the world. In this scenario the welfare loss associated with a terms of trade deterioration would have to be large enough to offset the welfare gain resulting from increased trade creation. Earlier we noted that only a small share of domestic demand for nonagricultural goods is currently met by domestic production in the new member countries, implying a low potential for trade creation by joining AFTA. This, coupled with the relatively minor expansion in the size of AFTA, suggests that any terms of trade improvements are also likely to be minor, if not negligible. This again points to little change in welfare between the expanded and the original AFTA. It also reaffirms the view that unilateral liberalization is Pareto-superior to either the formation of the original AFTA or its expansion.

Noneconomic effects

The accession of the SEATEs will increase ASEAN's diversity and heterogeneity and change its geopolitical character. This widening will pose challenges to ASEAN's cohesion. Much has been said about how ASEAN must avoid a two-tier system emerging when the SEATEs become members. The reality is that a two-tier system was always going to be inevitable, at least initially, if the SEATEs were to be accepted as full members. In other words, a two-tiered ASEAN already exists. What is required at this point is a focus on measures to address this problem, rather than more rhetoric that denies that this fragmentation has already occurred. Note, however, that the ASEAN–6 countries have initiated some minor programmes of technical and financial support to assist the SEATEs in their development pursuits. Although on a small scale, this move is unprecedented on the part of ASEAN, which has always operated on the basis of equal partnership. The 1997 Asian financial crisis is likely to have made the task of retaining cohesion within an expanded ASEAN much more challenging, as the crisis-affected ASEAN countries will no longer be able to provide the level of technical and financial support to the new members as planned before the crisis.

ASEAN is a body that is governed by consensual decisionmaking. It is an extreme case of the asymmetric decisionmaking rule, implying that its weakest or most conservative member will govern the pace of change. If ASEAN retains this rule, then the pace of change will probably have to slow down to accommodate its new members. To avoid this, ASEAN will have slowly to abandon its consensus rule in favour of a less rigid system, such as a system of majority voting (a first step has already been taken with the introduction of majority voting for dispute settlement). While a shift toward majority voting could prevent the more advanced countries from having to reduce the pace of reform to meet the standards of the transition member countries, it could lead to one or more new members feeling somewhat marginalized in the decisionmaking process. This could happen if the new members find themselves frequently disagreeing on issues where the incumbents share a common position after 30 years of communal and consensual decisionmaking. Another risk is that of administrative unwieldiness resulting from widening, particularly given ASEAN's complex institutional setup (Arndt 1996).

AFTA-PLUS: ATTEMPTS TO DEEPEN

AFTA is not just about reducing intra-ASEAN tariffs on traded goods. Following the trend in RTAs elsewhere, AFTA has various measures to deepen regional integration by extending the agenda beyond the liberalization of barriers to trade in goods. This agenda is referred to as AFTA-Plus. In an earlier review of AFTA, Lee (1994, p. 4) noted that 'In order to achieve the goals of AFTA, ASEAN would need to go beyond tariff reduction to include nonborder issues ranging from NTBs to investment policies ... in other words, what is needed is not AFTA *per se*, but an "AFTA-Plus".'

The Framework Agreement on Enhancing ASEAN Economic Co-operation concluded at the Fourth ASEAN Summit Meeting in Singapore in January 1992 contained provisions to increase co-operation in banking, finance, transport and communications. Other AFTA-Plus measures include harmonizing standards, instituting reciprocal recognition of tests and certification of products, harmonizing customs procedures, removing barriers to foreign investment (as part of the proposal for an ASEAN Investment Area), engaging in macroeconomic consultations, abiding by rules of fair competition and promoting venture capital. AFTA-Plus also aims to deal with such issues as trade-related investment policies and trade-related intellectual property rights, as well as with the protection of copyrights, patents and trademarks.

This is quite a long list, and agreements on co-operation have yet to be concluded in many of these areas. Co-operation or liberalization agreements have been reached in the following areas: NTBs; services; foreign investment; intellectual property; and customs.

NTBs

While quantitative restrictions on products in the inclusion list must be eliminated immediately, a programme to reduce other NTBs has been initiated. The CEPT Agreement requires that NTBs on a product are eliminated within five years of enjoying CEPT concessions. The Eighth AFTA Council in 1994 called on member countries to eliminate NTBs before this five-year period ended, and no later than 2003. The Interim Technical Working Group on the CEPT scheme identified the following NTBs as the most prevalent in intra-ASEAN trade: customs surcharges; technical measures and product characteristics requirements; and monopolistic measures (particularly in relation to exclusive import rights of state-controlled enterprises).

Services

The ASEAN Framework Agreement on Services was signed in December

1995 at the Fifth ASEAN Summit Meeting. This agreement was ambitious, and had two main objectives. The first was to eliminate virtually all restrictions (discriminatory and market access measures) to trade in services among member countries. The second was to liberalize trade in services by expanding the depth and scope of liberalization beyond that undertaken under the General Agreement on Trade in Services, with the aim of realizing a free trade area in services. The agreement explicitly identifies the potential for using the regional approach to achieve a deeper level of integration than that pursued at the multilateral level, that is, with the General Agreement on Trade in Services. The Framework Agreement deals with 'mutual recognition' and encourages member states to recognize, for the purpose of licensing or certifying service suppliers, their education or experience obtained, requirements met or licences or certifications granted in another member state.

Foreign Investment

In the declaration of the 1995 Summit Meeting, the ASEAN leaders agreed 'to establish an ASEAN Investment Region that will enhance ASEAN attractiveness and competitiveness for promoting direct investments'. The promotion of foreign direct investment in ASEAN is viewed as a critical objective of AFTA, particularly in light of the investment–trade nexus in the region (Athukorala and Menon 1997). The promotion of foreign investment is viewed as perhaps an even more important objective of AFTA than promoting intra-ASEAN trade.

The Framework Agreement on the ASEAN Investment Area was signed in October 1998. Arguably the most significant aspect of this agreement is the preferential or discriminatory treatment afforded to ASEAN investors in member countries. This preferential treatment will take the form of access to investment in particular sectors within manufacturing available only to ASEAN member countries on a reciprocal basis. That is, ASEAN members will be asked to list sectors in which they will allow only foreign investors from ASEAN to participate. This access is provided through national treatment provisions within six months of the date of signing the Framework Agreement on the ASEAN Investment Area. These exclusions are to be progressively phased out by 2003 instead of 2010 as initially agreed. Myanmar will join the six ASEAN countries to progressively phase out the exclusions by 2003 instead of 2015 as originally envisioned. Vietnam and Lao PDR are to 'exert their best efforts' to achieve early realization of the ASEAN Investment Area, and will do so no later than 2010, instead of the original deadlines of 2013 and 2015, respectively. From then on, preferential access to ASEAN members will be eliminated and the Investment Area will operate on a nondiscriminatory MFN basis.

Intellectual Property

The ASEAN Framework Agreement on Intellectual Property Co-operation was signed at the Fifth ASEAN Summit Meeting in 1995. This agreement stipulated that member states shall explore the possibility of setting up an ASEAN patent system, including an ASEAN Patent Office, to promote the regionwide protection of patents and an ASEAN trademark system, including an ASEAN Trademark Office, to promote the regionwide protection of trademarks. Apart from patents and trademarks, other areas of co-operation identified include copyright and related rights, industrial designs, geographic indications, undisclosed information and layout designs for integrated circuits.

Customs

Three areas of co-operation relate to customs: tariff nomenclature; customs valuation methods; and customs procedures. The ASEAN Experts Group on Tariff Nomenclature undertakes work on tariff nomenclature, while customs valuation methods and customs procedures are under the purview of the ASEAN Working Group on Customs Procedures.

ASEAN is in the process of simplifying and harmonizing its tariff nomenclature. It is preparing an ASEAN harmonized tariff nomenclature at the eight-digit level, based on the six-digit level of the harmonized commodity description and coding system of the World Customs Organization. The ASEAN harmonized tariff nomenclature will be a common nomenclature to be used in all ASEAN countries by 2002. As signatories to the Final Act of the UR, however, ASEAN members were committed to implementing the GATT transaction value method by 2000. In 1994 the ASEAN economic ministers mandated that customs procedures in ASEAN be harmonized so as to facilitate trade within ASEAN.

HOW SUCCESSFUL HAS AFTA BEEN AT DEEPENING?

It is often claimed that agreements on some nontariff and nontrade issues are more likely to be concluded at the regional rather than the multilateral level. Economic and social diversity across a small group of countries concentrated geographically is likely to be low, it is often argued, and thus less likely to impede progress toward harmonizing standards and procedures or reaching agreement on other trade-facilitating measures. Both the degree and scope of harmonization policy, for instance, may also be enhanced in the context of reduced diversity, and so regional efforts may be able to surpass the extent of integration possible at the multilateral level. With these potential advantages over the multilateral approach, the regional approach is also sometimes defended on the grounds that it can be a building rather than a stumbling block toward multilateralism: the argument is that once agreement is reached at the regional level, the opportunity exists for it to be offered on a multilateral MFN basis. Thus in principle, RTAs have the potential to achieve a deeper level of integration than that possible through the multilateral approach alone. Even if it is not any deeper, it is argued that we might be able to get there more quickly using the regional approach. The question then is basically an empirical one: how likely are RTAs to achieve these objectives? In particular, how successful has AFTA been in achieving deeper integration?

The first point to note is that economic and social conditions may be diverse even when countries are geographically proximate, as the ASEAN case clearly demonstrates. Even the ASEAN-6 vary significantly in economic and social conditions. The expanded ASEAN is substantially more diverse. Indeed, the economic, political, cultural and linguistic diversity within ASEAN is greater than that within the EU. Second, the provision of regional public goods is also complicated by economic and social diversity. Thus the conditions that might favour regional, as opposed to multilateral, approaches to integration do not appear to exist with AFTA. In many cases differences in views among the member countries have limited progress in reaching agreement on liberalization or harmonization, but even when some progress has been made, the regional approach may be subject to complications. In particular, incomplete liberalization, in terms of either geographic or product coverage, could result in distortions that undermine the very purpose of the policy accords.

Nontariff Barriers

What of AFTA's approach to dealing with NTBs? While various NTBs have been identified, the wording of the CEPT agreement puts the focus on the product, rather than on the NTB. This could raise problems in relation to NTBs that cover or cut across a number of products. If one or more of these products are not yet in the CEPT scheme, and if the NTB cannot be selectively removed, then the programme's success will depend on countries' willingness to exceed the minimum requirements of AFTA. That is, if the NTB cannot be selectively removed, then dismantling it might require removing it from some products that are not in the Inclusion List. Relying on goodwill alone in implementing reform is precarious, particularly when governments might be under pressure from lobby groups to defer or delay change. This is demonstrated by ASEAN's slow progress to date in dealing with NTBs. Nevertheless, there have been a few achievements in the dismantling of NTBs, for instance, customs surcharges have been phased out on a number of selected

CEPT products, sanitary and phytosanitary measures on various crop and livestock products have been harmonized, and an ASEAN standard for 28 types of animal vaccines has been finalized.

The widening of ASEAN is likely to affect progress with the harmonization of standards in the future. Harmonization within ASEAN generally involves all participants agreeing to a common set of standards. In most of the SEATEs many sanitary and phytosanitary measures do not exist or do not cover the full complement of products. In this context any attempt at harmonization through ASEAN is likely to be problematic for the SEATEs, because it could result in selective harmonization. For example, if sanitary standards are applied to fish but not to meat, this could raise the price of fish and, all other things being equal, shift consumption away from fish toward meat (assuming that there are imperfections in the market's assessment of food safety, which is not unusual in developing or transition economies). This not only distorts consumption patterns, but has the potential of increasing rather than reducing risk levels associated with food safety (Leebron 1996). In other words, selective harmonization could actually induce the outcomes that the policy is intended to inhibit.

Thus the current status of standards development in most of the SEATEs relative to the ASEAN–6 countries could result in one of two outcomes. The first, and perhaps more likely, scenario is that the SEATEs might simply be left out of many aspects of ASEAN's harmonization programme. This is not a good outcome, particularly for ASEAN. Ironically, however, it could be better than the alternative, which is that the SEATEs could be brought into the harmonization programme, which might leave them in a situation where they are worse off.

Services

ASEAN countries have chosen to wait for negotiations under way at the WTO in relation to some areas of professional services, construction, tourism and transport. The value of waiting was demonstrated by the December 1997 WTO Agreement on the liberalization of financial services. Also, the ASEAN transport ministers have agreed to develop a competitive air services policy with a view to eventual realization of an open sky policy. This policy, however, has yet to be formulated. This general wait-and-see approach might reflect recognition of the difficulties associated with negotiating sensitive and complicated issues among a small and diverse group of countries. It may also reflect the lack of value added in pursuing these issues regionally when multilateral negotiations are already under way.

Market access issues in some service sectors are being negotiated within ASEAN on a bilateral level. ASEAN is keen to push ahead with arrangements, also currently being negotiated on a bilateral basis, which provide for mutual recognition of educational and other qualifications and certifications. However, the diversity within ASEAN, exacerbated by its recent widening, could result in either drawn-out negotiations or, if individual agreements at a bilateral level are reached, in distortions. To illustrate the potential for distortions, consider the case where two countries agree to mutually recognize professional certification, but the standards in the two countries are significantly different. In this situation the country applying the lowest or least onerous standard will become the favoured place to gain the qualification. That is, an internal regulatory problem not dissimilar to trade deflection could arise, where entry to the RTA is sought via the member imposing the lowest barrier.

Foreign Investment

The promotion of foreign direct investment is viewed as an important objective of AFTA and AFTA-Plus. Projects implemented under the programme to implement the ASEAN Plan of Action on Co-operation and Promotion of Foreign Direct Investment and Intra-ASEAN Investment include joint training programmes, high-level strategic planning meetings, a survey on promoting foreign direct investment into and within ASEAN, and a protocol to amend the 1987 ASEAN Agreement for the Promotion and Protection of Investment. This protocol contains measures to simplify investment procedures and approval processes, to increase the transparency of rules governing investment, and to improve accessibility to information on a timely basis. ASEAN members will benefit by adopting measures such as these.

As discussed earlier, however, the most significant initiative in the ASEAN Investment Area relates to preferential access for ASEAN investors. Such preferences are bad policy for a number of reasons. First, preferential access would involve back-tracking in relation to current policy toward foreign direct investment in a number of ASEAN countries, which already effectively provides MFN and national treatment to investors (the only discriminatory aspect in some countries relates to restrictions on the foreign ownership of land). In addition, preferential access arrangements are likely to lead to investment diversion. Furthermore, given that the definition of an ASEAN investor is less than 100 per cent ASEAN ownership, there will be an incentive for non-ASEAN investors to incorporate the minimum ASEAN share in their investment package if the rents associated with the preferential access are significant. By deliberately incorporating a minimum ASEAN content to secure preferential access, the quality of the investment, and thus the benefits to the host economy, are likely to be lower than they would have been without this distortion.

The benefits of preferences will be lopsided in that they will accrue to ASEAN countries with the capacity to invest abroad. The main beneficiary would be Singapore, and perhaps the other original members of ASEAN after their full recovery from the financial crisis. The SEATEs are unlikely to have the capacity to invest abroad even by 2010. Thus while rules of reciprocity may be in place in theory, in practice they are unlikely to matter to the SEATEs. Thus if the SEATEs abide by the proposal to provide preferential treatment to ASEAN investors in particular sectors, this will be a one-way arrangement in which ASEAN investors will extract above normal rents at the expense of the SEATEs.

Intellectual Property

The removal of barriers occurs on the presumption that such liberalization is mutually beneficial. In the case of intellectual property, however, countries that do not innovate but copy innovations without offering compensation to the originator could end up worse off because of rules that protect intellectual property rights (Bhagwati 1994; Lawrence 1996). The ASEAN countries are, by and large, noninnovating countries. What then is their motivation to pursue regional agreements on the protection of intellectual property? The main reason would be the belief that such protection would encourage foreign investment in particular, but also trade. The relevant question is not whether intellectual property rights should be protected, but whether this protection is more likely to be successfully negotiated through regional or multilateral means. The multilateral approach (TRIPs) has one key advantage over the regional approach. This is the ability to trade concessions across disparate interests, that is, to weigh the costs to noninnovating countries of conceding on intellectual property protection against the benefits from increased market access for agricultural goods, textiles and apparel as part of the UR package (Maskus 1997).

Furthermore, a multilateral approach based on minimum standards and disciplines is preferable to competition between groups of countries or between RTAs in terms of protecting intellectual property rights so as to attract foreign direct investment and technology. For these reasons an ASEAN agreement on intellectual property is unlikely, or if it does occur, is probably going to be superseded by TRIPs. ASEAN can play a complementary role to the multilateral effort, however. The ASEAN Intellectual Property Association, established in December 1996, could focus on enforcement and administration issues associated with TRIPs. Enforcement of intellectual property rules has been a major concern with respect to developing countries (Konan et al. 1995).

Customs

In areas such as harmonizing customs procedures, tariff nomenclature and customs valuation methods, the progress achieved under AFTA-Plus has been impressive. Differences in customs procedures across ASEAN countries interfere with the flow of goods across borders and act as NTBs. Historically the ASEAN-6 countries have used different methods to value traded goods, such as the Brussels definition of value, home consumption value, valuation based on prevailing export market price or true market value in the importing country. The situation in the SEATEs with respect to customs valuation is even worse. These new ASEAN members are moving from either no system or an arbitrary and complicated hybrid system of valuation to a uniform system that will apply in all ASEAN countries. AFTA-Plus has been successful in moving the deadline for implementation of the common GATT transaction value system ahead of that agreed to in the Uruguay Round. This process will remove a significant impediment to trade within ASEAN.

INTERRELATIONS BETWEEN WIDENING AND DEEPENING

Widening has the potential to either slow the process of deepening within AFTA or to further fragment AFTA. With the EU debates, for instance, 'wideners' such as Margaret Thatcher were keen to use the expansion in membership to limit the extent of integration and the resultant loss of national autonomy with respect to various aspects of social and economic policy (Weintraub 1994). The widening of AFTA to incorporate SEATEs could slow the pace of deepening, because the new members are not yet in a position to match the reforms that the ASEAN-6 countries might want to achieve. The ASEAN-6 countries may not be willing to slow the pace of deepening to accommodate AFTA's new members, in which case they will have to proceed with arrangements that exclude them, at least temporarily. This will add to the fragmentation of AFTA. A further sign of the fragmentation within AFTA is the active pursuit of bilateral free trade agreements by Singapore. Although these agreements are not incompatible with AFTA, they do reflect the growing differences across members of the widened AFTA.

Widening may also affect some of the core aspects of AFTA, such as the monitoring of rules of origin associated with implementing the CEPT preferences. Current customs procedures in the new members, and perhaps in some of the original ones, do not permit accurate measurement of the domestic content of imports. That the process of 'measuring' domestic content in the new members is based purely on the certificate of origin is an open secret. In other words, a product may qualify for CEPT preferences even if its content does not meet the minimum 40 per cent ASEAN requirement as long as the certificate of origin identifies an ASEAN country as the exporting country. This is another reason for providing the CEPT reductions on a nondiscriminatory MFN basis.

The next question is whether the pace of deepening within the ASEAN–6 has affected widening in any way. One could argue that the lack of success in achieving deepening within AFTA has facilitated its widening. Without significant progress in many areas of AFTA-Plus, and with agreements still pending in other areas, it has been easier for the new members to satisfy, if not accept, the conditions of membership. The slow pace of deepening within the ASEAN–6 may actually have paved the way for the widening of AFTA.

IMPACT OF THE FINANCIAL CRISIS ON WIDENING AND DEEPENING

The rhetoric suggests that the financial crisis will have hastened the process of deepening co-operation in ASEAN. This mood was reflected at the 30th ASEAN Ministerial Meeting in Kuala Lumpur in October 1997. In his opening address, Malaysian Prime Minister Mahathir raised the need to deepen AFTA: 'Are we setting our sights to be a single market or an economic union *à la* EU? What is certain is that we need to make the bold move towards greater economic integration as we will have to face an uncertain environment' (*Bangkok Post*, 17 October 1997). Prime Minister Mahathir has also spearheaded a proposal to use a regional currency in intra-ASEAN trade.

Although such proposals have been discussed recently, they appear unlikely to materialize in any significant form. One bilateral payment arrangement between Malaysia and the Philippines has been concluded, and two more – between Malaysia and Thailand and Malaysia and Indonesia – are at different stages of discussion. Even if the two proposed multilateral payment arrangements come to fruition, they are unlikely to be significant economically because of the low volumes of bilateral trade between these pairs of countries. Indeed, intra-ASEAN trade as a whole is low, and therefore any move to introduce the use of a common currency for intra-ASEAN–6 trade is unlikely to be worthwhile. For this reason, and because of vast differences across ASEAN countries in terms of their stage of development, institutional structures and political systems, any attempts at increasing regional integration by moving towards an economic union is unlikely to succeed in the foreseeable future. Not only is further deepening unlikely, but ASEAN integration through its core medium of preferential tariff reductions has also been hampered as recently as 2000, when ASEAN ministers agreed to Malaysia's request to defer the transfer of automobiles from the temporary exclusion list to the inclusion list until 1 January 2005.

Little more than rhetoric supports the case that the crisis hastened the process of deepening within ASEAN. The first round of crisis-induced reforms in most of the ASEAN countries, some of which were reinforced by IMF programmes, suggests that the prospects for regional deepening have been hampered, because the reforms were essentially unilateral in nature, not regional. Indeed, the unilateral reforms have overridden prospects for a regional, and thus potentially discriminatory, arrangement in many areas. In the financial sector of the crisis-affected countries, the reforms focused on rationalizing the banking industry and created pressure to open markets to foreign banks in a nondiscriminatory manner. This action implicitly recognized that the financial sector in, for example, Thailand would not have been assisted before the crisis by the presence of Indonesian banks competing in its market, or vice versa.

If the crisis is unlikely to have deepened co-operation within ASEAN, did it fuel attempts to widen ASEAN further? The answer is yes: the crisis created the impetus to pursue further widening of ASEAN, at least in an informal way, and was one of the significant driving forces behind the ASEAN+3 concept (along with the failure of the WTO negotiations in Seattle and APEC's lacklustre performance in pursuing liberalization). If ASEAN+3 is formalized, or, failing that, if the informal links are significantly strengthened, then the potential for deepening does exist. An ASEAN widened to include these important trading and investment partners would make deepening co-operation arrangements both worthwhile and mutually beneficial.[3] If this occurs, then the crisis may have contributed to both a widening and deepening of ASEAN.

CONCLUSION

Two recent developments among RTAs have been the tendency to both widen and deepen. Widening involves either increasing the number of countries participating in the RTA or establishing substantive links with other RTAs. Deepening involves extending the liberalization agenda beyond just trade to include such issues as NTBs, services and intellectual property rights. AFTA has been widening, from six members in 1992 to ten now. The new members are likely to benefit from AFTA membership, with the main benefits coming from improved access to markets in the region and increased foreign investment flows. The widening has increased AFTA's diversity, made it more heterogeneous and, though regularly denied, created a two-tier system consisting of advanced and transition countries.

AFTA's attempts at deepening integration, largely though the AFTA-Plus programme, have had only limited success thus far. Apart from harmonizing customs procedures and tariff nomenclature and fast-tracking a common customs valuation method, progress in other areas has been limited. In the area of foreign investment, the establishment of the ASEAN Investment Area is a setback and runs counter to the free, open and nondiscriminatory investment regimes that have been the hallmark of ASEAN countries in the past. The Investment Area is not only unnecessary, but is also likely to be inefficient and unfair. In areas such as services and intellectual property rights, the multilateral rather than the regional approach would appear to be both more effective and less likely to be subject to distortions.

The Asian financial crisis is unlikely to have directly contributed to deepening within ASEAN. It has, however, highlighted the weakness of ASEAN as it currently stands and has added pressure to pursue further widening. The ASEAN+3 concept, although currently informal and in its infancy, may hold out the potential for a widening that would significantly enhance regionalism in East Asia. Should the ASEAN+3 idea or some other link-up of ASEAN with its major trading partners materialize in any formal way, then the potential for further deepening in a meaningful and mutually beneficial manner would emerge. However, ASEAN must first widen before it is likely to be able to deepen.

NOTES

1. In their assessment of Vietnam's accession to AFTA, the ASEAN Secretariat (1996, p. 38) noted that: 'The accession to the CEPT Agreement and Viet Nam's participation in many other areas of ASEAN economic cooperation ... sends a strong signal to foreign investors of the direction of her economic policies. They strengthen the perception that Viet Nam is firmly committed to the continuing liberalization of her trade and investment regime.' There are other examples of developing countries using membership in an FTA to send similar signals. According to Lawrence (1996, p. 31), 'A key Mexican motive for NAFTA [the North American Free Trade Area] was to ensure that its economic reform policies would be credible and permanent.'
2. Indeed, some of the increases in trade among the ASEAN–6 countries are attributed to the increase in the reporting, rather than the volume, of trade (Menon 1998).
3. In a recent empirical analysis, Tan (2000) finds that the gains from liberalization in terms of growth in real gross domestic product and exports are about four times higher in ASEAN+3 than in the current ASEAN.

REFERENCES

Arndt, Heinz (1996), 'AFTA and After', in Joseph Tan (ed.), *AFTA in the Changing International Economy*, Singapore: Institute of Southeast Asian Studies, pp. 42–9.
ASEAN (Association of Southeast Asian Nations) Secretariat (1996), *AFTA Reader: The Fifth ASEAN Summit*, vol. IV, Jakarta, Indonesia.

Athukorala, Prema-chandra and Jayant Menon (1997), 'AFTA and the Investment–Trade Nexus in ASEAN', *World Economy*, **20** (2), 159–74.

Bergsten, Fred (2000), *Towards a Tripartite World*, Washington, DC: Institute of International Economics.

Bhagwati, Jagdish (1994), 'Comment' on Hoekman, in Susan Collins and Barry Bosworth (eds), *The New GATT: Implications for the United States*, Washington, DC: The Brookings Institution, pp. 111–17.

Bhagwati, Jagdish (1997), 'The Global Age: From Skeptical South to a Fearful North', *World Economy*, **20** (3), 259–84.

Cooper, C.A. and B.F. Massell (1965), 'A New Look at Customs Union Theory', *Economic Journal*, **75** (300), 742–7.

Konan, Denise, Sumner La Croix, James Roumasset and Jeffery Heinrich (1995), 'Intellectual Property Rights in the Asian-Pacific Region: Problems, Patterns and Policy', *Asian-Pacific Economic Literature*, **9** (2), 13–35.

Lawrence, Robert (1996), *Regionalism, Multilateralism and Deeper Integration*, Washington, DC: The Brookings Institution Press.

Lee, Tsao Yuan (1994), 'The ASEAN Free Trade Area', *Asia-Pacific Economic Literature*, **8** (1), 1–7.

Leebron, David (1996), 'Lying Down with Procrustes: An Analysis of Harmonization Claims', in Jagdish Bhagwati and Robert Hudec (eds), *Fair Trade and Harmonisation: Prerequisites for Free Trade?*, vol. I, *Economic Analysis*, Cambridge, MA: MIT Press, pp. 41–118.

Maskus, Keith (1997), 'Implications of Regional and Multilateral Agreements for Intellectual Property Rights', Policy Discussion Paper no. 97/10, University of Adelaide, Centre for International Economic Studies, Adelaide, Australia.

Menon, Jayant (1997), 'Australia–Asia Economic Diplomacy: Regional Economic Cooperation in the Asia-Pacific', in Mark McGillivray and Gary Smith (eds), *Australia and Asia*, Sydney, Australia: Oxford University Press, pp. 81–99.

Menon, Jayant (1998), 'The Expansion of the ASEAN Free Trade Area', *Asian-Pacific Economic Literature*, **12**, 10–22.

Menon, Jayant (1999), 'Transitional Economies in Free Trade Areas: Lao PDR in AFTA', *Journal of the Asia-Pacific Economy*, **4** (2), 340–64.

Mundell, Robert (1964), 'Tariff Preferences and the Terms of Trade', *Manchester School of Economic and Social Studies*, **32**, 1–13.

Tan, Kong Yam (2000), 'Regional Trading Arrangements in the Asia-Pacific Region: Strategic Options for a Weakened ASEAN', in P. Petri (ed.), Regional Cooperation and Asian Recovery, Singapore: Institute of Southeast Asian Studies.

Than, Mya (1997), 'Economic Co-operation in the Greater Mekong Subregion', *Journal of Asian-Pacific Literature*, **11** (2), 40–57.

Weintraub, Sidney (1994), *NAFTA: What Comes Next?*, Washington, DC: Praeger.

10. Trade policy reforms, growth and poverty reduction*

Ramesh Adhikari

One of the remarkable occurrences in the history of economic development over the last five decades is the success of East and Southeast Asia in achieving faster growth and poverty reduction than that achieved by other developing countries (ADB 2000; Collier, Dollar and Stern 2000; OECD 1999). In the early 1990s a World Bank (1993) research report categorized them as high-performing Asian economies. The report indicated that many factors were responsible for their success, but the most important was the economies' greater openness or outward orientation of their trade policy, coupled with macroeconomic stability and the development of human and physical capital. In general, these economies have grown significantly faster than other developing economies and sustained that growth over time. The faster growth has been associated with reductions in poverty and a more equitable distribution of the gains resulting from the rapid growth. Their core labour standards have improved, and they have been able to take much greater advantage of their labour forces. In addition, they have achieved high literacy rates. Some of these successful economies have experienced rapid convergence in their income levels to that of the industrial countries, thereby leaving the closed economies even further behind (Dollar and Kraay 2000). However, ADB (2000) reports that in most Southeast Asian economies, such as Hong Kong, the Philippines, Malaysia, Singapore and Thailand, while high and steady economic growth reduced poverty, this growth was not associated with improvements in income inequality, as Gini coefficients remained high at 0.41 to 0.50.

In contrast to the impressive performance of the East and Southeast Asian economies, many of the poorer developing countries in Asia as well as in other regions have not as yet been able to integrate successfully into global markets, and hence reap the growth-inducing and poverty-reducing benefits of trade (World Bank 2000b). The literature suggests that trade policy reforms involving greater openness to foreign trade and investment can benefit the

---

*This chapter has benefited from comments by Prema-chandra Athukorala and John Weiss.

poor as much as they benefit the national economy (ADB 2000; Dollar and Kraay 2000; Winters 2000). There also appears to be a general agreement that trade reform may result in some social costs, with potentially negative effects on poverty reduction, at least in the short run. While openness is an important precondition for faster growth, and possibly for poverty reduction, its success will depend on other accompanying policy reforms at both the national and sector levels, on institutions and on good governance. Externally, the success of an open trade and investment policy will depend on the global trading environment.

OPENNESS AND ECONOMIC GROWTH

In this chapter openness implies liberal policies towards external trade and foreign direct investment, which are the main components of trade policy reforms as practised in the newly industrialized and developing Asian countries. The relationship between openness and economic growth is founded on the standard comparative advantage model propounded by Heckscher, Ohlin and Samuelson, which postulates that developing countries generally have a comparative advantage in the production of relatively labour-intensive products (Adhikari 2000; Adhikari and Weiss 2000). Through their specialization in the areas of their underlying comparative advantage, they will achieve higher economic efficiency and faster growth rates. In this context, economies with open trade and investment policies can specialize in what they are best at; create competitive industries; stimulate domestic and foreign investments; exploit economies of scale; and benefit from transfers of knowledge, technology and managerial skills, access to foreign savings and marketing networks. This would also allow countries to attain the dual objectives of faster growth and poverty reduction by maximizing the trickle-down effects on the poor.

The last three decades have witnessed countries with more open economies growing more rapidly than those with closed economies. Observers have claimed many benefits for greater openness, including a reallocation of resources in line with comparative advantage, improved economic efficiency and faster growth and additional employment opportunities resulting from the expansion of labour-intensive industries. The work of a number of eminent economists supports this viewpoint. In the synthesis of a multicountry research project on trade and employment in developing countries, Krueger (1993) notes that despite factor market conditions, developing countries' manufactured exports tend to exhibit the factor intensity consistent with their endowments, and that the scope for further increasing their demand for labour through both trade policies and a realignment of domestic factor market incentives is sizeable. Bhagwati and Srinivasan (1983, 1999) emphasize the efficiency and the welfare-enhancing role of outward orientation in national development policy, in addition to its superior equity outcome. Openness also produces other efficiency benefits, for instance, the removal of unintended policy distortions such as anti-export biases and the unwanted growth of economically inefficient import substituting investments, thereby avoiding what is referred to as immiserizing growth (Bhagwati and Srinivasan 1983; Brecher and Diaz-Alejandro 1977). Furthermore, openness to trade and investment implies the potential for increased transparency and procedural simplification, which reduce opportunities for high transaction costs, associated administrative inefficiency and leakage.

In the short run, trade openness essentially leads to static gains, for example, as a result of changes in the prices of goods and/or technology shifts resulting in a reallocation of resources. It may also lead to dynamic gains, such as those brought about by factor accumulation, innovations and technology diffusion, leading to higher growth in the long run (Panagariya 2000).

Considerable effort has gone into empirical investigation of the consequences of trade policy reform. Nordström (2000) lists 20 studies devoted to trade and growth and summarizes sources and country coverage, trade orientation indexes and results. A vast number of cross-country studies test for a link between measures of openness to foreign trade and capital flows and economic growth. The literature has expanded considerably with the use of alternative data sets and proxies for openness and improved econometric tests. While some remain sceptical of the merits of an exercise that contains radically different countries in a single sample and may explain only a modest proportion of growth differences, several authoritative studies now show that, allowing for a range of other factors, openness does tend to be associated with higher economic growth (Dollar 1992; Edwards 1992; Greenaway, Morgan and Wright 1998). These findings are consistent with Bhagwati and Srinivasan (1999) (see also Chapter 2 in this volume), who highlight the positive contributions of trade openness to economic growth. Dollar and Kraay (2000) also confirm the positive relationship between openness and economic growth.

Empirical studies examine the impact of removing or lowering tariff and nontariff protection of domestic industries on economic efficiency (for instance, in terms of returns on capital) and on productivity performance (for example, on the growth of total factor productivity) for different activities usually in the manufacturing sector. Higher total factor productivity growth will be one of the important mechanisms through which trade reform can generate higher economic growth. While the results are not always uniform in this case, it is clear that the stimulus generated by trade reform will be only one of several factors influencing productivity growth. Investigators have found positive productivity effects of trade policy reform for various countries, including those as dissimilar as Korea (Kim 1994), Mexico (Iscan 1998) and Sri Lanka (Athukorala and Rajapatirana 2000). The economic efficiency of manufacturing industries improves when protection is lowered or removed as part of policy liberalization relating to trade and investment (Adhikari 1988).

The findings of the IMF (1987, 1993), Summers and Heston (1991) and the World Bank (1987, 1991, 1993) support trade policy reforms by emphasizing the positive association between trade openness and faster economic growth. Furthermore, investigators have studied various measures of trade and economic growth, and their results consistently support the credibility of the positive association between trade openness and faster economic growth. For example, they have examined trade to GDP ratios (Barro and Sala-I-Martin 1995), trade protectionism (Sachs and Warner 1995), more indirect techniques designed to control for reverse causality and other statistical anomalies (Frankel, Romer and Cyrus 1996) and growth as measured by per capita GDP growth or by productivity measures (Coe and Helpman 1993).

Edwards (1998) is an extensive empirical study of the relationship between openness and total factor productivity and found that more open countries experienced faster total factor productivity growth. The study used comparative data on 93 countries to analyse the robustness of the relationship between openness and total factor productivity growth. Nine indexes of trade policy were created to investigate the relationship. Meanwhile Wacziarg (1998) investigated the impact of trade policy reform on economic growth using data from a panel study of 57 countries from 1970–89. His study was probably the first attempt to evaluate empirically, in a cross-country context, the respective roles of various theories of dynamic gains from trade in explaining the observed positive impact of trade openness on economic growth. Wacziarg used a new measure of trade openness, based on the effective policy component of trade shares, to identify the effect of trade policy on several determinants of growth. His results suggest that a policy of trade openness has a strong positive impact on economic growth. In general, an improvement of 10 percentage points in a trade policy index is associated with a 0.71 percentage point increase in economic growth. Furthermore, his findings indicate that when the effect of trade openness on growth is decomposed and attributed to the various channels of transmission, increased investment is by far the most important channel of transmission, followed by productivity and government policy.

Economic theory generally implies that trade liberalization and economic growth are positively correlated, but the connection is not well substantiated in numerical general equilibrium models. Rutherford and Tarr (1998) developed a numerical endogenous growth model applied to five developing countries and estimated the impact of tariff changes in those countries as part of UR commitments. A lump sum revenue replacement that reduces a tariff from 20 per cent to 10 per cent would produce a welfare increase of 5 to 11 per cent of the present value of consumption (equivalent to a 0.4 and 1 per cent permanent increase in terms of growth rates), depending on the assumption about the kinds of taxes used to replace revenues and whether or not a country has access to international capital. Because of the dynamic effects, the estimated gains appeared considerably larger than those found in the literature on the impact of the UR.

While extensive empirical research has demonstrated the strong link between trade openness and faster economic growth over an extended period, they are not free from criticism. For example, Rodriguez and Rodrik (1999) highlight several limitations, namely: (a) the lack of conclusive evidence on the direction of causality between openness and growth; (b) the use of an openness measure in the literature that does not reflect purely trade phenomena, but includes other policy variables that are more macroeconomic in nature (for example, the Sachs–Warner openness measure); (c) the sensitivity of results to the choice of time period and/or sample countries; and (d) a number of other econometric shortcomings.

OPENNESS AND POVERTY

Dollar and Kraay (2000) argue that the acceleration of economic growth through greater openness also reduces absolute poverty. Based on the evidence from individual cases and from cross-country analysis, they demonstrate that an open trade regime leads to faster growth and poverty reduction in poor countries. Trade liberalization is generally a strong positive contributor to poverty reduction, because it allows people to exploit their productive potential, assists economic growth, curtails arbitrary policy interventions and helps to insulate against shocks (Winters 2000). Dollar and Kraay (2000) support this line of thinking.

As exemplified by the experience of East and Southeast Asia, discussed earlier, openness has worked better when accompanied by a coherent set of growth-oriented macroeconomic and structural policies, institution and capacity building, adequate social policy and good national governance (see ADB 2000; Demery and Addison 1987; IFAD 2000 for details on various poverty reduction measures). Winters (2000) tries to explain the channels of the impact of trade liberalization on poverty by looking at likely behaviours of individuals and households, enterprises and governments.

In short, any sets of policy measures that enhance the wage income and asset income of the poor are poverty reducing. In addition, direct cash or in-kind transfers during internal and external shocks are poverty reducing, but only for a short period. Most of the world's poor live in rural areas. Some are concentrated in remote areas and confined to ethnic communities, implying that they lack ready access to physical and social infrastructure and are almost totally cut off not just from international markets, but also from domestic markets. These groups will need a different set of policy measures, as trade openness alone will be insufficient to address their problems.

Thus understanding of how the channels of transmission work, where trade policy reform may not be particularly poverty reducing, and where and when the poverty reduction effects of trade policy reform may be negative is important. One way to address these questions is by looking at the effects of trade policy reform on major economic sectors such as agriculture and manufacturing; on households and individuals; on government revenue and expenditure and on the timing, duration and costs of adjustment.

Effects on Agriculture and Manufacturing

Once a policy shift from a closed economy to an open one takes place, the trade orientation of productive sectors such as agriculture and manufacturing changes. They become more export oriented, assuming no infrastructure constraints. This happens in response to changes in demand structures and supply potentials. Once trade barriers are reduced or lifted, the border prices of traded goods will become closer to their domestic prices. Imports will be relatively more expensive and exports will be more competitive (cheaper) in international markets, largely because of implicit devaluation, which would reduce or remove pro-import substitutes or anti-export biases. Previously protected economic activities will be exposed to outside competition, and some of them may fold. In general, economic efficiency in terms of resource allocation and use and firm-level productivity may improve as a result of increased competition and increased access to foreign markets, technology and capital. This will also affect the nontraded sectors in the same way. However, how long after such changes in trade orientation and the ensuing reallocation of resources, labour turnaround and adjustment in the nontraded sectors take place and the poor are likely to benefit is unclear. Empirical evidence to date is scanty.

Effects on Households and Individuals

In the immediate and short run, workers in previously protected sectors may lose their jobs because of closures or downsizing, and the government may lose revenue from import tariffs. However, export activities will be encouraged to expand, which will provide additional job opportunities and encourage backward linkages. Final consumers may or may not face higher prices than before, depending on the types of imports and the extent to which they were protected or subsidized. For example, imported inputs and foodstuffs may be costlier following the removal of implicit import subsidies or government-administered prices. However, under an open trade policy regime, an increased flow of goods at more competitive prices is likely, which would enhance consumers' welfare.

The most commonly discussed sources of poverty are lack of income and assets to attain the basic necessities of life, a sense of 'voicelessness' and an inability to influence the state and societal institutions and a vulnerability to adverse shocks linked to an inability to cope with them (World Bank 2000a,b). The extent of poverty reduction at the household and individual level will depend on many factors, such as country or location, initial conditions, socio-political structure and governance, in addition to trade policy reforms. The main assets, and therefore the main income sources, of the poor are labour and land. Trade openness can provide the poor with employment (new jobs, higher wages) as well as market opportunities for their goods and services, which can enhance their incomes. For example, households will benefit from trade liberalization if it results in increases in real income, for example, an increase in the prices of labour, goods and services that households sell, or a decrease in the prices of goods and services that households buy. The price of their labour may rise because of increased demand for unskilled labour-intensive goods as a result of trade liberalization. However, the income the poor can derive from their assets will also depend on their access to other assets, such as physical infrastructure, credit and empowerment. Furthermore, while trade liberalization will provide larger and more stable markets for local producers, at the same time it will subject them to the variability of world markets.

The rural sector in developing countries, where small-scale farming is one of the major sources of livelihood, has the largest share of absolute poverty. This implies that increased incomes in rural areas should derive from the agriculture sector or related activities. Thus trade liberalization should extend to rural areas and provide them with opportunities to enhance rural household incomes, particularly those of small farmers. Logically, farming and farm-related activities should be made more productive and efficient through commercialization. However, trade openness will also expose small farmers to risks in terms of price fluctuations, and to opportunities in terms of better technology and improved supplies of inputs.

The positive effects of trade liberalization on poverty reduction may not be realized if bottlenecks exist in domestic markets, including problems in the provision of physical infrastructure and utilities, in access to credit, in links with international markets and/or in global trading environments being unfavourable. Consistent reform of domestic markets is important to maximize the benefits of trade openness. For example, in Nepal in the early 1980s, allowing the private sector to supply imported inputs, such as raw wool and metals, part of the policy reforms initiated under a small-industry development project, helped to expand exports of rugs, carpets and traditional handicrafts enormously compared with the previous situation, when a state trading company maintained a monopoly over such inputs.

Openness to trade and investment has also helped to provide employment opportunities for women. For example, in Bangladesh and Sri Lanka a high proportion of the workers engaged in garment factories are women from rural areas, as are most Nepalese weavers. A similar trend is apparent in other Asian countries such as Cambodia, the Philippines, Thailand and Vietnam.

Thus, on balance, trade reform is likely to have a positive impact on poverty reduction. However, recent cross-country analysis that goes beyond GDP figures to consider their internal distribution casts some doubt on this optimistic conclusion. Lundberg and Squire (1999) find that openness, as proxied by the Sachs–Warner index (Sachs and Warner 1995), is correlated negatively with income growth among the poorest 40 per cent of the population and positively with the income of the remainder. This has the worrying implication that while openness is good for growth in the aggregate, that is, as previous studies have found, the majority benefit, it has a negative effect, at least in the short run, on the incomes of the poorest. While the authors themselves caution that this result is suggestive rather than definitive and needs to be tested by specific country studies, it none the less provides useful tips to researchers. Furthermore, ADB (2000) reports a finding that runs counter to Lundberg and Squire's controversial and unexpected results. In a simple regression between change in openness (as proxied by the share of imports and exports in GDP) and change in poverty reduction (based on national poverty lines) for a sample of 40 countries during 1970–92, the relationship was found to be negative and significant, implying that growing openness to foreign trade reduces poverty. More recent empirical work in this regard substantiates the positive link between openness and poverty reduction (Dollar and Kraay forthcoming).

Effects of Trade Policy Reform on Industrial Employment

While the employment effect at the sectoral level varies across countries, many empirical studies conclude that the negative effects of trade policy reforms on employment are at best modest. Michaely, Papageorgiou and Choksi (1991) reviewed liberalization episodes in 18 countries and found that in only two – Chile and Spain – did a major fall in employment occur following liberalization. The authors suggest that in both these cases factors other than trade reform were at work, specifically, exchange rate overvaluation in Chile and wage rigidity in Spain. While this study is widely cited, it had methodological limitations. A number of studies that have employed superior empirical procedures, for example, Hanson and Harrison (1999) have corroborated for Mexico and Morocco the weak unemployment consequences reported by Michaely, Papageorgiou and Choksi (1991). Furthermore, evidence indicates that the fear that smaller firms are likely to be disproportionately hit by trade reform is also misplaced. A study of the impact of trade reform on industrial structure in employment terms by Aswicahyono, Bird and Hill (1996) finds that in Indonesia reform had little impact in terms of changing the size distribution of firms.

The experience of East and Southeast Asian countries is perhaps more convincing as far as it concerns the potential impact of openness-led economic growth on poverty reduction. Fields (1994) reports on the experience of Hong Kong, Korea, Singapore and Taiwan, and shows that the entire working population benefited from labour market institutions during the period of rapid, export-led growth and economic transformation. Labour market repression was neither necessary nor desirable for outward-oriented economic development. The countries attained and maintained generally full employment, improved their job mixes, raised real earnings and lowered their poverty rates. Their openness to foreign trade and investment seems to have resulted in higher growth performance and a considerable reduction in absolute poverty (Athukorala and Menon 1999).

For South Asia Dev (2000) shows that, at the aggregate level, the impact of economic liberalization on employment and labour income has not been as severe as for Sub-Saharan Africa or Latin America, but neither has it been as good as for East and Southeast Asian countries. The evidence on changes in unemployment following economic opening is mixed, and in some cases underemployment increased or continued to remain high. However, whether some of the concerns regarding increasing inequalities, particularly between skilled and unskilled labour in terms of reduced growth of real wages, are due to liberalization as such or merely reflect the half-hearted nature of policy reforms remains unresolved. Furthermore, the available evidence does not support the view that liberalization adversely affects employment growth in the formal sector, and also shows that employment growth picked up despite labour rigidities after liberalization. The results appear to be valid at least in the case of India and at the aggregate level. Nevertheless, more research needs to be undertaken in this regard, especially at the microeconomic level. In Sri Lanka, where reforms have been far more comprehensive and sustained for a longer period (since 1977) than in most other latecomers to outward-oriented reforms, the evidence of a significant increase in employment in domestic manufacturing throughout the post-reform period is unambiguous (Athukorala and Rajapatirana 2000).

The evidence and inferences are not immune to criticism, however. First, adjustment may entail significant costs in the short run when domestic factors, in particular labour, are immobile. Hence, when they are no longer required in contracting (economically unviable) activities, a long time lag may occur before they are absorbed in expanding (economically viable) activities. Second, experience in many developing countries almost always suggests that short-term 'once-and-for-all' gains from resource reallocation are the only gains if they are at all successfully achieved. Most developing countries do not seem to have realized long-run employment benefits through dynamic changes in comparative advantage or technological progress. Third, openness could also bring in advanced technology that requires highly skilled labour, which is not usually available in developing countries; thus the likely employment benefits may be small. Fourth, according to Rodrik (1997), openness could mean an elastic demand for labour, leading to higher labour standards, greater volatility in earnings and working hours and less bargaining power, all of which could hurt unskilled labour. However, Panagariya (2000) examines the validity of this proposition and finds it to be unjustified.

Finally, small, remote and poorly endowed countries and/or regions within countries do not necessarily benefit from openness alone in terms of employment or efficiency gains. For example, the Kyrgyz Republic and Mongolia are open and liberal, but they have not yet been very successful in promoting trade and investment, which could benefit their poor. Similarly, island countries that are open and liberal, but are remote and have limited resources have not succeeded in improving growth and prosperity for reasons other than open trade policy. Openness alone may not, therefore, help these countries. For trade policy reform to work, concurrent, complementary macroeconomic and structural reforms in other sectors are necessary.

Effects on Government Revenue and Spending

Trade tax revenue, particularly from import tariffs, is one of the main sources of tax revenue in many Asian countries. One major concern of national governments in these countries, and hence a major rationale for donor support to them, has been the revenue implications of trade policy reforms. Trade policy reforms can be revenue enhancing, but in the immediate term it may not be so (Deacon 2000; Greenaway and Milner 1991; Prichett and Sethi 1994). Whether governments lose significant revenue will depend on the extent of tariffs and associated exemptions and the degree of compliance. For example, it is generally believed that trade policy reforms that replace nontariff barriers, including quantitative restrictions, and reduce high tariff rates and multiple tariff bands, are likely to enhance revenue following their implementation, or at least be revenue neutral. This would occur because of a higher degree of compliance as a result of a more efficient tariff structure and simplified tariff administration. If the tariff cuts relate to the bulk of imports or free trade arrangements are agreed, this might result in lower revenue to the government. In the latter case consumers may benefit because the increased and duty-free flow of goods will lead to more competitive prices. Note also that this kind of import liberalization may lead to higher volume of imports, and hence to a broader tax base and more revenue.

In the case where the government's revenue loss is considerable, the government might introduce new taxes or increase the rates of existing taxes to make up the losses, borrow from abroad or cut government expenditures. In the case of new or increased taxes, the impact on poverty will depend on whether the new taxes or higher tax rates fall disproportionately on the poor. Borrowing from abroad to finance the deficits will not have any welfare costs, at least in the short run. Cuts in public expenditure, particularly in spending on the social sector, rural infrastructure and utilities, will worsen poor people's welfare.

However, as trade reform typically raises aggregate incomes, the government should generally be able to raise tax revenue from among groups other than the poor. In many cases governments implement trade policy reform, particularly the reduction of import tariffs and the removal of export taxes, in tandem with the introduction of reform programmes for tax policy and administration. Such programmes often include the introduction or strengthening of value added tax.

On the positive side, increased growth of national income induced by trade policy reform will give more financial resources to the government, which are likely to lead to additional government expenditure on primary health, education and public utilities, which would benefit the poor, and hence provide a longer-term contribution to poverty reduction.

However, the empirical literature is thin in this regard. Abed (1998) provides probably the most comprehensive study of the revenue implications of trade reform. Following a survey of 36 of the least developed countries, the study reports that trade taxes accounted for nearly one-third of total tax revenue, or around 5 per cent of GDP. Ebrill, Stotsky and Gropp (1999) reviewed the revenue implications of trade reform in six countries: Argentina, Malawi, Morocco, the Philippines, Poland and Senegal. Trade reforms in these countries included the tariffication of quantitative restrictions, the reduction of tariff levels and their dispersion, and the removal of some export taxes. Trade taxes were an important source of government revenue. However, experiences varied, and in several cases poor revenue performance or a weak macro-economy seem to have compromised trade policy reform. Most of these cases illustrate the importance of successful revenue-enhancing reforms to domestic taxes in tandem with trade policy reforms to offset likely adverse revenue effects.

Adjustment Experience: Poverty Reduction, Time and Costs

The development outcomes of the 1980s and 1990s (Table 10.1) lead to several observations. First, trade openness, in terms of the trade to GDP ratio, is lower in low- to moderate-growth countries than in high-growth countries, and correspondingly, GDP growth follows the same trend. Growth rates declined in the 1990s compared with the 1980s. Poverty is not only high in low-growth countries; it increased significantly from the 1980s to the 1990s. Higher-growth countries have less poverty, and poverty reduction appears to be faster. Low-growth countries also have higher illiteracy and infant mortality rates. Progress in these areas also seems slower in the low-growth countries.

In the immediate term trade liberalization may negatively affect the income growth of the poor, and governments will have to provide appropriate social safety nets. In the short run, expected once-and-for-all reallocation of

Table 10.1   Development outcomes by growth class, 1980s and 1990s

Indicator	Period	High growth	Moderate or improved growth	Low growth
Trade/GDP (%)	1980s	82.0	71.0	59.9
	1990s	92.1	77.0	70.2
GDP growth	1980s	6.5	2.3	2.1
(% per year)	1990s	5.3	4.2	0.3
Poverty (percentage	1980s	31.0	32.1	30.2
living on less than	1990s	24.1	31.4	36.9
US$1/day)				
Infant mortality	1980s	41.0	66.6	71.0
(% per 1000	1990s	29.2	54.3	60.7
live births)				
Illiteracy (%)	1980s	22.9	37.6	38.8
	1990s	17.2	31.2	31.4
Number of countries	n.a.	13	53	39

n.a. = not applicable.

Source: World Bank (2000a, tables 1.2 and 1.4).

resources should affect the income of poor people depending on the nature and duration of labour turnaround. Empirical evidence is generally lacking in the case of labour turnaround subsequent to trade policy reform (Matusz and Tarr 1999). However, Milner and Wright (1998) report the success story of Mauritius. According to them, Mauritius combined trade liberalization and poverty reduction programmes, which resulted in increasing unskilled and female wages as exports boomed. A similar story is evident in Athukorala and Menon's (1999) account of Malaysia. According to them, Malaysia has succeeded in achieving its development objectives by adopting pragmatic policies in line with changes in the global economy since the early 1970s. Rapid and sustained growth through export-led industrialization has been accompanied by rapid employment growth, reduced poverty and across-the-board improvements in living standards.

In the long run, openness may bring about technological advancements and innovations, which will create new areas of comparative advantage and benefit the poor. Labour turnaround will depend on market flexibility and education and skills. Workers' education level may be an important influencing factor in this respect. Evidence on the distribution of education suggests the existence of a positive relationship between education and income inequality. Lopez, Thomas and Wang (1998) found that the Gini coefficients of countries such as India and Pakistan (0.64 to 0.67) were higher than that of China, Korea, Malaysia and Thailand (0.22 to 0.42) for 1970–90. Thus inequality in terms of education seems to follow the same trend as poverty.

In other countries the adjustment experience has been mixed. A World Bank study (Dollar and Kraay forthcoming) reports that 18 rapidly opening developing countries – including Bangladesh, China, India, Nepal and Vietnam – have achieved higher than average growth rates as a result of increased openness. However, in terms of poverty reduction these countries do not seem to have been successful, because they still house the majority of the world's poor.

China and India both have a high concentration of absolute poverty despite high and stable economic growth averaging 6 to 7 per cent per year. Both are large economies with regulated domestic markets. While they are not fully open to the outside world, they have benefited considerably from foreign trade and investment. Population growth, while lower than in the past, is still high in India, but in China it is low and underpinned by the one-child policy. Recent figures suggest that there are about 270 million people under the US$1 a day consumption level (ADB 2000). Urban unemployment and poverty are emerging as China's new challenges. Furthermore, the reform of state-owned enterprises is likely to result in additional layoffs of workers in coming years. The social safety net needed to prevent many of the laid-off workers from becoming extremely poor has yet to be developed.

Transition economies, particularly in Central Asia, have not been able to break through their poverty net. The increase in poverty in Central Asia appears to have stabilized in response to the levelling off of the downward trend in GDP. However, prolonged recession in the region and the effects of the 1997 Asian financial crisis and the 1998 Russian crisis worsened the poverty scenario. For example, the Kyrgyz Republic was badly affected by the crisis, which resulted in a depreciation of its currency by about 50 per cent. In terms of policy orientation, the country is open, and also the first republic to join the WTO. However, because of its geographical remoteness, its relatively less favourable endowment of natural resources such as oil compared with, say, Kazakhstan, the prolonged recession in regional markets, and its poor physical infrastructure and relatively weak institutions, the Kyrgyz Republic has not been effective in bringing about faster economic growth and associated poverty reduction. The lack of sufficient economic growth and direct poverty reduction measures in Central Asia has meant that many of the transient poor who emerged following independence about a decade ago have graduated to the group of 'chronically poor'.

HOW CAN TRADE POLICY REFORM BE MORE POVERTY REDUCING?

While there is no simple answer to this question, it may be said that both internal and external factors having the potential to reduce poverty could be more carefully designed and implemented. More substantive actions, rather than rhetoric, among donors and stronger will and commitments of national governments would help in this process.

Targeting and Sequencing Trade Policy Reforms

Careful targeting of trade policy reforms may maximize the resulting benefits to the poor. Trade policy reforms could start by removing unintended anti-poor policy biases against the sectors in which the poor work and the goods that they need. Similarly, domestic policy reforms could also be aimed at removing policy and institutional measures that hurt the poor most.

In particular, careful sequencing of macroeconomic reforms, domestic sector reforms and public sector reforms may minimize costs and maximize benefits to the poor. There is a body of literature on the sequencing and pacing of trade policy reforms to minimize the costs of reforms and/or adjustments (see, for example, Adhikari, Kirkpatrick and Weiss 1992; Thomas and Nash 1992) on the experience of trade policy reforms under the World Bank's adjustment lending during the 1980s). The reform programmes should include all the complementary policy measures, institutional reforms and infra-structure improvements whose absence or deficiency may impede the benefits that could otherwise flow from trade policy reforms. As discussed earlier, trade policy reforms alone may not be effective in benefiting the poor, hence complementary measures should go hand in hand with reform programmes in a properly sequenced manner. The key requisite is that trade policy reforms must reach rural areas to benefit the poor, for which complementary policy measures to improve awareness, infrastructure, utilities, production technologies, marketing networks and skills will also be necessary.

Making the Global Trading Environment Pro-Poor

Thus far, trade liberalization has not been sufficiently inclusive to achieve poverty reduction through pro-poor growth, and problems are apparent in both the industrial and developing countries. Increased exports of labour-intensive products, such as agricultural products or textiles, would help poorer people, but such exports are currently highly protected in the industrial countries. Furthermore, technical barriers, social labelling, labour standards and expected compliance with environment-related standards are constraints to market access by developing countries (see Chapter 6 in this volume). Another problem is that the bulk of agricultural activities in many developing countries are largely subsistence activities, and are not commercialized, and lack easy access to markets both within and outside their countries. In many cases the agriculture sector in developing countries is also protected from external competition, mainly for political reasons. Some developing countries clearly fear possible competitive pressure from countries with advanced agricultural production systems, which might wipe out their agricultural activities, on which most poor people depend.

Over the last decade, the share of developing countries' exports of goods in total goods exports grew from 15 to 20 per cent, and their share of the services sector rose from 13 to 16 per cent. Their manufacturing exports grew from 20 to 70 per cent of their total exports, which implied the relative importance of manufactured exports compared with agriculture exports. Recent improvements can be attributed to declining tariff barriers to manufactured trade in both the industrial and developing countries. For example, the average import tariff in industrial countries is 4 per cent and in developing countries it is 13 per cent. However, in the case of the former, it conceals the tariff peaks and escalations on products in which developing countries have a comparative advantage. The position is substantially worse in the case of agricultural products. On average, the tariff on agricultural products is higher in the developing countries (18 per cent) and slightly lower in the industrial countries (15 per cent). However, nontariff barriers, restrictive quotas and antidumping and other forms of contingent protection, including competition from subsidized agricultural exports in the industrial countries, are many times higher and/or prohibitive. For example, effective import tariff rates on agriculture and textile products such as processed foods, fruits and vegetables, rice and footwear in the EU, Japan and the United States range from more than 100 per cent to 1000 per cent.

Quantitative analysis suggests that complete liberalization of global agricultural trade could yield benefits to both the industrial and the developing countries (see also Chapter 3 in this volume). The industrial countries would save billions of dollars if they removed farm subsidies. Thus a win–win situation apparently exists for both the industrial and the developing countries, but the agriculture sector is traditionally an extremely sensitive sector from the political point of view. In addition, some developing countries fear that their agriculture sector would not be able to compete with that of the industrial countries, and hence believe that agricultural trade liberalization might not work in their favour. While this has some elements of truth, actual effects might not be as bad as feared. Furthermore, targeting and sequencing with appropriate provisions for meeting adjustment costs could help. Politically, it may not be easy to arrive at general agreement on the liberalization of agricultural trade. Even if it happens, it will take time. However, the industrial countries could start opening up, which might encourage the developing countries to do so.

Could Donor Assistance be More Poverty Reducing?

Major donors have been emphasizing their operational support to poverty reduction in the developing countries, although this is not really new, as donors had also supported poverty reduction in developing countries in the past. For example, one of the five strategic objectives of the medium-term strategic framework of the Asian Development Bank was poverty reduction, and the World Bank, particularly during McNamara's time in the 1970s, together with other donors, supported a series of integrated rural development projects for poverty reduction. In many cases this approach did not lead to the expected success. There were many problems, of which the main ones could be attributed to the lack of beneficiary consultation and participation and weak governance. The recent emphasis on poverty reduction attempts to ensure sustainability by addressing the issues of better resource allocation; stronger institutional capability and governance; increased transparency and accountability; and partnerships with the private sector, nongovernmental organizations and communities.

There are certainly a number of initiatives that donors can take towards reducing poverty. To start with, they could provide guidance to the developing countries in formulating policies and strategies and strengthening institutions and governance, and realign their own operational activities along these lines. When it comes to trade policy reforms, donors could start with providing assistance for further trade policy reforms, domestic market reforms and related institutional strengthening in the developing countries, and at the same time open up their markets more liberally. This could also be extended to WTO-related issues, where donors could be instrumental in improving WTO deals and promoting a genuinely pro-poor, rules-based multilateral trading system. On the question of preparing for a new round, Schott (2000, p. 76) wrote:

> Industrial countries should indeed be criticised for their miserly offerings. International financial institutions should also be directed to co-ordinate their efforts more closely with the WTO to enable developing countries to take advantage of the opportunities created by trade pacts; there have been many hortatory declarations in support of such policy coherence, but so far little action. Extending trade preferences to the poorest countries is also commendable, even though such measures usually offer only marginal and temporary support. As a rule the benefits for key products to assuage domestic lobbies can be revoked without contravening WTO obligations. Moreover, gains for some poor countries come at the expense of losses for others.

Recent development reports of the multilateral and international development agencies list a number of measures for reducing poverty in developing countries. For example, the Asian Development Bank (2000) lists the following as necessary to address poverty issues in Asia and the Pacific: improving the global trading environment, for example, by making labour and environmental standards less restrictive; increasing the flows of foreign assistance; and providing international public goods, such as medical research on tropical diseases and agricultural research. While the World Bank (2000b) emphasizes foreign aid and debt relief, it also highlights four key areas of international action for poverty reduction: expanding market access for developing countries' goods and services in the rich countries; reducing the risk of economic crises; encouraging the production of international public goods that benefit poor people; and ensuring a voice for poor countries and poor people in global forums.

In the context of openness to foreign trade and investment, the proposal to expand market access in high-income countries is a good one, and is also consistent with the Asian Development Bank (2000). As indicated earlier, various forms and extents of trade barriers in the industrial countries on exports such as agricultural goods and labour-intensive manufactures from the developing countries can place huge constraints on poor countries' efforts to grow and to reduce poverty through openness to trade and investment. The implicit cost of these trade barriers to the industrial countries' governments is also estimated to be large (as highlighted earlier on), and thus phasing out such barriers would save considerable resources for them. However, reducing trade barriers will require bold political will on the part of industrial countries' leaders.

CONCLUSIONS

Economic growth is a necessary condition for reducing poverty. Trade policy reform leading to openness to external trade and investment is useful for accelerating growth, and also for poverty reduction, because it enhances returns to the main assets of the poor. However, country- and location- or time-specific factors or needs may alter the combination of policy measures and their outcomes, as there does not appear to be a universally acceptable or appropriate model of poverty reduction for all developing countries and for all times.

Benefits arising from trade policy reform may vary depending on the type and extent of the reform and country-specific situations. Note also that trade policy reforms could hurt poor people in the short run because of some unavoidable costs during the adjustment period in the form of losses of jobs, traditional businesses and subsidies and reduced public investment in the social and infrastructure sectors. However, there is a dearth of empirical evidence on the likely adjustment or the turnaround time and costs subsequent to trade policy reform. Proper sequencing and careful timing of the reform process and sufficient provision to mitigate the social costs will be necessary.

Although there is no straightforward answer as to how to make trade policy reform more poverty reducing, some areas of reform that could affect the incomes of the poor have been highlighted. In addition, trade policy reform is only one of several important policy variables that can induce poverty reduction. It works more effectively when the reform is comprehensive, markets are liberal and functioning and institutions are sufficiently strong and market friendly. As poverty reduction issues are multifaceted, they should be addressed systematically under the framework of an overall development strategy of the country concerned and should be co-ordinated in a comprehensive, cohesive and integrated manner. National governments should start by removing those policy measures, institutions and practices that hurt the poor the most. Similarly, the global trading environment could be made more favourably disposed towards the poor.

REFERENCES

Abed, George (1998), *Fiscal Reform in Low Income Countries*, Occasional Paper no. 160, Washington, DC: IMF.

ADB (Asian Development Bank) (2000), *Asian Development Outlook*, Manila.

Adhikari, R. (1988), *Manufacturing Industries in Developing Countries - An Economic Efficiency Analysis of Nepal*, Aldershot, UK: Gower.

Adhikari, R. (2000), 'Trade Liberalization and Poverty Reduction', paper presented at the seminar on Trade Policy Issues, 17-21 July, Asian Development Bank Institute, Tokyo.

Adhikari, R. and J. Weiss (2000), 'Poverty Reduction Issues', background paper for the seminar on Poverty Reduction Issues, 3-11 November, Asian Development Bank Institute, Manila.

Adhikari, R., C. Kirkpatrick and J. Weiss (1992), *Industrial and Trade Policy Reform in Developing Countries*, Manchester and New York: Manchester University Press.

Aswicahyono, H., K. Bird and H. Hill (1996), 'What Happens to Industrial Structure When Countries Liberalise? Indonesia Since the mid-1980s', *Journal of Development Studies*, **32** (3), 340-64. Available at http://www.francass.com/jnls/jds_v32.htm.

Athukorala, Prema-chandra and Jayant Menon (1999), 'Outward Orientation and Economic Performance: The Malaysian Experience', *World Economy*, **22** (8), 1119-39.

Athukorala, Prema-chandra and Sarath Rajapatirana (2000), *Liberalization and Industrial Transformation: Sri Lanka in International Perspective*, Delhi: Oxford University Press.

Barro, Robert J. and Xavier Sala-I-Martin (1995), *Economic Growth*, New York: McGraw-Hill.

Bhagwati, J. and T.N. Srinivasan (1983), *Lectures in International Trade*, Cambridge, MA: MIT Press.

Bhagwati, J. and T.N. Srinivasan (1999), 'Outward-Orientation and Development, Are Revisionists Right?', Columbia University, New York, processed.

Brecher, Richard A. and Carlos F. Diaz-Alejandro (1977), 'Tariffs, Foreign Capital, and Immiserizing Growth', *Journal of International Economics*, **7**, 317-22.

Coe, David T. and E. Helpman (1993), 'International R&D Spillovers', Working Paper no. 93/94, IMF, Washington, DC.

Collier, Paul, David Dollar and Nicholas Stern (2000), *Fifty Years of Development*, Washington, DC: World Bank. Available on http://www.worldbank.org/poverty.

Deacon, B. (2000), *Globalization and Social Policy: The Threat to Equitable Welfare*, Occasional Paper no. 5, New York, United Nations Research Institute for Social Development.

Demery, I. and T. Addison (1987), *The Alleviation of Poverty Under Structural Adjustment*, Washington, DC: World Bank.

Dev, Mahendra (2000), 'Economic Liberalization and Employment in South Asia', Discussion Papers on Development Policy no. 9, Centre for Development Research, University of Bonn, Bonn.

Dollar, D. (1992), 'Outward-Oriented Economies Really Do Grow More Rapidly', *Economic Development and Cultural Change*, **40** (April), 523-44.

Dollar, D. and A. Kraay (2000), 'Growth Is Good for the Poor', World Bank, Development Research Department, Washington, DC, processed.

Dollar, D. and A. Kraay (forthcoming), *Growth, Trade and Poverty*, Washington, DC: World Bank.

Ebrill, L., J. Stotsky and R. Gropp (1999), *Revenue Implications of Trade Liberalization*, Occasional Paper no. 180, Washington, DC: IMF.

Edwards, S., (1992), 'Trade Orientation, Distortions and Growth in Developing Countries', *Journal of Development Economics*, **39**, 31–58.

Edwards, S., (1998), 'Openness, Productivity and Growth: What Do We Really Know?', *Economic Journal*, **108** (March), 383–98.

Fields, G. (1994), 'Changing Labor Market Conditions and Economic Development in Hong Kong, the Republic of Korea, Singapore, and Taiwan, China', *World Bank Economic Review*, **1** (1), 391–414.

Frankel Jeffrey A., David Romer and Teresa Cyrus (1996), 'Trade and Growth in East Asian Countries: Cause and Effect?', Paper no. 5732, National Bureau for Economic Research, Cambridge, MA.

Greenaway, D. and C.R. Milner (1991), 'Fiscal Dependence on Trade Taxes and Trade Policy Reforms', *Journal of Development Studies*, **27**, 95–132.

Greenaway, David, W. Morgan and P. Wright (1998), 'Trade Reform Adjustment and Growth: What Does the Evidence Tell Us?', *Economic Journal*, **108** (September), 1547–61.

Hanson, G. and A. Harrison (1999), 'Who Gains from Trade Reform?: Some Remaining Puzzles', *Journal of Development Economics*, **59** (1), 125–54.

IFAD (International Fund for Agriculture Development) (2000), 'Ending Rural Poverty in the 21st Century', Rome.

IMF (International Monetary Fund) (1987), *Trade Liberalization in Fund Supported Programs*, Washington, DC.

IMF (1993), *World Economic Outlook*, Washington, DC.

Iscan, T. (1998), 'Trade Liberalisation and Productivity: A Panel Study of the Mexican Manufacturing Industry', *Journal of Development Studies*, **34** (5), 123–48.

Kim, K. (1994), 'Trade and Industrialisation Policies in Korea', in G. Helleiner (ed.), *Trade Policy and Industrialisation in Turbulent Times*, London, Routledge, pp. 317–63.

Krueger, Anne O. (1993), *Political Economy of Policy Reform in Developing Countries*, Cambridge, MA: MIT Press.

Lopez, R., V. Thomas, and Y. Wang (1998), 'Addressing the Education Puzzle: The Distribution of Education and Economic Reform', Policy Research Working Paper no. 2031, World Bank, Washington, DC.

Lundberg, M. and L. Squire (1999), 'The Simultaneous Evolution of Growth and Inequality', World Bank, Washington, DC, processed.

Matusz, S.J. and D. Tarr (1999), 'Adjusting to Trade Policy Reform', Policy Research Working Paper no. 2142, World Bank, Washington, DC.

Michaely, M., D. Papageorgiou, and A.M. Choksi (1991), *Liberalizing Foreign Trade: Lessons of Experience in the Developing World*, Oxford, UK: Basil Blackwell.

Milner, C.R. and P.W. Wright (1998), 'Modelling Labour Market Adjustment to Trade Liberalization in an Industrializing Economy', *Economic Journal*, **108**, 509–28.

Nordström, Hakan (2000), *Trade, Income Disparity and Poverty: An Overview*, Geneva: WTO. Available on: http://www.wto.org.

OECD (Organization for Economic Co-operation and Development) (1999), *Trade, Investment and Development*, Paris.

Panagariya, Arvind (2000), 'Trade Openness: Consequences for Poverty and Income Distribution', paper presented at the Third Anniversary Symposium, 8 December, Asian Development Bank Institute, Tokyo.

Prichett, L. and G. Sethi (1994), 'Tariff Rates, Tariff Revenue, and Tariff Reform: Some New Facts', *World Bank Economic Review*, **8**, 1-16.

Rodriguez, Francisco and Dani Rodrik (1999), 'Trade Policy and Economic Growth: A Skeptical Guide to Cross-National Evidence', Working Paper no. W7081, National Bureau for Economic Research, Cambridge, Massachusetts. Available on: http://www.nber.org/papers/w7081.

Rodrik, Dani (1997), *Has Globalization Gone Too Far?*, Washington, DC: Institute for International Economics.

Rutherford, Thomas F. and David G. Tarr (1998), 'Trade Liberalization and Endogenous Growth in a Small Open Economy: A Quantitative Assessment', Working Paper no. 1970, World Bank, Washington, DC. Available on http://www.econ/worldbank.org.

Sachs, Jeffrey and Andrew Warner (1995), 'Economic Reform and the Process of Global Integration', *Brookings Papers on Economic Activity*, **1** (April), 1-118.

Schott, Jeffrey (2000), 'After Seattle', *The Economist*, 26 August, p. 76.

Summers, Robert and Alan Heston (1991), 'The Penn World Table (Mark 5) and Expanded Set of International Comparisons, 1950-88', *Quarterly Journal of Economics*, **106**, 327-68.

Thomas, Vinod and John Nash (1992), 'Trade Policy Reform: Recent Evidence from Theory and Practice' in R. Adhikari, C. Kirkpatrick and J. Weiss (eds), *Industrial and Trade Policy Reform in Developing Countries*, Manchester and New York: Manchester University Press, pp. 186-97.

Wacziarg, Romain (1998), 'Measuring the Dynamic Gains from Trade', Working Paper no. 2001, World Bank, Washington, DC. Available on http://www.econ/worldbank.org.

Winters, L.A. (2000), *Trade and Poverty: Is There a Connection?*, Geneva: World Trade Organization. Available on: http://www.wto.org or http://www.worldbank.org/trade.

World Bank (1987), *World Development Report 1987*, New York: Oxford University Press.

World Bank (1991), *World Development Report 1991*, New York: Oxford University Press.

World Bank (1993), *The East Asian Miracle: Economic Growth and Public Policy*, New York: Oxford University Press.

World Bank (2000a), *The Quality of Growth*, New York: Oxford University Press.

World Bank (2000b), *World Development Report 2000/2001*, New York: Oxford University Press.

Index